CONVERSATIONS
OF SILENCE

CONVERSATIONS of SILENCE

S. Harold Nickerson, M.D.

Santa Fe
New Mexico

© 1995 by S. Harold Nickerson

All Rights Reserved

No part of this book may be reproduced in any form or by any electronic or mechanical means including information storage and retrieval systems, without permission in writing from the publisher, except by a reviewer who may quote brief passages in a review.

First edition

Printed in the United States of America

Library of Congress Cataloging in Publication Data

Nickeron, S. Harold.
    Conversations of silence / S. Harold Nickerson.—1st ed.
      p. cm.
    ISBN 0-86534-231-8   (paper)
    I. Title.
PS3564.12878C65   1995
813'.54—dc20   94-45897
                                                          CIP

Published by Sunstone Press
        Post Office Box 2321
        Santa Fe, New Mexico 87504-2321 / USA
        (505) 988-4418 / *FAX: (505) 988-1025*
        orders only (800) 243-5644

FOREWORD

Plato, in his Republic, engages in philosophic discussion concerning the recognition of essential truth. He leads his listeners down the road until they come to a divergence — where a dichotomy takes place. One path leads to the state of basic truth; the other, to opinion cloaked in the substance of truth. He teaches his students to distinguish the difference, to avoid confusion between what is fact and that which is fact-like but not truthful, that is fictitious.

Stanley Baldwin, the British statesman, once described truth as "many-sided."

Any resemblance in this novel to anyone living or dead is entirely coincidental.

THE AUTHOR

CONVERSATIONS OF SILENCE
6

7

THE COLLEGE CAMPUS

The original campus was created in 1813 by a generous bequest from the founder whose name was given to the university, and whose remains are entombed in front of the Arts Building which faces a wide expanse of land roughly rectangular in shape, and on which rugby encounters occasionally took place.

It was gradually changed from what was originally a little more than forty acres of fields and pasture land into the campus where Elena, in the Language Department, and Edward Rankin, a medical student, worked and played and met, more than a century and a quarter later.

The campus was somewhat unusual in its arrangement since all the faculty buildings were on the college grounds and were within a fifteen-minute walk from each other, including the R.V. Women's College, just around the corner. The college grounds were crisscrossed everyday by the several thousand students going to their various classes. It was inevitable that many friendships should begin.

Students from every nation gravitated toward the university which had by then achieved an enviable record of national and international prestigious accomplishments. A roster of its graduates included many names of men and women who returned to all parts of the world, to accomplishments and achievements which have found their place in the history of progress in the fields of science and letters.

The world economy, at the time Elena and Edward studied at the university, was in the doldrums. Political parties in all countries were unstable and collapsed with dreadful frequency, only to have other "prophets" or "leaders" rise, like the phoenix, from the ashes of their predecessors' political overthrow. The United States of America was still struggling in its effort to break loose from the shackles of the Great Depression.

The University—it is where the odyssey of Elena, Ed, and the others, begins. It was a different time from the present—and yet, it was the same.

◆◆◆

CONVERSATIONS OF SILENCE
8

The hospital routine was a new and strange experience for Ed. Added to a lost feeling was a homesickness for the way things used to be—for the familiar faces and places—for Elena. His longing was almost unbearable as he remembered how they had made hungry, desperate love the night before he had to leave her.

His nights were often troubled by a recurring dream of wandering naked through a crowd of people, nobody noticing him or his nudity, as if he did not exist, had no presence. The dream was often invaded by erotic visions of Elena.

A particularly restless night left him listless and brooding. He went about his morning duties and activities with a complete lack of enthusiasm and was glad to finally escape to the doctors' lounge. He stared out of the window moodily thinking of Elena and remembering the others. How were they? What were they doing?

His mind drifted back to the time to when he was newly arrived from England quite alone. His lodgings near the University became the only "home" he knew . . . .

CHAPTER I

"Cramming" for examinations was a way of life in those days at medical school. Cramming was the literal word for it on that particular night. Ed, Thomas and Crandall were physically crammed into Ed's room, soaking up as much information as possible into their heads for the morrow's "spot exam." It was one of those cruel tests where rows of anatomical specimens—muscles, nerves, organs and every other conceivable anatomical structure—are laid out in rows like items in a grocery store. The student starts with the first specimen, identifies the structure, and, when the buzzer sounds, moves on to the next specimen. George, the anatomy assistant, acting as the monitor, would fastidiously count off the previous number of seconds before pressing the buzzer and grin at the hapless medical students staggering from one specimen to the next like a chain gang.

All this on one day's notice. The simple fact was that the student knew his work or he did not. There was very little time for real study, only the desperate cramming to pick up loose ends or anticipate trick questions. But students who made the grade were assured of a sound foundation in anatomy.

Ed's brow was furrowed as he studied the pages before him. Even Crandall with his phenomenal memory was apprehensive. Thomas returned to his room to get some milk. During these sessions he had the habit of consuming enormous amounts of shredded wheat and milk. He returned with the milk, also his meerschaum pipe and tobacco pouch. Settling back into his corner, he grunted in peaceful contentment. Ed and Crandall eyed his pipe with foreboding and apprehension.

"Not again!" muttered Crandall. Thomas peered at him over the top of his glasses and smiled benignly. His optical problem necessitated thick corrective lenses which somehow made him arch his eyebrows when looking directly at one, giving him a look of perpetual surprise.

"Do you have to smoke that stinkweed now?" Ed complained. "My brain is fuzzy enough as it is."

Thomas, safe behind the barricade of milk, cereal and piled-up books, lifted his shoulders deprecatingly. He waved his hand in a gesture of peace and reached for the pipe. He inherited the meerschaum pipe from his grandfather and was forever stuffing the bowl with a brand of tobacco which Ed swore was "a mixture of seaweed and cabbage leaf."

"More like skunk cabbage," Crandall growled. "How you can smoke the stuff and live is beyond me." Thomas, the connoisseur, insisted that it was his own special blend from his tobacconist on St. Catherine Street, prepared according to his own refined taste. Crandall held his nose, indicated that the contents of the tobacco pouch should be slurred down the toilet. Thomas continued to tamp down the tobacco. He applied a large wooden match and soon had a nice glow in the bowl.

The smoke settled into noxious layers. Ed periodically hacked, coughed, and threw baleful glances at Thomas. Crandall was silent for an unusually long time.

Ed raised his head and looked at the genius. He sensed a subtle change in Crandall's expression. Then it happened. A slight twitch appeared at the corner of Crandall's mouth, rapidly spreading over his cheek to his eye. The eye blinked for a fraction of a second; the twitch disappeared. Ed pretended to read. It happened again. The twitch

CONVERSATIONS OF SILENCE
10

appeared at regular intervals.

Crandall did not seem aware of the "tic." Ed remembered the incident at the "Pig and Whistle" less than a fortnight ago where he and Crandall were drinking beer. Without warning, Crandall ducked under the table. Since the "Pig and Whistle" was off limits to students, Ed figured Crandall was afraid of being seen in the place. But Ed saw nobody. And now . . . this twitch. Was the class genius pushing too hard?

A chair scraped. Ed looked up. Thomas was heading for the pantry again, this time for some cookies. As he left, Ed whispered gently, "His shredded wheat . . . and the tobacco pouch . . . quick, before he comes back."

"Huh? Shredded wheat and . . . ."

Ed leaned over Crandall and grabbed the pouch. Crandall stared as Ed emptied a third of the pouch into the wastebasket. He then ground some shredded wheat between his palms, letting the fragments fall into the pouch. He brushed all evidence of crumbs from the table.

Crandall, catching the spirit of the intrigue, replaced everything in Thomas' corner. He gave the pouch an extra pat, placing it exactly as Thomas left it. They quickly regained their places as Thomas returned and ambled to his corner. Ed and Crandall feigned deep study.

Comfortably settled, Thomas reached for his pouch. Without lessening his concentration, he refilled the pipe, tamped the mixture, and struck one of his wooden matches. With an exaggerated sucking-in, he pulled on the pipe.

Ed and Crandall could hardly contain themselves, but neither moved a muscle.

The first billow of blue-black smoke crackled from the bowl and a small bright spark of shredded wheat sailed through the air, igniting in a miniature parabola. The two conspirators ducked involuntarily. Thomas did not budge.

The fireworks continued. Thomas appeared absorbed in his notes. The sparks erupted, sailing about Thomas' nose like Roman candles. The acrid smell of burning toast filled the room. Thomas concentrated on his book. Ed and Crandall were beyond study. Crandall's face twitched spasmodically; Ed fought off a strong urge to cough. The cataclysmic activity continued until the adulterated tobacco burnt itself out. No one said a word. The entire situation precluded any further useful study that night.

Thomas yawned deeply and snapped his notebook shut. He gathered up his books and the remains of his snack with great deliberation.

"Guess I'll hit the sack. See you two in the morning." He left.

Ed and Crandall just looked at each other.

"What do you suppose happened?" Crandall finally asked.

"I don't know," Ed shrugged, "unless . . . unless he knew all along. Do you suppose he somehow saw us? He must have seen us, the sly bastard." Again the two looked at each other.

Crandall muttered, "Even so, the smell wasn't half as bad as the stuff he usually smokes."

Although it was late, there was no sleep in him. After Crandall left him, he pulled out his diary and wrote:

Crandall must surely be aware of his "tic" but he seems unconcerned. His conversations are logical, lucid. He makes good sense in his answers during clinic. Still, what happened a few days ago in the surgical amphitheater is fresh in my mind. He dozed off and I had to nudge him awake. Dr. Jonathan was looking in his direction.

Could it be that he is trying to learn all things too quickly and too soon? Is he reaching a critical point, depleting some kind of mental and emotional reserve? There is still so much to learn—it will take a lifetime for me. But Crandall is not waiting.

Tommy seems to be doing well—he and his damnably benign disposition. He will make a good family doctor and counselor, be liked by his patients, have many friends. Thank goodness he does not smoke that evil pipe in public.

Ed dropped his pen, stretched, turned out the light. Lying in the dark with his eyes open, his thoughts returned to Crandall. There was really nothing he or his classmates could do. Acquisition of medical knowledge came first for all of them. All else was secondary. But his close friend was a potential casualty . . . He remembered a question from Kant, "Can we isolate reason? Is it a source of conceptions and judgments which spring from it alone?"

He had no answer. He turned on his side and fell asleep.

CHAPTER II

Edward Rankin was annoyed at the world in general, Giselle in particular. Tommy Hutchison mentioned her to him last night and what he told him was responsible for his present mood. In fact, he was beginning to regret his interest in hypnotism. It was creating altogether too much publicity for one who was still a neophyte with much to learn about its burgeoning ancillary applications to medical problems.

Giselle was his girlfriend, his closest and dearest—although Aline ran a close second in his affections and interest—but her promise to Tommy to have Ed perform (perform? How dare she call it that!) before a group some time in the near future was too much to accept, without even consulting him beforehand.

In his exasperation, he dove into the pool with an extremely ungraceful flop, did many furious laps and pulled himself up pool side.

He wiped his eyes on the towel draped around his shoulders. Chlorinated water. He was tired after the strenuous workout. The weariness, however, did not soften his frustration over his swimming performance. It was not good enough. It had to be better—if he was to make the relay team. He was sure to be chewed out by Coach Hatcher because he was doing something wrong.

He gazed moodily into the olympic-sized pool. The raucous shout from a fellow swimmer, amplified in the vaulted enclosed building, startled him out of his abstraction. He waved to his teammates as he started for the showers.

Edward Rankin was compulsive in the matter of sports. His purpose was not only to succeed, but to excel. And excel he generally did. He possessed a driving force which, in competition and intense physical activity, found an outlet for the emotions and deep feelings he kept within himself. If one were to suggest to him that he was taking out his aggressions, he would deny that he harbored aggressive feelings toward anyone about anything. The same drive poured into his studies, as well as his extracurricular activities. Hypnotism, for example. He was a good student and possessed a receptive mind with a retentive memory—a memory that would pursue and prod him . . . that would influence his entire life. A memory that would become a burden toward the latter years of his career.

Edward lost his parents when he was quite young. They were killed in a railroad accident while traveling through Europe. He went to live with his uncle, Matthew Rankin, a widower without children, whose main interest lay in an English woolen mill of which he was part owner. Ed spent most of his early and adolescent years with teachers and masters of the old classical school in England and Scotland. He acquired a sound academic education, but little in the way of the softer things in life. He grew into a man of reserve and sensitivity.

Matthew Rankin died during the worldwide Great Depression. The residual estate left barely enough for Edward. In his young mind, Ed became increasingly determined to be a doctor—perhaps a surgeon. He knew little about what the study of medicine entailed, but he was sure this was what he wanted to be. His reasons were vague, but were perhaps influenced after a teenage illness. After a strenuous game of rugby while in Public School, he was seized with chills and fever. The doctor who visited him was kindly, sympathetic. Edward took to him almost instantly. Long after he fully recovered, he continued to visit the old gentleman, who was kind to him and treated him almost like a son.

McGill University, in Montreal, was world renowned for its high standards of learning. Its reputation in medicine was the highest. After reviewing his finances, Ed decided he would be able to swing it for lodging, tuition, and at least some personal necessities. He applied to McGill University. He was accepted.

Ed balanced his load of obligatory pre-med and liberal arts courses with French and German. He already spoke French fluently and he had an aptitude for languages. The medical courses were just beginning.

It should have been difficult for him, with the shyness and reserve, to cultivate intimate relationships with young women, but somehow this quality in him proved attractive to them. Though no one would suspect it, Ed was a romantic sentimentalist at heart. Perhaps women intuitively felt this hidden sensitivity and found it warm and exciting.

CONVERSATIONS OF SILENCE
14

As he made his way from the gym, Ed decided that he would have to follow a much more rigorous training schedule for the swim meet. Early to bed, more training, no drinking, no partying, no smoking. There would have to be a period of comparative celibacy. He groaned; he was supposed to see Giselle tonight.

On a weekend some time ago he got to know the girl better. A serious student, she had always seemed quiet, reserved. But one night he discovered another side to Giselle. Passion hardly described it. It was after this bout of lovemaking that he mentally gave her the nickname of Grasshopper. It was only a thought, but apt, he decided. Still, he had to make a decision about Giselle's promise to Tommy.

As he crossed the campus, he recognized a classmate sprinting in the distance. The fellow waved and Ed waved back. This simple gesture proved decisive, in his young mind. He opted for the swimming team tryouts, more rigorous training, no alcohol or smoking, abstinence from late hours—and Giselle. It would be a sacrifice, he decided, not without a sigh.

He met her at the usual place—a news stand not far from the Women's College. They hugged and walked away arm-in-arm. Soon, Ed thought, soon I will have to tell her. She was not her talkative self. To break the silence Ed began to hum, sotto voce, a popular tune. As they walked, her preoccupation increased. Ed waited. "Ed," the girl broke in, "I hope you won't mind terribly, but I promised the crowd you would try some hypnotism at the party." His irked expression left no doubt how he felt about her announcement.

"It seems," he said archly, "you have arbitrarily assumed the duties of a theatrical agent."

"I couldn't help it, Ed," she begged, "I was telling Crandall and Thomas and the others about your talent. They think I am spoofing them." The words were now coming fast. "Honest, I just had to do it. I couldn't let anyone say anything against my Eddie." She stepped forward and turned in front of him, stopping him in his tracks. She began to pout and purse her full lips, looking up at him with her large green eyes. Ed's look of reproof slowly gave way to a begrudging acquiescence. Giselle could always manipulate him that way. In his more rational moments he believed that all women were endowed with

Machiavellian instincts purely by virtue of their gender. Her pleading eyes held the unspoken promise of joyful things to come. He succumbed completely.

Giselle hastened to press her advantage. "Tell you what, Ed," she said cheerily, "I'll be the first subject. I promise to be good and cooperative, just so you do not suggest lovemaking before the group while under hypnosis." She giggled at the thought.

"You know better than that," Ed answered mildly. "People just don't do things like that under hypnosis if it goes against their normal moral behavior and aesthetic values."

"I know that, Eddie darling, but with *you* making the suggestions, who knows . . . I might do anything."

They both exploded into loud laughter at the thought of performing a public copulation. Without warning, the thought of *Grasshopper* entered Ed's mind. He was terrified that some day he might blurt the name out loud.

Ed was born to be a surgeon. He knew it early in his medical studies; he could not think of being anything else. He possessed an enterprising, innovative, inquisitive nature that would prove to be the most important quality in his career as a surgeon. It was the thirst for a variety of clinical subjects which carried him into fields outside the required courses. In Chemistry, he studied writings on the pulp and wood industry. His curiosity even led him into the improbable field of hypnosis.

His dabbling in hypnotism began rather innocently. He became interested after watching a proficient staff doctor, who demonstrated on several patients. What excited the young man most was Dr. Bramson's avowal that hypnotism would prove very helpful in medicine in the future. After a particularly engrossing session, he approached Dr. Bramson with some trepidation.

"Doctor, do you suppose I could learn more about the art, by watching you, for instance. I would like to know more about the technique."

Dr. Bramson eyed the young man before him. "You're a med student, are you not? Don't you think you are still a bit young and immature for this sort of thing?"

Ed had no ready answer for the doctor who continued to study him. "Tell you what," Bramson continued, "come to watch me whenever you can, listen to what I say. We'll talk some more at a later date. There is nothing really mystical about it. The technique is quite simple."

It was how it began. He continued to discuss and consult with the doctor and, with increasing practice under Bramson's supervision, he was rewarded with a reasonable measure of success.

He always remembered Bramson's words: "You have the ability, Ed. You merely need to learn the routine of the spoken words and how to present them. Most of the art depends on the hypnotist's personality and self-assurance."

Ed was careful never to attempt to place subjects in deep hypnosis, a possible hazardous state, especially in the hands of an inexperienced person, Dr. Bramson had warned him. At that time, hypnotism was little known by lay people, much less understood.

Edward enjoyed a measure of popularity by virtue of this odd talent. However, he performed only among his friends at the university, carefully choosing the occasion. Though he did not choose tonight, he felt better when Giselle volunteered to be the subject. She was perfect, partly due to the great rapport and the close relationship she enjoyed with Ed.

The party was at the home of Janet Gordon, a biology major who lived in the city with her parents. Ed remembered seeing her once or twice in anthropology class. As the couple entered, they heard violin strains of the Barcarolle from *Tales of Hoffman*. Giselle and Ed looked at each other, wondering if another talent had been recruited for the evening. Ed was beginning to hope that the burden of his performance had been lifted from his shoulders. He simply was not quite in the mood for hypnotizing anyone. Besides, he frequently left such sessions with a headache.

Just then Aline came bouncing into the foyer. Ed's eyes lighted up. Giselle's closest friend was completely different from her in most respects. Aline was blond, blue-eyed, bubbly and buxom. For some obscure reason the two girls were dubbed "the opposite twins," by their friends. Perhaps it was because Giselle and Aline took the same courses at the university, inseparable, even seemed to think alike, also felt the same attachment for the same man.

Aline looked—appetizing. It evoked a look of jealousy in her friend.

"Come on in," she said, smiling. "I want you to meet some new people."

Ed groaned inwardly. New people. He disliked performing in the presence of many strangers. Giselle and Aline both knew that. He sighed. Aline and Giselle both knew how to manipulate him.

Aline hooked a possessive arm into Giselle's and Ed's and pulled them into a large living room. The violinist turned out to be Janet's father. He was a member of a string quartet. It took a few moments of gentle persuasion on Janet's part to convince him that, although everybody loved his playing, it would be a proper gesture if he would leave the room to the younger folks. Her father left reluctantly amid scattered applause.

Giselle and Ed were introduced to the group and they all began to enjoy soft drinks, beer and Canadian cheese. He noticed Berlow Crandall talking to a newcomer to the group. She was a student at the Agricultural College which was affiliated with the university. Crandall was the genius in Ed's class in Medical School. Ed liked him for his modesty and "fairness."

Aline ebulliently announced that Ed was going to hypnotize a subject, and that if they would stop playing the gramophone, Giselle was willing to be the first subject. Giselle looked at Aline with disapproval. It irked her that Aline was taking over. However, she decided against getting too upset with her friend.

Ed had developed a flair for the theatrical on these occasions. He built up the performance by describing the hypnotic state. Then he took Giselle's hand. She bowed and curtsied to the group. Ed ceremoniously led her to a couch. This was old hat for Giselle, too; she was under hypnosis in short order.

Aline, who had witnessed this several times, whispered, "She's under, Ed. She's under, I'm sure." She looked lovingly at Ed. It was always exciting to Aline no matter how many times they witnessed it. She was Ed's biggest fan.

"Now, Giselle," intoned Ed, "I want you to hold out your right arm. Hold it very stiff." Giselle did so. "That's it. Very good. Your arm is now becoming rigid like a steel rod. No one can bend it."

CONVERSATIONS OF SILENCE

Crandall rose from his chair and approached Ed. "Would you care to let me try, Ed," he asked genially.

"Well," said Ed, "a man can be too forceful, Berlowe, and since Giselle will resist fully, something could be broken or injured. Why not let one of the girls try instead?"

"Sure. Only, I thought—"

"Why not let Janet try. She was good enough to let us use her home, so—come here, Janet; see what you can do."

Janet demurred. She was a bit overawed by the entire proceeding.

"Oh, go on, Janet." Aline gave her a friendly shove. "She won't do anything. What's more, you will not be able to do anything." Aline sounded like a veteran.

Janet approached Giselle and gingerly tried to bend her elbow. She tired again with greater effort. And again. She found that Giselle resisted her in spite of all her huffing and puffing.

Crandall could not resist coming over to test Giselle's arm. The muscles were all in a spastic state. This corroboration by one whose intelligence they all admired served to heighten the group's awed suspense. Ed gave a few additional commands, then decided it was time to bring Giselle out of hypnosis.

"Now, Giselle, when I count up to ten and snap my fingers, you will rise from the couch and say, ' My goodness, how thirsty I am.' You will then drink half a glass of water. Following this, you will wake up, but you will forget everything that has transpired. Everything. You yourself will feel in tip-top shape."

Ed wandered about the room talking to his friends as he meanwhile ticked off the numbers up to nine. Then, to heighten the effect, he walked to a far corner of the room, paused, whispered, "10." Giselle rose to the couch. "My goodness, how thirsty I am," she said. She went over to a glass of water on a nearby table, picked it up and drank half the water. She then stepped over to Thomas and engaged in a conversation about a popular book. Crandall followed her around like a sleuth trying to detect any abnormality in her behavior. He was impressed. He approached Ed.

"This hypnotism is very interesting. I would like to be able to do some of it myself. Do you suppose I could learn how to work it?" he asked.

"There is more to it than meets the eye, Crandall. It isn't

something that one can *work*, like a formula or a machine. It's something that comes from within the performer. It is—" Ed was groping for the proper words, "—tell you what—get in touch with Dr. Bramson and tell him that you are interested and that I suggested you speak to him. That would be the best way. He is a decent fellow; he will be frank with you."

Crandall seemed satisfied. He returned to the girl from Agricultural College.

The group had fun as Ed continued the performance with different subjects. He had one fellow kiss everyone in the room, but only on the left ear. He had a girl drinking water which was to taste "like very tart lemonade." She grimaced and puckered her lips in distaste. Everyone laughed. All clean fun. No harm.

"We should have had Elena here tonight. It would be wonderful to see how she behaved as a subject," some suggested.

"I second the motion," Thomas added.

"Elena," Ed queried. The usually voluble "opposite twins" became strangely silent but everyone else had something nice to say about her. There arose a chorus of voices, male and female, all trying to talk at once. Elena was a foreign exchange student majoring in languages. It was apparent she was very popular with the boys. It was also obvious she was equally popular with the girls—but not with Giselle or Aline, judging from their expressionless faces.

"If you can get her to be still long enough," Giselle remarked with some asperity. Ed studied her, trying to interpret the remark. She returned his gaze with a baby-like look of innocence.

Ed sighed. The prospect of temporary celibacy from her loomed more and more like a real deprivation, but the face of Coach Hatcher loomed much larger to him at the moment. A sacrifice—a bloody sacrifice, that is what is was. He would have to tell her later . . . or maybe tomorrow. Soon.

He was roused from his self-pity.

"Why not take Sharon here. Danny brought her. Redheads are supposed to be assertive and fiery—or something." This brought a good deal of laughter, especially from the boys, but stony silence and a look of apprehension from Sharon.

Sharon was new to the group. She resisted emphatically, but two pairs of strong hands grasped hers and pulled her to her feet. Realizing that she was the focus of all eyes and not wanting to be called a poor sport on her first visit, she reluctantly consented.

She reclined cautiously on the couch. Ed proceeded with his usual patter of persuasive words, the preliminary formula of suggestions including the manner in which she should assume the relaxation of her body and limbs.

Ed quickly realized that she was fighting him. He was getting nowhere; she was throwing up a mental barrier. After the usual arbitrary two minutes, he informed the group, "Sorry, but this is not going to work. Sharon is fighting me." This was followed by "ohs" and "aws." The boys, in particular, were disappointed. What did they expect? A nude provocative dance and moral abandonment! They were disappointed because they wished to find out how redheaded Sharon would behave under hypnosis. She was the first redhead to be introduced into their group. Sharon was keenly aware of what was happening. She sat bolt upright. "I knew you couldn't do it, Ed," she crowed, looking around the room triumphantly. Ordinarily, Ed would have given it up as a bad job, a lost cause, but the triumphant gleam irked and nettled him more than a little.

Sharon swung her legs over and was about to get up when Ed offhandedly suggested, "Sharon, if you are agreeable, I am willing to give it another go."

Sharon was so cocksure that she could cope with anything that Ed could try that she willingly lay back comfortably and relaxed even before Ed instructed her to do so. As Ed had speculated, she was so willing, so receptive that she actually proved to be one of his best subjects. Too good!

In a rather short period of time Ed had her behaving like the popular Greta Garbo. She imitated the actress's body gestures and speech. When Ed suggested that she "vanted to be alone," a favorite Garbo trademark, she had the group in stitches, as she tried to assume the serious, haunted look of the beautiful woman. A few more antics and Ed decided that it was time to bring down the curtain on this little performance. Ed felt satisfied. Too smug!

After the preliminary suggestion that she would awaken when he snapped his fingers at the number ten, he went through the usual routine of slowly counting to ten. He went about the room in the usual manner. "... nine ... *ten*" He snapped his fingers. Nothing happened! This was unexpected, unusual. The others, unaware of Ed's dilemma, watched expectantly. Ed bent over Sharon and with some urgency, instructed her, speaking closely and distinctly into her ear. Again, he counted to ten. Again nothing happened.

Ed belatedly thought of why a foolhardy neophyte hypnotist like himself had somehow gotten a subject deeper than he had intended. He felt sick. The others looked at Sharon and waited. Ed promised himself that if he extricated himself from this predicament, without injury to anyone, his abbreviated career as a hypnotist would be terminated. He had visions of being called up before the Dean of the Medical School for carrying on what some considered weird practices. He pictured the headlines of the local newspaper:

"MEDICAL STUDENT AT THE UNIVERSITY RESPONSIBLE FOR DEATH OF REDHEADED BEAUTY DURING FORBIDDEN RITES."

From the back of his mind, Ed heard Dr. Bramson:

"One may bring a subject out of the hypnotic state in two ways. One may leave them alone and they eventually drift into a natural sleep, out of which they ultimately awaken. Or, one may have to use careful force; a physical painful stimulus such as a slap across the face is often effective." Ed opted for the latter measure. It was more practical, he decided. Fewer explanations and no waiting around.

"This had better work," Ed muttered to himself as he sent up a silent prayer. He swept his right hand across her cheek rather sharply. A moment later the eyes of Sharon, the redhead, who was sure that "Ed couldn't do it," fluttered open. She sat up, looked around, confused. For a full minute, she silently surveyed the room and the group. Someone came over and gave her a glass of beer, which she drank soberly. She tried to straighten the events out in her mind, but, as Ed had suggested, she experienced a complete amnesia of what had transpired. She felt her hot cheek and looked in the mirror beside the entryway door and puzzled over the marks on her left cheek . . . marks as red as the color of her hair. His friends at the gathering never realized what nervous strain Ed had been under.

The party began to break up. Crandall came over to Ed and queried, "Did you say, Ed, that the name was Dr. Bramson? There is a Dr. Bramson in the ENT Department."

"One and the same," Ed replied.

Aline, Giselle and Ed were the last ones to leave. As they prepared to go, Janet said soberly, "My father watched the whole thing through a partly open door. He wonders if it was not all make-believe; that your subjects might have been in—er—er—collusion with you." She paused, only to hasten, "That is what he says."

"And you, Janet, what do you think?" asked Ed. His "professional honesty" was being questioned.

"Oh, I think that Dad is old-fashioned. I certainly am impressed, but confused—I know so little about it. Ed, do you suppose that I could be a subject sometime?" She saw him hesitate before answering. He looked dubious. Ed was still recovering from his encounter with the redhead. It was fresh in his mind. Also, his resolve about no further experimenting.

"Please?" pleaded Janet.

"Well—maybe," Ed answered.

The foursome sat down and proceeded to drink to "the evening just past" and to the "evening to come." They consumed a considerable amount of good Canadian beer. They all made trips to the bathroom in staggered traffic fashion. Aline soon developed uncontrollable hiccups. Ed delightedly watched the blond's bosoms upthrust with each hiccup. Giselle became quiet, her usual bibulous reaction. Janet's eyes drooped. Ed was thinking of the morrow.

Aline stood up. She thought the fresh air might help her hiccups. The others followed. Outside, Ed had a girl on each arm. The fresh air seemed to have a salutary effect on Aline, as her hiccups became much less frequent. Giselle was silent, almost morose. Both girls were ready for any change in mood on Ed's part. It was close to midnight. Ed felt unhappy about the training schedule he had resolved to follow. The "opposite twins" had been a source of joy to him. He sighed . . . tomorrow he would tell them. Hell, the night was still young and full of promise. Tomorrow, for sure, he would tell them. Early hours, no partying, etcetera, etcetera. The "etcetera" would be the saddest part. He would console them by saying that it would be only for awhile.

Only for a while—but he would kick himself silly if, after this real sacrifice, he would not qualify for the swim meet. He qualified.

One of the few possessions that Ed inherited from his late uncle was a leather-bound diary his uncle had never used. From time to time, he would jot down his thoughts about university happenings, campus life, his friends and professors. The handsome book eventually would become old and dog-eared with use. The habit of keeping a diary became a permanent part of his daily life. It served as a repository of his private feelings and innermost thoughts.

The book lay open before him as he thought back to Sharon, remembering every detail about his scare and her behavior. He decided that further hypnotic sessions were not for him; not worth what he went through. His career as a hypnotist was terminated. He wrote:

The Sharon affair still troubles me. If only she had not goaded me with her taunts. I sometimes wonder what impels me to do such things; to go off half-cocked on something like hypnotism. "C'est peu necessaire." I wonder what new foolish project will intrigue me.

Ed raised his eyes as Thomas appeared in the doorway struggling with an armful of books and a large bowl of shredded wheat which he dearly loved. Without glancing at Ed, he wordlessly sat down on the couch and settled in, to study and to eat.

Ed slowly turned his head, mantis-like, and studied Thomas for a long moment before returning to the diary:

Tommy just dropped in. A good sort. Friendly, no malice in him. I can picture him in years to come, not only as a dedicated family doctor, but as a confidant and advisor. He will surely be loved by all his patients. He's stable and plodding. Sometimes I wish I had his patience and sense of contentment instead of this restlessness and feeling of lack of fulfillment which drives me and gives me no rest.

He wrote a few more lines, but finally gave up with a shrug, his attention span interrupted. He turned to Thomas. "I'm going out for awhile. Get some fresh air. How about you?" Thomas lazily agreed.

Later in life, driven by the same innovative spirit, Ed would become the originator of new and important techniques in surgery. That he would achieve international recognition would be incredible, even incomprehensible, to the young man who had, that night, so regretfully abjured any further dabbling in hypnotism.

CHAPTER III

Ed would have denied the biological possibility of love at first sight. That sort of thing, he argued, was for poets and songwriters. As for him—impossible. Romance, on the other hand, was something quite different; pleasurable and exciting, without depth.

He was attending a French play, sponsored by the Alliance Française, accompanied by Giselle. Aline joined them a little later. They were chatting in the foyer during intermission when the girls espied one of their friends. Aline began to wave excitedly and motioned to the girl to join them. As she drew near, Aline excitedly introduced her to Ed. "Ed, please say hello to Elena. Elena . . . Ed Rankin. He's from England." It was all spoken in French, the usual custom at these meetings.

Ed and Elena exchanged the usual pleasantries in French which she spoke as fluently as he did. When she later reverted to English he was surprised to detect a mild Slavic accent. It disappeared completely when she reverted to French.

The girl was striking.

Her Slavic beauty was enhanced by high cheekbones and violet-dark eyes. She had full lips which always seemed to be smiling.

He knew he loved her that first day.

He spoke to her with his eyes: 'Elena I find you enchanting. After these few moments I feel I have known you a long time. I am in love with you.' He was in a trance. Although he remained silent he felt quite happy with the inexplicable feeling that they were communicating and understanding each other in their silence. A feeling of elation surged through him the intensity of which he had never experienced before.

Aline nudged him back to reality. She pouted, "Now that you two have met I hope you will not do things to make us jealous."

"Insanely jealous," echoed Giselle, who had not taken her eyes off Ed.

Elena laughed a musical trill. She again looked at Ed. She saw a sensitive face which could mean an underlying gentleness and reserve, a capacity for deep feeling. Probably a romantic sentimentalist as well. She knew she wanted to see him again, to know him better. They looked at each other with frank open gaze.

Far from home she had constantly missed her parents although the University milieu was exciting and she had made many friends. The young men she met were pleasant enough, but her Slavic temperament impelled her to seek someone else, in whom she would find a kindred spirit, whom she could love, enough to give herself fully and know that she would find complete understanding in return.

CHAPTER IV

Ed and Elena often attended the same group gatherings. In spite of his deep feelings, some uncontrollable perversity would sweep him into an inarticulate corner. At the sight of the beautiful girl he felt the flow of words dry up within him while his mind and heart opened up to her. His love and desire for Elena transcended the use of words. He did not know that he had the words that Elena yearned to hear. Thoughts of her intruded into his studies. Her face constantly appeared before him. He was possessed with pleasurable fantasies which left him with a greater love for her. Deep within him there grew a curious melange of sensations; a sense of longing, of great solicitude, joy and sadness. The sadness puzzled him, but he instinctively knew that the sadness belonged with the others. It had to be.

He and Elena moved within a large circle of friends. They had drifted together from disparate and diverse departments. They formed a less sophisticated time. In those years academia enjoyed a high priority for liberal education and the classics. The students valued them as a preparation for the more advanced specialized courses which would prove essential for the productive lives to come.

Sex carried a different connotation in the coed community. In those days, simpler forms of enjoyment, group entertainment, music, discussions, dancing, and outings gave the young men and women mostly everything they wanted. Occasionally, when a boy and girl were overwhelmed by their intense attraction for each other and crossed the

CONVERSATIONS OF SILENCE
26

usual accepted social bounds, their lovemaking was often intruded upon by unbidden fear and self reproach. There was no "pill" in those days and pregnancy was unthinkable. Was this the fear for Elena that Ed instinctively felt during his fantasies of her?

He sought every opportunity to be in her company when his studies allowed him the time. Her vivacity touched everyone around her. They played together and laughed a good deal. There were other moments of awkward silence when they looked into each other's eyes.

It confused and distressed him when she seemed to show no particular preference for him although she appeared to be happy in his company. She always hugged him in greeting... but she did the same to all her friends. He could not know that it was her way—the way of a woman-child excited by strange and confusing stirrings within her.

There were occasions when Ed walked her to the women's dorm. Elena seemed to enjoy these walks, chattered all the way. Once, in late fall, when the leaves were piled high in mounds across the campus grounds, Elena suddenly broke away, scampered like a child through the leaves, kicking them in all directions. Ed, smiled broadly as he watched her cavorting. He felt he should join her... but... it would just not be like him. Elena would have been mildly surprised if he had.

Like a child who was caught misbehaving, she returned to Ed's side and, with an exaggerated sense of contrition, resumed her walk. She rolled her eyes up at Ed with such impish and carefree insouciance, he burst into laughter. She joined him.

Occasionally their eyes met, lingered. Ed's heart flopped like a flounder. His face warmed, reddened. If only, during these moments, he could have the free flow of words he enjoyed at other times with his friends.

His love and desire for Elena was too intense. The words would not come.

The seasons changed. University life brought subtle, but indelible, changes in all who came to learn. It was a progressive self-enrichment, not only with academic knowledge, but with a new way of life's perceptions as well.

It was a beginning.

Elena was an only child. Her father was a wealthy importer. His distributorship included parts of Scandinavia and the Baltic countries. Her early exposure to her father's business generated in her a desire to travel, to visit foreign countries and cities with their strange-sounding names. She was a bright child, had academic accomplishments in languages, including French and English. She was a brilliant student; when the time came, she was offered the opportunity to attend one of the finest universities as an Exchange Student. Her parents decided that she should go to McGill on the recommendation by an alumnus, a well-known writer whom the father knew well.

Her father had other reasons for encouraging her to leave home. He was becoming increasingly aware of early rumblings of world dissension and coming change. Besides, he argued, she was a well-balanced young lady, self-reliant, independent. He convinced her mother that she would learn to tone down her excessive exuberance as she acquired a wider horizon of knowledge and understanding about others as well as herself... they both would pray to their patron saint for her safekeeping; they would light a special candle in church for her.

CHAPTER V

It was Ed's senior year in medical school. He became increasingly occupied with securing a good hospital appointment, after graduation, for an internship followed by a residency in a good hospital. During the summer recess, Ed learned about an available externship in one of the surrounding community hospitals. It was to be for about two weeks. He mentioned it to Elena and described the duties which were not more than dressing cuts, burns and bruises. Also, notifying the doctor on duty for hospital emergencies.

"Isn't there a resort area where you are going, Ed?" asked Elena.

"It is close to a large lake where the summer people go," he answered. "I'm going to miss you, Elena. Miss you a lot."

She looked at him for a long moment, remaining silent, waiting for him to say more.

In those days each hospital, large or small, was an independent facility with its own "elite" medical staff. Each served the local community needs.

Some of the communities radiating from Montreal consisted of

CONVERSATIONS OF SILENCE

large farming areas run by families. Early each morning, the farmers trucked their produce into the city some distance away. The farmers were a hardy lot, educated just enough to suit their needs. Most of them spoke just enough to communicate. Their wives attended to bearing children, especially sons who would grow up to help the father. On Sundays, which they rigidly observed as the Sabbath, the family members seated themselves on the front porch of the homestead, the patriarch in his rocker, followed in line by the oldest child all the way down to the youngest. They usually sat in silence, facing the road. The mother brought up the end of the line, often holding an infant in her arms. She looked washed-out, much like the frequently laundered dress she wore. Her hair was pulled into a bun.

Not infrequently there were two grandfathers, one maternal, the other paternal. They had their own individual rockers, their ancient pipes filled with the strong tobacco grown on their own land.

They were a proud people with an unswerving faith in the church and hard work. Charity, in any form, was demeaning, abhorrent. Their way of life was rooted in their land, nourished in part by their own sweat.

He presented himself at the hospital front desk and was told to wait for Dr. Steve. Ed found it difficult to qualify his first impression of the doctor. He came through the door like a whirlwind. He was thin, wiry, and in constant motion, moving from one foot to the other, hands in and out of his pockets, head turning this way and that, all the time talking. He told Ed to call him only for emergencies—that the city people at the lake were working him blind, with all their damn fool activities; to expect a lot of dispensary work on account of "this crazy weekend crowd." Oh yes—one more thing. Ed would be called upon to do blood counts and urinalyses after he learned the routines. Dr. Steve then dashed through the door and was gone.

After Ed was settled into his cubbyhole office, he went over to the equally small lab. Blood exams in those days were much simpler, less expensive then. Miss Curley, the technician, was a cheerful girl of undetermined age.

"I saw you talking to Dr. Steve," she said. Her voice was laconic. "He's something."

"Yes?"

"To him, everything is an emergency. I've never seen such an excitable man."

"Yes?"

"'Loose as ashes' Steve, we call him."

Ed already knew that in many small community hospitals the medical and nonmedical staff members were a closely-knit group, often related. They could be rather blunt with each other. They possessed the impervious skins that were essential to maintain their obvious friendliness toward each other.

"Loose as ashes?" he questioned, mystified.

She was pouring a reagent into a small graduated flask, eyes fixed on the level. "You'll see." She went on with her work, and Ed went down to the emergency room area.

The staff was limited. Usually, one nurse doubled for emergency as well as operating room duty. Appendectomies, hernia repairs, and various minor surgical procedures were carried out in the O.R. Any major problem was transferred to the city.

Hello, young lady. I am Edward Rankin." He smiled at the nurse who was a few years his senior.

"You're the medical student from the university? Things are quiet for the moment, but I heard there is a fractured ankle coming in. I've called Dr. Steve. Have you ever given an anesthetic?"

"No, I haven't, I—"

"Never mind. He'll probably use local. Here comes Sally. Sally, meet Edward Rankin—our extern for the next two weeks."

"Hello there." She extended her hand. "I'm in x-ray," she explained.

A vehicle pulled up and two husky local men helped a young man ease into a wheelchair. The man was still in his swimsuit. Sally wheeled him away to take the necessary x-rays.

"By the way, my name is Meg. Meg Small." She moved around to arrange the lights over the table. She disappeared momentarily and returned with a trolley laden with neatly arranged padding, splints, plaster cast material, sheet wadding and a pail of water.

Dr. Steve flew in. Before the swing doors stopped moving, he disappeared in the direction Sally had taken.

He soon returned with Sally. Dr. Steve was holding up the wet, dripping film, studying it while walking back into the E.R. Ed could see that it was a simple fracture needing minimal manipulation. The bone fragments were still in good position.

"Sally, Meg, and you—uh—uh—Rankin, help me get this man up on the table." They all helped him out of the wheelchair and onto the table. He was a good patient, did not complain much. The swollen ankle was cleansed and injected with a local anesthetic. When the lad said, "The ankle is good and numb," Dr. Steve manipulated it carefully back and forth.

"Hmmm. Loose as ashes. Very unstable. A form-fitting cast should hold it. Meg, let me have some sheet wadding. I'll also want some four-inch rolls, some reverses, and a walking iron." Ed had to give the man credit. The cast was a work of art. And he worked fast. "We'll keep him here awhile. Rankin, watch the toes. I'll be back to tell him when he has to see me." Before any of them could say much, Dr. Steve had his jacket on and was gone.

In a few days, Ed was setting up the necessary equipment and laying out the usual dressings and medications himself. There were so many minor injuries coming in from the "summer people" that Meg appreciated his help. On one occasion, he assisted at an appendectomy. He merely held the retractor, but he considered it an event.

Almost daily a fractured arm or elbow or wrist came in. Dr. Steve would usually say, "Loose as ashes." He seemed particularly insensitive to the fact that the staff had heard that many times before. He was always in a hurry, coming and going.

About ten days after Ed's arrival, a farmer with a possible abdominal injury and a fractured right wrist was brought in. He had been struck by a truck. Ed felt that he should be admitted for observation on account of possible internal injuries. He called Dr. Steve and informed him about the fractured wrist. Dr. Matthias was available to give the anesthesia.

The patient came down on a stretcher. Everything was ready when Dr. Steve telephoned in to say, "Get him under, Matthias, so I'll be ready to go ahead as soon as I get there." Ed noticed that the wrist showed little swelling.

Before Dr. Steve arrived, a child was brought in. In his limited way, Ed diagnosed the child's problem as "summer diarrhea" with marked dehydration. He went upstairs to do the blood counts and urine specimens. He was getting good at analyses.

He came back downstairs, surprised to learn that Dr. Steve had already come and gone. "The left wrist was 'loose as ashes,' but he handled it well, and it was cast in quick time," Meg commented.

"You mean the right wrist," Ed said.

"No, it was the left wrist. Wait, I'm not sure now, but–I think ..." she said slowly, "... he did the left wrist. It must be the one. I remember him even saying 'it's loose as ashes.'"

Ed decided to go upstairs and see for himself. He could have been wrong of course.

The farmer was sitting up in bed. He was groggy and could hardly focus his eyes on the cast on his left arm. He turned his unsteady head and studied his right wrist; it was beginning to swell considerably. He was puzzled but still too narcotized to feel anything.

An odd feeling came over Ed. He got on the telephone and called Dr. Steve. He tried to give him the news gently.

Probably for the first time in his life, Dr. Steve was speechless, but not for long.

"I don't believe it. It's impossible. Why, that wrist was loose as– Rankin, I hope this isn't just a big joke of some kind. I'm coming over a little later. The office is jumping right now."

Ed checked the x-rays again. No mistake. Later, he found Dr. Steve talking to the injured farmer, Emile Gioffrion. In a mixture of French and English, the farmer expressed stubborn incredulity. Steve's face was a study. He worked his mouth furiously, as if something painful and sharp were caught in his dentures. Grimaces played across his reddening face like a panorama of bad dreams.

"No Emile, my friend," he finally protested. "You do not understand. We did it this way–the–er–*kind* way."

"How so, the kind way? How can it be kind to put the cast on the wrong arm? I ask you that." Emile waved the cast at Steve.

"Your internal injuries Emile; that's what it was. It would have caused too much of a shock to manipulate your broken wrist on top of a serious injury. So what do we do? We make a model of the good wrist. It is like a negative film before you make the positive picture. Now we know what your wrists should look like. All that is necessary is to put a cast on your right wrist and you can thank us for probably saving you from a deep shock."

Ed listened to Steve in disbelief. Steve was beginning to assume an air of innocence. Emile wavered, but chose to believe him. After all, the tradition in his family was to trust the doctor, yes?

CONVERSATIONS OF SILENCE

What a virtuoso~Dr. Steve.

Ed would always recall the incident with mixed feelings, not without a smile.

The time passed quickly enough. Ed was glad to return to his lodgings, to Elena. After relating the "wrong-arm" incident to her, she asked, "This doctor Steve, did you not like him, Ed?"

It surprised him that he did not have a ready answer.

CHAPTER VI

One weekend Ed was busy filling out applications to some of the more prestigious hospitals. He knew tardy applications could result in failure to obtain an internship at the proper time.

After writing steadily all morning and into the early part of the afternoon, he grew bored and weary. He looked at his watch—1:15—gazed out the window. The day was too nice to be wasted, he decided. He yawned, stretched, clasped his hands behind his head, lazily drinking in the outdoor scene. It would be a beautiful day for a picnic. A picnic with Elena.

He went out to the hallway phone, dropped a coin into the box and called her number.

The phone rang many times. Ed knew this meant very little. The girls could all be in for that matter, but each one expected the other to answer the phone; it practically rang off the wall. Finally someone picked it up. "Is Elena there?" he asked. The voice answered, "No, she isn't in—oh, wait a moment. She might be. She said something about getting a paper finished. Hold on, I'll see." She accidentally dropped the receiver which clattered against the wall with such force it almost shattered his eardrum. The girl picked it up, said, "Sorry," and put it down again gently.

A few moments later Elena's voice came over the phone. "This miserable thesis I am working on is making me very unhappy. Here I am, literally enslaved and driven by this ideé fixe. Who is this?"

She could have been talking to the professor or to the janitor. She seemed to take everyone into her little confidences. Ed smiled at hearing Elena's voice. Her accent was always slightly more pronounced over the phone; Ed wondered if she used less restraint in her speech when she was less conscious of a listener's physical presence.

"Elena," he began, "it's a beautiful day. I'm tired. You're fed up. Let's have a picnic. We'll take the bus out to Playfair. We'll bring our swimsuits . . ." Ed left it hanging in mid-air. Elena seemed to be thinking it over. "Dear sweet Eddie. My thesis . . ." She paused. Then, with a spontaneous laugh, "All right, let's go Eddie. It will be fun. Come by in 15 minutes. I'll be ready."

A breeze blew across the Playfair picnic island which they had to reach by a small ferry from the mainland. They swam and frolicked in the water like porpoises. Ed was intrigued and refreshed, as always, by Elena's free-spirited, happy laughter. After the swim, they walked, stopping at times to gaze out over the water. They skipped stones. Elena chatted incessantly. They stopped at a stand and ate hamburgers dripping with garnish.

Elena wore a peasant dress with a wide surcingle and a low-neck blouse. She preferred the dirndl styles which were reminiscent of her European origin. She was beautiful, vital. Ed could not remain silent any longer.

His feeling of deep love welled up within him. It overcame his shyness and reserve. An uninvited sense of ill-defined concern mingled with his love—nagged at him. He had to speak. Elena studied him, aware of the subtle change; she turned toward him.

"Elena," he said softly, "stop bubbling long enough to look at me. There, that's better." He held her chin gently. "You are the most beautiful girl in the world. Surely you have been told that many times."

She looked at Ed for a moment, thoughtful. Then with a pleasant little cry, she leaned forward and kissed him squarely on the mouth. Perhaps it was only a friendly gesture of thanks for the compliment. She started to pull away but found herself trapped by his encircling arms. She gave him a long searching look. At last, she thought, he's saying the words I have been waiting to hear. Slowly she brought her lips to his. They embraced hungrily. They finally separated. Elena, breathless, silent. She studied his face intently. To feel her closeness was enough for Ed. He knew that Elena was soon to reach a change of direction in her life. She was trying to sort things out. As he looked at her he thought of Cowley's words:

> "Today is ours. We have it here!
> Let's treat it kindly, that it may
> wish, at least, with us to stay.
> To the Gods, belongs tomorrow."

But, for us, Ed hoped, there will be all the tomorrows to come.

He was entering Elena's fragile world. In many ways she was still a woman-child. Ed had witnessed enough relationships at the university to know what happened in many such cases. The lightheartedness and fun were always there before a love affair began. Soon the friendly joviality gave way to sad, pensive sweetness and secret whisperings. As if the joy had to be drawn off to vitalize the passion.

Gazing at Elena, he prayed silently, "Elena my sweet and joyful carefree daughter of the Baltic mists. You are beautiful. I desire you with all my being. You were made to be loved. If you let me, I will love you with gentle tenderness. I will do whatever it is in my power to keep you happily dancing and singing. I want you. But you must decide."

A siren blew twice—the last ferry back to the mainland. It was nearly dusk. Hand in hand, Ed and Elena walked toward the dock, meeting picnickers converging from all parts of the island. On board they leaned over the stern rail watching the wake of the boat. Elena turned her back to the stern and leaned on her elbows to let the breeze blow through her hair. Ed felt an intermingling of great joy and thoughtfulness. He wanted to shout, to laugh, to be silent, to cry. Most of all he wanted to be close to Elena. Just to be close. The miracle of the day filled his body and mind.

It was early twilight when the bus dropped them off at campus. On their walk home, they often stopped to look at each other, as if they were discovering each other for the first time. Elena spoke little. When they reached her dormitory, she again studied his face, for a long time. Her eyes moved as if she were imprinting every detail of his sensitive features on her mind. There was a pleading look in her eyes. Ed understood. She was thinking, "Be gentle with me. I am entering your world; much of it is strange to me. But I trust you. I love you."

As if in answer to her silent thoughts, Ed whispered, "I loved you from the first moment we met, Elena. Your world is beautiful, but fragile. Your laughter and gaiety, as well as your joy and happiness are precious. I understand this, Elena." He kissed her eyes gently.

Elena mounted the stone steps. Ed watched until she disappeared. "Elena," he thought, my world is a bittersweet place, you will find. You will not always be singing or laughing. Your smile will often be wistful and sad—but you will be loved. How you will be loved!"

That night, shy, introspective, sensitive Edward Rankin slept the troubled sleep of all young men at such a moment in their lives.

Ed and Elena often had to plan their time carefully in order to meet each other. When they met, they walked and talked. They often stopped to kiss, holding each other closely. When the opportunity presented itself by some happy chance, they made love. Ed was not surprised to find that Elena's Slavic heritage had endowed her with an overwhelming passion that wholly possessed her when they lay together.

Their lovemaking was gentle, tender, long-lasting. He treasured his beautiful Elena as something fragile, although Elena's responses were robust enough to convince him that she would not break.

The lovers gradually withdrew from their usual haunts. Their friends understood, but missed them. Elena's vivacity had always lifted their spirits.

The "opposite twins" pined openly for Ed; however, his absence did not seem to affect their appetites or health. "He isn't much fun anymore," they complained.

Whenever Ed or Elena made love they discovered new and exciting things to laugh about. They gloried in their youth and their union. For hours they would lie studying each other's faces, kissing with barely touching lips. He often teased her about a small dark spot on her lower lip—her only imperfection.

Ed noticed a subtle change coming over Elena. Her demeanor suggested greater insight. She had softened her joyous outbursts. She looked fulfilled and happy. Elena had become a woman in every sense of the word.

The days passed and graduation was near. Ed was appointed to a prestigious hospital in the East. Thomas was going to a hospital in California. Crandall had suffered a mental breakdown and left medical school in his third year for neurological care and had not been heard from since. Elena had come into her semester later than usual, so she still was working hard on her thesis which would require two to three months longer. She would stay close to the university.

When Elena heard about Ed's appointment, she was overjoyed at first, but soon grew thoughtful. The prospect of separation loomed before them; they discussed it many times during their walks.

The night before Ed's departure, they made desperate, passionate love. Afterwards, each retreated into a silence which hung heavily between them, a barrier which neither could lift. A new sadness filled their minds. For the first time the young lovers were facing the future.

Elena spoke first. "Ed, I am saying good-bye here. Not tomorrow. I cannot bear seeing you go away. Tonight the pain is tolerable. The warmth of your closeness and your love is still within me, but tomorrow—do not ask me—"

She rose and started to dress as Ed studied her thoughtfully. He finally rose and dressed hurriedly.

They walked slowly back to campus, their arms around each other. Next morning would be Convocation Day. The day afterward the campus would be deserted. A chill went through Elena. Ed gave her a comforting squeeze. They said little. It was beyond words, this feeling of tenderness and of loss, of hope and despair, of complete companionship and impending separation. It was love, a mutual identification with each other, a giving and receiving, a merging of two minds. It would never die; it was indestructible. It would live.

CHAPTER VII

Convocation Day was exciting, inspiring, confusing, and above all, a day of jubilation.

Ed and his classmates addressed each other as "doctor" without pretext or excuse. The newness of the word filled them with pride and a sense of achievement after the countless hours of study and loss of sleep. It was a good feeling. It carried the promise of still more learning and experience yet to come. For most of them it was but a beginning as there would always be another beginning. Another and another.

Ed was saddened by Elena's decision not to come. He would have liked her to see him in his cap and gown. Thoughts of her subdued an otherwise perfect day. The letdown came later when he discarded the gown and made his solitary way back to his room. Elena filled his mind.

The following morning Ed sought out Thomas who was also packing. They exchanged goodbyes, promised each other that they would keep in touch. After more than four years of close friendship and sharing experiences, their goodbye was rather abbreviated and embarrassing. Each knew that the curtain on university life had dropped, that the next scene would be the beginning of their own and their classmates' professional lives. The fledgling doctors would travel to places far away. Few would keep up correspondence with their medical school friends. "Too bad about Crandall," Ed said. "Yes—too bad," Thomas replied.

Ed returned to his room to make a final check. Strange, he should have considered it his home. He thought of the friends he found, the joy of loving and living; this had been the happiest period in his life. Giselle, Aline, the others—and Elena. He had been happy here; it truly was his home. He looked around the room where he had lost his loneliness for the first time in his life. Its memories would be a source of reminiscence for a long time to come. Yet he knew that most in time would become dim in his memory. All but Elena. What he would miss most about her was not her striking beauty or their lovemaking or all those things that young lovers revel in. It would be the "conversations of silence" he found possible with her. Her complete understanding of him, his compassionate great love and concern that no unhappiness should ever touch her. The full giving and taking of each other.

His room was bare. There was little more to do. He'd shipped some boxes of books that morning. He sat in his old chair and planted his feet on a suitcase. He *was* filled with excitement looking forward to his hospital appointment. It would be the beginning of the life he was born for, the life he was meant for. He fantasized himself in the future as an accomplished surgeon—performing expert operations in the amphitheater surrounded by students and other medical men eager to learn from the "master."

CONVERSATIONS OF SILENCE

He came out of the daydream with a start; it occurred to him that Elena was not included in his fantasy.

ELENA! A chilly loneliness spread through him as his fantasies quickly dissipated. He was leaving a part of himself behind as surely as if he'd employed a fine scalpel to accomplish the cut. Would he be the lesser for it?

She would not come to say goodbye. There would be no warm embrace, no soft whispering, no Elena. "Goodbye, Elena, my love," he whispered. "You will always be a part of me."

It was a conversation of silence. He could not know that, as the years passed, such conversations of silence would often by repeated.

He picked up his suitcase. He turned at the door for one last look at the room and left.

In the years to come, Aline will meet an attorney whom she will marry. The man will prove to be a womanizer and some time after her daughter is born, Aline will divorce him and will subsequently marry a wealthy owner of rich mines in Northern Ontario and will happily bear him two sons. Their marriage will last and Aline will grow into a beautiful buxom matron happily cherished by her husband. Ed will become a faint memory as the years pass.

Giselle will stay on at the University and earn her Master's degree. She will subsequently be granted her Ph.D. in Romance Languages. To Giselle the university milieu will be a constant reminder of Ed. She will join a group of intellectual and literary people all of whom smoke excessively and who drink too much at times. Giselle will occasionally have an affair with one of the men in her group, but will always keep it casual. She will return to England later, carrying with her many wishful living memories of Ed. She will feel a disinclination to correspond with her Canadian friends and will, in due time, become lost to them. She had loved Ed.

Tommy took a one-year internship in a Pennsylvania Hospital where he met a tall, young and pretty nurse named Cindy, from the midwest. She stood taller than Tommy, but he looked up into her beautiful blondness and immediately fell in love. When he completed his internship, Cindy persuaded Tommy to return with her to her hometown to put up his shingle for general practice. Specialization in medicine was to come years later.

He practiced a bit of everything as most doctors did in those days. Cindy worked by his side in the office except when she took time off to have his children. After the third child (all girls) Tommy took on a girl to take Cindy's job in the office and Cindy went back to housekeeping and childbearing.

When the fourth child was also a girl, Tommy became thoughtful but was lifted to sheer happiness when the fifth, and last child was a boy. There was plenty of room for the family in the new mansion he built in Midwestern style. It stood on the lone elevation in town which they capriciously called The Hill. His practice was extensive since it covered a wide area of the surrounding countryside. He kept late hours and worked hard. He prospered. The community honored and loved him. He never gave up his meerschaum pipe, but did change the blend of tobacco after an ultimatum was laid down by Cindy. The years were to treat him and his family kindly.

Elena will . . . but more later.

Ed's first day at the hospital did not quite measure up to a triumphant arrival. He was greeted in a manner bordering on disinterestedness which abraded his sensitive nature. He had yet to realize that in large institutions, personal relationships take time to develop; especially for a newly-arrived intern fresh out of medical school.

Introductions, assignment of living quarters, a proffered brochure on general hospital rules were accomplished in short order.

Sitting alone in his room completed the letdown feeling. "Well, I'm here," he glumly muttered to himself.

CHAPTER VIII

Ed found it difficult to believe that he, a grown man, could become so homesick. He yearned for the way things used to be . . . for the familiar faces and places . . . for Elena. He often spent troubled nights, dreamed that he wandered naked through a populous labyrinth. Nobody noticed him or his nudity. It was a though he had no presence; the people were indifferent. His dreams were often invaded by erotic visions of Elena whom he could never reach, never touch.

The beginning of his internship was a strange new life for him. He was constantly subject to the supervision and impersonal criticisms of both junior and senior residents. Through his inherent ability to listen and to comply with orders, he gradually began to formulate his own direction and to acquire the special training he needed. The appellation "surgeon" had a nice ring to it, but Ed knew the title had to be achieved only through increasingly difficult stages of training. The hospital training would consume five years of his young life.

Many years later Ed would look back to that time. It was before the era of the sophisticated and extensive laboratory complex with its team of specialized technicians, before the expenditure of millions of dollars on computerized equipment into which one could feed a few drops of blood and a printout of multiple and accurate readings would be available in record time. He would realize that during all his professional years, he had in some way lived the whole gamut of progress of modern medicine and surgery. He would know he had helped to alleviate some of the human misery and pain. That is what it was all about.

Ed and Elena corresponded frequently. She decided against returning to Europe. It was fast becoming embroiled in political unrest. She had finally been granted her Ph.D. and was appointed to the Language Department of a western university. In a chatty letter to Ed, she occasionally mentioned members of the male faculty. Ed had no illusions about Elena's social life. She could charm anyone, simply by being—Elena. He suffered pangs of jealousy mingled with great yearning.

He never lost the tenderness, his prayerful solicitude for her well being.

The feeling that she was vulnerable, fragile, never left Ed. He instinctively prayed that, whatever happened to her, she would be spared any real hurt. His concern for her future, even a future not shared with him, transcended his own jealousy and deprivation.

During the latter part of the summer, Ed and Elena were overjoyed to obtain vacation time, finally, synchronizing their schedules for a meeting place. They chose a resort which was a few hours' drive out of Montreal. They had been there before, there would be few guests; it was out of season. The fall foliage coloring would add to their enjoyment.

Ed arrived first.

After registering, he instructed the boy to take the luggage to his room while he went outdoors to drink in the familiar splendid view of the mountains and the lake. He toured the chalet's balustraded balcony which encircled the building, watched a family of raccoons busily foraging nearby. He looked out over the lake for a long time, lost in a limbo of memories until the present intruded. Confused, he found that he could not relinquish his work entirely behind.

He retired early since he had to drive down to Montreal at six o'clock in the morning to meet Elena. The thought of her quickened his pulse, filled him with all the old mixed emotions.

It was a beautiful drive into the city. He parked the car in the square and went through the doors of the Bonaventure Station. As he walked down the long platform, excitement and trepidation grew in him. He saw her first as she hopped down from the lowest step. His throat tightened; his heart hammered. He began to wave wildly, running toward her.

She wore a loose coat which made her look smaller than he remembered, so vulnerable.

Elena searched the faces in the crowd, until she saw Ed waving like a wild man, running toward her. She began to wave in return. When he tried to speak, no words came. How could he put into words all that he felt at the sight of her who was a part of him? He held both her hands in his, looking at her with pride and adoration, drinking in thirstily of her beauty. She tilted her head in her odd little way and gazed at him, also speechless. There was a slight quiver to her lower lip. As if on a given signal, they came to each other in a tight embrace. He held his love in his large arms, methodically kissed her eyes, nose, chin, her parted lips. Elena made chirp-like sounds—she was speaking words of love in her native tongue. The sounds of love brought the flood of memories to both of them. They were submerged on the railway platform in their own private world. It was as if they had never parted.

Ed picked up her bags, excitedly led her out into the square and

CONVERSATIONS OF SILENCE

helped her into the car.

Each realized the other had subtly changed. Each knew that the other knew. Ed was tender. Flashes of the carefree Elena surfaced at the most unexpected moments. They walked and climbed the mountain paths and never seemed to have enough of each other. The days passed quickly. Laughter came easily.

One day, when the autumn sky was clear and the mountain lake reflected the surrounding trees and foliage like a mirror, Ed took the canoe out. Elena was settled in the bow, facing him. The moment was too beautiful for words. They both felt it—and retreated into their own thoughts as he paddled at a leisurely pace. The silence was complete. It was broken only occasionally by the lonely cry of a wild bird; its sound spread across the lake, flying like the bird itself, to finally die in the growth on the opposite bank.

Elena broke the silence first. "You must love your work, Ed. More than anything else." She swished her fingers through the water, creating miniature wakes.

Ed groped for the right words. He finally answered, "Elena dear, I feel I was born to be a surgeon. I cannot think of myself being anything else." Divining the direction of Elena's thoughts, he added, "But that, of course, will take a few more years of training."

She continued to play her fingertips through the water.

When the sun began to drop behind the mountain crest, the autumn chill rapidly developed. Elena shivered and hugged her sweater tightly to her body. Ed paddled vigorously toward the boat landing which was just around the bend. He welcomed the physical exertion. It helped to brush aside his troubled thoughts.

Jean-Paul, the caretaker, was waiting for them at the landing to help them out of the canoe. It was his silent way of admonishing them for being out on the lake so late in the gathering dark.

Tree-trunk logs were burning in the lobby's huge stone fireplace. The flames were reflected dull red in the timbered rafters of the cathedral ceiling. The couple enjoyed a robust wine and delightful Canadian cheese. They were regaled by an accordion player who sang many humorous French verses of a song entitled, "La Grenouille in which the last line of each verse carried a double entendre and was applauded by the few people there, with typical good humor.

Ed and Elena were comfortable and warm. They drowsily wished that this could go on indefinitely, this living in a womb-like insulation. If only the present could stand still. Elena was almost kitten-like in her complete self-abandon to snug comfort. As Ed looked down at her, his solicitude and concern for her future continued to nag at him. He gently pulled her closer, surrendering himself to the fulfillment of their present moments together.

Their lovemaking later, was gently deliberate and slow. They wanted to prolong it forever. Afterwards, they slept a dreamless sleep, barely stirring during the night. The days passed quickly. Just being together was enough for them. They loved and played each day with an almost child-like abandon, heedless to the faint sense of desperation deep within them.

The leave-taking at the station was the most difficult part. The tension in their conversation was barely controlled. When the "all aboard" was shouted through the station, it suddenly seemed that a thousand more words had to be said. Before he realized it, Ed was shouting to Elena through the train window, as it puffed out of the station. He remained transfixed until the last echoes of its departure faded and he was convinced she was gone.

They continued to write each other. But, it became increasingly obvious that intimate . . . even personal . . . news diminished. Ed progressively advanced in his training. His letters were full of his hospital experiences and his aspirations. Elena's letters contained tearful narrations about the plight of her parents amid the confusion of the spreading European turbulence. Her mother was seriously ill and her father was cautioning against coming home. To stay free in the "beautiful America" would be the finest thing she could do for her parents, was the message she received from her father over two months ago. She had not heard from him since then. She felt so helpless.

CHAPTER IX

Elena decided to have weak tea instead of the usual morning

coffee. The nausea abated. She carried Ed's child. It was as simple as that.

Dear Mother, where are you? I miss your arms of comfort, and your kind understanding. I need you.

For the hundredth time she fruitlessly reviewed those days with Ed in the mountains. They had taken the usual precautions. All her thinking was academic and futile; she was undeniably pregnant. She sat before the mirror, started to apply her make-up—a little more around the eyes to hide the puffiness. She had not slept well.

She caught herself applying the make-up hurriedly, carelessly. It was an effort to control the trembling of her hands. She was meeting her class at nine and had to appear normal. Although she could not be more than two months pregnant, certainly showed no visible sign of her condition, she was certain that everyone in her class would immediately know.

Stop it Elena! You are letting things get out of hand. You are becoming illogical.

She steadied herself enough to finish dressing. By the time she closed the door behind her, she looked reasonably calm.

It was the late '30s. To Elena her pregnancy was a personal catastrophe with many ramifications. She desperately wished she could talk to her mother. It was something that one did not put in a letter; besides, the mail was being opened and censored, she thought. Also, it would kill her father if he knew. She moodily recalled how much she had changed from the Elena who left her home to come to the university as an exchange student. Strange, she felt no real regret.

Although Ed was always on her mind, she was determined to keep this from him. She had decided to keep the child. There was really nothing he could do. Warmth and deep love filled her when she thought of the past. Such a short time ago! She allowed the sweet memories to wash over her. Ed would always remain a part of her no matter what happened. This belief transcended the sensual. It gave her joy that she now carried a part of him within herself. It sustained her when she felt friendless, with no one to talk to, to confide in.

There were moments when she felt a dull, heavy loss of the luster of living. IT was like looking down into a black bottomless crevasse, too deep for even an echo. No friends. Except—except George Waverly of the Engineering Department. He was older, admittedly of high intellect and gentility. He often invited her to dinner and was an interesting host. He did not hide the fact that he had strong feelings for Elena. She was attracted to him by his sophistication and his kind consideration of those things Elena professed to like. She had not encouraged his rather decorous advances. But now she desperately needed help and direction. George Waverly–that kind, gentle . . . and yes, attractive man, might take her from this purgatory of insecurity and indecision. After much soul-searching she resolved to turn to him for whatever help he had to offer.

>Goodbye my darling Edward, my love. I know that you will never *forget me as I will never forget you*.

Her first thought was to send George a note inviting him to drop by. Instead, she picked up the phone and dialed his number. When his voice came over the phone, the calmness, she thought she possessed, left her. She realized she knew little about the man and what she was about to do could create a drastic change in the direction of her life. George Waverly could hear the tremulous voice, so unlike Elena's usual buoyancy. Without hesitation he spoke, "Elena, you are obviously in some deep distress. Don't say anything over the phone. I'll be right over. You know I want to help you and I am sure that we can straighten out whatever is troubling you." He hung up without waiting for her to reply.

Elena looked dumbly at the receiver in her hand. "You're sure that you can straighten things out" she repeated. "Dear George, how little you know. How little you can guess." She remembered she still held the receiver and hung up.

CHAPTER X

In some of her letters, Elena had mentioned an engineer; that the engineer was interested in her. She never mentioned whether she reciprocated this interest. Ed's days and nights became crowded with hospital duties. In one letter he reminded Elena that her last letter was received one month ago. She replied, about three weeks later, that she and George, the engineer, were planning to marry, and asked for his best wishes. Ed was distraught for a long time, but he realized that marriage for him was still out of the question.

When his later letter was finally returned—"Moved; left no forwarding address"—he felt the loss deeply. The emptiness would always remain. A niche in his mind was carved out for Elena. It belonged to her alone. It was her private shrine. No matter what course the rest of his life was destined to take, Ed knew that he would never forget her. His memory of what she had meant to him went far deeper than the physical union of two young lovers. They had achieved a union of a different kind. It was the total lack of holding back from each other in all things. The quiet joy, the wordless contentment they had felt in each other's company was the feeling that Ed would miss most. In the quiet moments of the years to come he would find himself "talking" to her, still thanking her for their "conversations of silence."

> *If Elena could have seen into the future, she would learn that George was a very wealthy man and headed one of the largest contracting engineering corporations in Michigan; that he lectured at the university purely as a hobby; that he would worship the ground she walked on; and that she would bear him a first-born, Lyle Edward, and subsequently, a second son.*

Ed was now chief resident in the fourth year of his training. He was hoping to gain a fellowship to round out a fifth year of specialized study. His post-graduate training had taken as much time as medical school. Memories of his college days were becoming faint, except the memory of Elena.

He had developed a cheerful and attentive bedside manner and a dry sense of humor which seemed to be effective with most patients. Emotional cases did not influence his professional objectivity. Still, he always thought of the patient as a whole, not as someone with an isolated physical disability. On occasion, he felt the urge to discuss his "feelings" with someone. Strange, how he felt he could bare his sensitivities to Elena. She had understood him. He would enter the Elena niche in his mind and reveal his deep feelings about his patients' emotions and anguish. Somehow "talking" to her helped. It crystallized his thoughts and helped him to help others in intangible ways. He began to keep his diary more regularly.

CHAPTER XI

Dr. Edward Rankin became adroit in his work. His department chief was aware of his resident's ability to listen and learn. Increasingly difficult cases were assigned to him under the guidance of his chief. There was no doubt that Edward Rankin someday would be what he had dreamed of all his life.

Edward Rankin's reputation as a dependable doctor of good judgment and technical skill gradually grew through the hospital. His quiet reserve were well known—particularly among the unattached nurses. He seemed to be oblivious to their physical charms, although his professional dealings with them were always courteous and pleasant enough.

One morning Ed was in the Private Pavilion talking to his chief. He was looking over the chief's shoulder when he noticed a nurse coming out of one of the private rooms. Her figure was perfect, even in her uniform. She carried the small medication tray as if she were preparing to present it to an august presence. Ed could hear the indistinct droning of the chief's voice, but his eyes were fixed on her. Without warning, her regal walk was shattered; she skidded on something on the floor and twisted desperately to keep her balance and the tray from falling. She barely succeeded, as she directed some inaudible remark toward the floor, then resumed her stately walk. Her cap tilted slightly askew over her ear.

Ed smiled at her unflappable composure. She had succeeded in providing him with a delectable picture. His smile spread into a wide grin. ". . . as I was saying," continued the chief, who had noticed the direction of Ed's gaze and who understood young men, "we'll work up Mrs. Delima's case with the tests I have outlined. She should be ready to discuss at rounds on Thursday, at the usual conference."

The chief wondered if Ed had been too distracted by the beautiful nurse, and felt it wise to check, "You do have them all listed, doctor, don't you? The tests, I mean."

"Yes—yes of course, doctor," Ed answered.

Ed left the doctor and hurried to catch up with the nurse. The cap was still resting on one ear. "How are you feeling?" he asked.

"How am I—what?" she asked in return.

"I saw you. You almost fell."

"It was a paper clip on the polished floor. Some nitwit dropped it and did not bother to pick it up."

"You gave yourself a nasty twist-Miss—er—Miss Brownell," said Ed, looking at the identification pin on her uniform.

"You are Dr. Rankin. I know. I am Peggy Brownell, and I thank you, doctor, for your solicitude." This was accompanied by a wide, friendly smile. It was mischievous and flirtatious.

"Er—Miss Brownwell—"

"You can call me Peggy if you wish."

"Peggy, I am headed for the cafeteria, and if this is your lunchtime, I was wondering—"

"Why not," she answered, before he had a chance to finish. She had a definite coquettish streak; she sidled up to him.

When they had filled their cafeteria trays, Peggy looked around until she spotted a resident from another department. Ed knew him. He wondered why Peggy had steered him toward Elmore's table.

"Randy, meet Edward Rankin. Randy Elmore."

"We know each other," said Ed dryly. "How is the mainstay of the Gynecology department?"

Ed's voice carried an obviously ironic tone. Randy was not Ed's most desirable acquaintance. Randy wore a perpetual toothy smile. He was chummy with most of the nurses, some of whom wound up in his bed. They recommended him highly to each other. Randy was independently wealthy, had a "roadster" with a "rumble seat" and knew the best places to go. His appearance after one of his hectic weekends attested to the general gossip.

It troubled Ed vaguely that Peggy and Randy were on such friendly terms. After a sandwich and a cup of coffee, he hurriedly excused himself and left them together.

A fortnight later they bumped into each other. He had duty that night. She glibly chose another date which was convenient, so he had no choice but to accept. She possessed an unconscious sensuality which stirred long dormant feelings in Ed. Feelings he'd not had . . .

since Elena. Peggy's speech was soft, full of unspoken promises. He marvelled at the paradox in her personality. The personal picture she presented was in incredible contrast with her appearance as the decorous professional nurse.

When Ed agreed to come, she laughed. "Wonderful. I'll be expecting you about seven-thirty." Ed watched her stunning receding figure. For the first time he did not think of Elena. He was finally grasping the present and relinquishing the ties to the past. It was bound to happen some time.

There were only four people at Peggy's—Peggy, Randy, Eustacia Newcomb and Ed. They all had drinks.

"Eustacia is a rather odd name, Miss Newcomb. I am rather curious about it. I hope you don't mind my asking."

"Yes it is. Daddy wanted a girl—and when I was born he chose the name Eustacia."

"It is reminiscent of the Gibson Girls era. I do know a little about it."

"That was it, Father is old-fashioned. They were his favorites. You can call me Stacy. Everybody does."

Peggy came over. "Hey, you two. Come into the kitchen and give me a hand with the drinks. Honestly, that Randy—"

They found Randy slightly bleary-eyed. He obviously had been drinking before he came. Peggy glared at him. Randy jumped to attention, bowed in a weaving sort of way, and in mock-waiter-fashion, burbled, "what will be your pleasure, ladies and—er—gentleman, I think."

Ed reddened but said nothing. Stacy bit her lower lip. Peggy's jaw dropped. Trying to gloss over the situation, she steered him by both shoulders into the living room and plopped him forcibly on the settee. "Now you just sit here, Randy Elmore, and not another word out of you."

He lapsed into a deep sulk.

Peggy came up to Ed two days later in the cafeteria. Randy was nowhere in sight. "I'm sorry about the other night," she started. "Randy was perfectly awful. He should have apologized to you. I'm not speak-

CONVERSATIONS OF SILENCE

ing to him until he does." Then, as an afterthought, "Why don't you come over. Just the two of us. I'll make it up to you, for him. I am sure there is a lot we can talk about."

Her physical presence aroused in him desire which had been long submerged. He responded physiologically, was visibly embarrassed. Nothing like this had ever happened until this sensuous woman came into his life. Up to now, the void that Elena had left in him proved much deeper than he knew. He could not help making comparisons whenever he met a different girl. Moreover, the arduous medical training and long hours over the years, coupled with his preoccupation and love for his work had left him little time for much else. Surgery was becoming his first love.

Now, as chief resident he had more time to spare since he could assign many of his former duties to the junior residents. He began to devote the additional personal time, to things of a social nature.

He harbored no illusions about Peggy; he felt no great moral compunction about the future relationship. Peggy was obviously well versed in the mechanics of love and could take care of herself. Ed was puzzled that a girl like Peggy could drive Elena from his mind. Yet the thought of Peg made his pulse quicken in anticipated pleasure.

She met him at the door in a negligee drawn over a gossamer something. He told her she looked lovely. Peggy was aggressive in her embrace and in the sensuous pressure of her body against him as he stepped through the door. His head pounded; his mouth went dry.

He had her there on the floor in front of the fireplace on a deep pile rug she had thoughtfully laid out. It was not exactly comfortable. Soon afterward, she gently took him by the hand and led him into the bedroom.

Peg was well versed in the art of love-making. It was wild and passionate, accompanied by little shrieks and a final unbelievable grunt at the end, followed by silence. Ed could not help but remember Elena's soft gentle murmurings as they had merged into each other, slowly and fully carrying out the act of love. With Elena, it had been as close to an actual physical union as possible. Elena had tears at the climax. With Peg it was a violent physical sinking into an indescribable act of two writhing bodies which culminated in a state of semiconsciousness and ecstatic delirium. Somehow, Ed felt, there was a destructive quality to this wild love-making—a death and silence following an encounter between violent forces. It left him depleted and empty. Yet he found he missed Peggy when she was not on a case at the hospital. After a few days away from her the wild images returned. He fantasized about their last time together. He called her and was delighted to hear her voice. She answered on the first ring.

"Peg, this is Ed—"

"Oh, Ed. I was just thinking about you—when can you come over? Can you make it now—?"

It was the beginning of an exciting relationship with Peg. She had a wild gypsy spirit. Ed often pictured her as a woman in history. She would have been the favorite courtesan at a royal court of France, or an accomplished, much desired, Hetiara in ancient Greece.

A fundamental appetite smoldered in her. She was driven by it. Some unkind person, using back-alley language, might have described it as something else. Perhaps she was greatly oversexed and could never get enough of love-making.

Regardless of the underlying drive, Ed was rapidly making up for his long period of celibacy. Peggy's professional nursing duties did not seem to suffer in any way. He would have been perfectly content to continue with the arrangement had it not been for a chance meeting with Stacy—in a museum, of all places.

Although he could not afford it, he was drawn to antique furniture, silver and glassware. Bronzes also held a fascination for him. He used to browse through antique stores on the avenue and occasionally visited the art museums, remembering how he and Elena had spent many enjoyable hours that way.

He had read about a special art exhibit at the museum and he was looking forward to seeing it. When he entered the building, he found the crowd dense, but it thinned out as the visitors gravitated into different alcoves and galleries.

Stacy was sitting on a folding chair in front of an easel copying a painting by Raphael. He stepped softly behind her and looked over her shoulder. She did not notice him. "Not bad, Stacy. As a matter of fact, very good," he commented. She was absorbed in her painting. Without turning around, she said, "Thank you," concentrating on her work. "Oh!" She realized she had been called by her name. "How rude of me. Why, it's Ed—Ed Rankin." She looked up at him, the concentration and absorption gradually replaced by a friendly, cheerful smile.

"Ed," she repeated, "this is a surprise. Do you come here often?" She remained perched on her folding chair, her paints and brushes on a small stool beside her. There was a subdued hum of voices as the crowd milled around them with the inevitable tour catalogues in their hands.

Ed looked at her long slender throat and beautifully shaped head. Her lashes were long and dark, her eyes a deep blue. She was beautiful. Strange he hadn't noticed that night at Peggy's apartment. Her voice carried the slightest trace of huskiness. She was frank and outgoing without affectation.

He found himself saying, "Stacy, we can't talk here with this crowd. Do you suppose we could have a bite of lunch together somewhere." When she seemed to hesitate, he continued in a more persuasive tone. "Please—I wish we could know each other better. I have been wanting to call you ever since the evening we met." The truth of the last statement was a bit slanted, but it served to convince Stacy.

She cleaned the brushes and neatly tidied up her work area. She removed her smock, put on a tailored jacket. "Ready?" she asked affably. As she spoke, she stood facing him. Her small feet were turned slightly outward. She reminded Ed of an old engraving of Carroll's "Alice in Wonderland." Ed was bemused. "Alice in Wonderland," he soliloquized.

"Were you speaking to me, Ed?" she asked good-naturedly.

The look of admiration in Ed's eyes was answer enough for Stacy. It reassured and pleased her.

The Plaza was not far away. It would probably strain his budget, but he wanted to have a quiet, leisurely lunch. He instinctively knew Stacy preferred quiet elegance over noisy music. Ed sensed depths to her personality and character which stimulated his curiosity.

They discussed many things. He found her well-read. She had traveled extensively. He was surprised to learn that her father was a professor of anthropology at an upstate university. His travels took him to many parts of the world to study cultures and tribal customs. Stacy, who was precocious in many ways, accompanied him on the less arduous trips, and into areas where health hazards were minimal. Without realizing it, or meaning to, she monopolized the conversation. Ed was quite happy to listen.

Sitting opposite her, he studied her face as she talked. The faraway look in her eyes, revealed she was re-living the experiences she related. He was sorry when lunch was over. "I really have to get back to the art gallery," she said regretfully.

Ed had tarried longer than he should have. The operative schedules had to be revised and posted. Particularly the spinal cases. They seemed to be the most challenging problem. A doctor. In Baltimore, through some of his findings, had opened up an additional field of study concerning spinal discs.

Walking back to the museum, Ed asked, "When can I see you again? I hope it will be soon."

Stacy wondered about Peg. "Do you like opera, Ed?" she asked at last. "I have two tickets to Tosca. My sister Kathy gave them to me. She and Peggy were classmates in nursing school—Kathy can't go—she was called on a case."

His interest in opera was marginal but his interest in Stacy was increasing. He was frank enough to tell her that he knew little about opera but would be glad to come. They would have a bite somewhere before or after the performance.

The evening turned out to be satisfying and enjoyable. She was easy to be with. She seemed to sense Ed's underlying reserve which struck a chord in her own emotional makeup. Ed revealed a sensitivity which surprised her a little. Her impression of a surgeon had always included the notion of a man of dispassionate objectivity, who would not be influenced by the intrusion of sensitive reactions. The fact that a man with a character such as Ed's could also be a cool, adroit surgeon in the operating room intrigued her. She wondered if future events would possibly have an abrading effect on his sensitive nature. She felt closer to him.

A few days after the opera, Ed called. "Guess what, a colleague of mine is letting me have his car. I know a good seafood place in Connecticut. How about it?"

A few days later Stacy called, "Ed, dear, my sister is bringing over her boyfriend. They seem serious about each other. Be a darling and drop by about seven. Can't wait to see you. Bye!!"

Soon they were seeing each other almost everyday. Their intellectual and aesthetic tastes overlapped or coincided. One evening he seemed to be noticing her legs for the first time. Her skirt crept up higher than usual. Ed decided that he had never seen more shapely legs. It was a strange phenomenon with Stacy—his increasing appreciation of her beauty, something that seemed to escape him at their earlier meeting at Peggy's place. The thought of Stacy began to haunt him at inopportune moments—when caring for patients, even in the operating room. She was becoming a part of him.

He remembered that he had not talked to Peggy in some time. The decent thing to do was to call and explain. He dialed.

Randy answered.

"Hello. That you, Randy?"

"Yup. What's on your mind?"

"Is Peggy there, please."

"She—er—says she's busy at the moment. Could you call back later--maybe tomorrow?"

"Oh—ok Randy. I'll do that."

He never did call back.

Ed was now in his early thirties. Soon he would have to weigh his decision for private practice against his acceptance of a teaching staff appointment at the hospital, affiliated with one of the city's medical schools. After much soul-searching, he considered the latter too confining from what he saw of it. Besides, he had no empathy for the more vocal, pragmatic staff members. His observations generated a healthy circumspection for the written or spoken word. As he attended the numerous conferences his own clinical impression guided him most.

When the time came, Ed decided, he would opt for private practice. It carried greater freedom and latitude. He had had enough of the confining institutional life.

CHAPTER XII

He was off duty that weekend. A dark mood hung over him when he rang the buzzer at Stacy's apartment. She had a plate of hors d'oeuvres and some Scotch ready for him. Ed took a generous swallow of whisky. He looked glum, as he reclined on the couch.

They had been making love in recent weeks. She was already in a negligee and looked highly desirable. It was a new negligee. Ed did not promptly comment on it. His preoccupation was not lost on her.

"Problems?" she asked.

Stacy looked down at Ed sprawled on the couch. He was gazing through his glass, studying it like a crystal ball.

"What is it, darling? Tell me. I'll listen."

Ed took another swig of Scotch, twirled the glass contemplatively, smiled at his lovely Stacy and gently pulled her down beside him. He took another swig.

"It's about Angelina, one of my patients," he sighed.

"Perhaps you already know, sweetheart, the good Lord has seen fit to endow the female of the human species with a longevity greater than the male. You and I have discussed it before; that all other factors being equal, the female will outlive—almost said *outlast*—her male spouse." They both smiled. Ed continued, "This, in part is due to the fact that husband and wife start out on their conjugal relationship with the man usually several years her senior. Actuarial statistics toll the bell on the man almost every time."

"How old are you, Stacy? I never asked." The question was rhetorical.

"Well, to continue—I know this Angelina very well. She is a cheerful little lady of 83 who suffered a broken hip. Did you know that women far outnumber men with broken hips? But, here I go digressing again!"

"Angelina did very well postoperatively, with the help of Giovanni, Alicia, Francesco, and Valentina, who alternately brought ' real home cooking,' including chicken soup, to the hospital. She has prospered to everyone's satisfaction, including mine and the chief's. This solicitude on her family's part has had its drawbacks, however. Ernesto took to calling me at the hospital twice a day, followed by other members of the family. The situation became intolerable, Stacy. I finally made it clear that only one family member could call me for a report, and only once daily. That family member could become the town crier for the rest of the community. After a short, noisy, sometimes violent debate, short of internecine mayhem, Ernesto emerged the victor.

"There was no question about Angelina being the matriarch of the family. In spite of hospital rules, they gather together around her bed, sons, daughters, in-laws and relatives of all kinds down to cousins twice-removed. They huddle and hover over her like a football team around the quarterback. From the midst of this congregation, sometimes with a bit of harshness, she emphasizes her wishes. She lets them know who is the boss. I wish you would meet her, my dear. She is a sweet old lady. I am an enthusiastic fan of hers.

"I can hear Angelina's voice above the others when I drop in daily to see her. I have finally become accustomed to the open stares of the members of her 'entourage' around me while I am examining her at the bedside. Just when I turn to leave, they open a passageway for me to go through. After I have made my 'egress,' it shuffles closed. Stacy, it is unbelievable. The hospital rules, as far as Angelina is concerned, are in a shambles."

Ed stopped talking and took another long sip from his drink. And then another. Stacy remained silent. Ed was becoming drunk. He sank further into the couch and looked morose. "Shambles—" he repeated musingly, more to himself. "My darling, there can be shambles of a more important kind; that is what I am coming to. Today, I was alerted by the Social Service office, as well as by the Visiting Nurse facility, that Angelina should make preparations to leave the hospital in the near future. So I dropped off on her floor to discuss it with her. When I approached, the usual conclave and hum of voices greeted me. The portal of ingress parted for me. I broke the news to Angelina directly, and indirectly to the 'loving' relatives around her. 'Now, Angelina,' I instructed, 'the Social Service lady who will visit you must know with whom you will live and she will obtain the necessary transportation for you. A nurse will visit you twice week. This is all you will now need in the way of care.'"

"The silence that followed my pronouncement was ominous, much worse than the usual noise. Angelina looked from one face to the other. They all seemed to be looking elsewhere, as if they were curiously attracted by some architectural anomalies they'd suddenly discovered in her room. Angelina's smile slowly faded and, what was more heartbreaking, the bright light in the matriarch's eyes gradually dimmed.

"I turned to Valentina, who was always able to shed tears at will for mama; then to Giovanni, the belligerent one–he always had it in for most doctors. He would always preface his aggressiveness with 'after all, she is my mother,' as if motherhood were a rarity. I shifted my gaze to Ernesto, the town crier. All of them—deeply silent. Angelina broke the silence herself. "Doctor, I will let you know. I will tell you soon."

"She slowly turned to the group and informed them that she was tired and asked them to please go. With forced gaiety she called after Valentina, 'Valentina, dear, don't forget to bring my chicken soup.' The clan filed out. I was about to leave when she called to me. 'Doctor, please come back. I would like to talk. Please wait uno momento.'"

"Yes, Angelina," I said.

Angelina reminisced, "When Mario, my husband, was alive and we had our own home, Mario worked hard. He made good money as a bricklayer. We saved. When Valentina married, we gave them money to help them get started. Also when her babies came. Ernesto was always losing his job and we helped him out. After Mario, my dear husband, died, my bambini still came to me for help. So I help them."

She continued, "I wanted to give them everything, doctor, because they are my children. They gave me precious grandchildren." She had a faraway look.

There was a long silence. I could study the little lady's face. It was not difficult to interpret the interplay of memories reflected in her face. Finally, Stacy, as if aroused from a deep reverie, she whispered, "Now I have nothing. They have what was once mine. If I kept it, doctor, would they still be around my bed now? Can you answer me that?"

"Angelina," I answered softly, stroking her wrinkled cheek, "I'll send up Mrs. Clarke, our Social Service worker, and I'm sure she will arrange something for you. She is very good that way." I knew that it was not the answer Angelina wanted. But I could think of no comforting words. I felt so useless. She absentmindedly played her rosary beads through her fingers. She has lived, I know, by the old unquestioning principles of faith and prayer. Stacy, Angelina possesses—oh, excuse me! What on earth made me hiccup like that? Where was I? Oh, yes—I was saying—Angelina's kind of faith, although unproven by logic, or dissected by intellectual theologians, is the true belief. There is no need for canonical interpretation by ecclesiastic officials for such as Angelina. Her belief is simple, unassailable. Stacy, you know I am not a religious man as far as church-going is concerned, but there are aesthetic and spiritual values which we must all hold. Or else we are nothing but empty shells."

Ed's head was bobbing a little with an effort to hold himself up. "Angelina is probably thinking of that other happening, almost two thousand years ago, when there arose the cry,

> 'Where are the apostles gone—the ones who pledged support and loyalty. Where are the apostles gone?'"

Ed closed his eyes and was silent.

Stacy placed his head on her breast. She kissed him, rocked him gently like a child. Tears welled up in her eyes.

Although her small frame seemed inadequate to the task, she draped his arm around her neck, and with her other arm around his waist, half dragged him into her bed. She removed his clothing. She then lay down quietly beside him, laying a protective arm across his body.

Ed stirred a little, half opened his eyes, and murmured "Dear heart, I love you. Marry me, will you? Be my wife."

"Yes, Ed," she answered. "We have been as one for a long time now."

That is how Ed proposed and Stacy accepted.

CHAPTER XIII

Ed and Stacy were married by a magistrate. Later, due to insistence from Stacy's father, they endured the formality of a church wedding. Satisfied that his daughter was truly married, her father returned to his anthropological studies.

Ed rented a ground floor apartment to start his office. The living room area was converted into a waiting room, the dining room into the consulting room, and the bedroom into an examining room. A small den was converted into the bedroom and a closet into a small laboratory equipped with gas and electricity—it also boasted of a hot plate on which light housekeeping was feasible.

The office equipment came in. His stationery had been printed. "Edward Rankin, M.D.C.M.," it read. His hospital appointment was granted. Ed was launched into private practice.

Ed and Stacy walked arm-in-arm from room to room, surveying their "estate." Ed smiled. "Well, what do you think of it, Stacy?"

She sighed, "The living quarters are not exactly sybaritic . . . but one year from now, Ed," she pointed to a wall at the end of a short corridor leading to the bathroom, "we are going to break through that wall there, and have the next apartment as well. You just wait and see, Ed. Just wait and see."

She was prophetic about that. Less than a year later he was able to accomplish it.

He was fortunate in being appointed surgical consultant to a hospital located 40 miles north of where he did most of his work. But it meant going out in all sorts of weather and time of day or night. Nevertheless, it proved in the long run to be a more reliable source of income to him than the larger hospital to which he was attached. The hospital was strategically located near the crossroads of two important highways, and all traffic casualties were funneled into its Emergency Room. At times he was very busy, with severe injuries following multiple car accidents.

One icy day he was on his way. He had an early schedule to meet at the hospital and was in hurry because he had started out late. He had taken this trip so often in the past that he swore his car "could find its way by itself, like a homing pigeon." He knew every twist and turn in the road. Suddenly, his car, traveling at 50 miles an hour, struck a patch of ice under an overpass. As the car hit the ice, its rear swerved to the left. Without thinking, he spun the wheel to the right. The car skidded wildly. It made a crazy 180 degree turn into the wrong lane. "Thank God it is early in the morning," he thought. "No cars coming from the opposite direction." His mind fell into a dull awareness, as the car turned in a mad merry-go-round, up and over to the opposite side of the parkway. He heard a crash. His eyes instinctively closed as he brought his arms up in a wrap-around instinctive gesture.

Then silence. Complete silence.

He slowly opened his eyes and squinted into the brightness of a winter-blue sky framed by the windshield. He felt no pain but made a rapid clinical assessment. He knew that he was all right—nothing broken or ruptured; he could move. Odd, how trained instincts take over in a mind tuned to encounter and handle emergencies. Car

CONVERSATIONS OF SILENCE

accidents with shattered limbs had been his daily fare. He realized the car was upended on its tail; he was looking heavenward—visually, at least. Then he wondered what was holding the car from dropping back into the ravine he could see reflected in the rear view mirror. He was afraid to so much as sneeze. Before realizing what he did, he carefully leaned toward the dashboard and turned off the ignition key. The possibility of a cracked block, and escaping oil and gas bursting into flames, occurred to him as an afterthought.

When the car struck, he was forced against the padded seat back. This had absorbed the shock of the impact. He had escaped without even a scratch! He experienced no nervous tremors, felt no nausea or shock, none of the expected symptoms. He was troubled by the absence of any other car on the parkway since he could not stay here indefinitely. Fear that the car would disengage itself from whatever was fortuitously holding it was constantly with him. Still, overall, he was calm, which mildly surprised him.

As if on cue, a car came toward him from around the bend. A guardian angel could not have arranged it better. It was a state trooper on an early tour of duty. He stopped his car about 20 feet away from Ed's, got out and walked toward the wreck with the usual gait that these men of authority assume as a prelude to writing out a speeding ticket.

Ed carefully turned to watch him. Soon, a number of cars appeared, with the drivers tumbling out and running toward his upended vehicle from several directions. It was like what happens at sea when a previously empty ocean is suddenly roiled by numerous converging wakes produced by the dorsal fins of sharks milling around the car, disregarding its sky-gazing occupant.

The trooper knew Ed was a doctor by the license plates. He signaled Ed to roll down the window.

"Are you okay?" he asked.

Ed was getting angry. "Will somebody get me out of this damn car before I burn to death or get carried with it down below. I am afraid to move or sneeze inside here."

The cop smiled tightlipped and admonished, "Take it easy, Doc. The transmission is jammed tight against an upright post you snapped off clean as a whistle." He paused. "How fast were you going, anyway?" Looking down into the ravine, he reflected, "You know what's down there, Doc? You are not far from Clifton. That's a cemetery down there." He continued, "You can come out; the car won't budge. Here I'll help you—"

Two bystanders held the door open. Ed was helped down from his high perch. He looked under the car and exhaled a soft whistle. He went pale; his mouth was suddenly dry. The posts that supported the rustic fences which extended along the parkway, measured approximately six to seven inches in diameter; they were heavy posts. In addition to the horizontal logs which were smashed, the upright posts were sheered off cleanly by the transmission of the car, which then came to rest on the stump. It was firmly braced, allowing the rear wheels to roll backward a few feet. The top of the post had carried about 10 feet of fence with it to the bottom of a hollow. Ed could see the cemetery.

While Ed was gazing down into the hollow, the trooper approached. "Doc, I am going up the road a ways to light some flares to alert any cars coming around the bend. Then we'll try to pull the front of the car down and see what happens." He returned a few minutes later and, addressing no one in particular, called out, "Will some of you guys help me get this car back down on the road."

A number of hands reached up and grasped the front bumper. For an anxious moment the car teetered backwards but it began to come down, gently at first. When the front reached about one foot from the ground, it gained momentum. Someone shouted a warning and the volunteers jumped back. The car came down with a loud noise, followed by a cloud of loosened rust and mud. A confusing cacophony of many voices gave free advice—"instant" mechanics. The engine and front end were intact, the rear bumper was bent, and the right rear wheel wobbly and out of line. The gas tank was undamaged. The car was tough.

Ed climbed into the car, turned on the ignition. No more than 40 minutes had elapsed. The engine turned over.

The trooper came over. "Doc, drive it across the road into your own lane. Where were you headed, anyway?"

"I am headed for Community—a hip repair," Ed replied. "I should have been there long ago. Could you please radio a message to headquarters and have them telephone the hospital? Tell them I'll be there shortly. I am sure they are trying to locate me. I'm glad the car can still run."

The trooper studied Ed for a long moment. "You mean you're going up there? To do the operation? It's none of my business, Doc, but with the shock to your nerves and your almost getting killed—I mean, you're sure you're up to it?"

Ed could truthfully say that he felt calm and "in control"—whatever that was supposed to mean. He answered, "Really, I am fine, just fine. I'm alive and intact. The car runs, so there is really no reason I shouldn't get going. I'm okay. Will you please get those messages out? I'll deeply appreciate it."

Shaking his head from side to side, the trooper gave in. "Okay. Just remember, the right rear wheel is badly out of line. You know these disc wheels are not that strong. So take it easy." His temporarily submerged professional duties resurfaced at this point. Like a character actor changing the timbre of his voice as the plot demanded, he spoke in his best "trooper" voice, leaning in through the open window. "The broken fence is the property of the state and you will probably get a bill for its repair or replacement."

Ed nodded and drove off. He was puzzled by his sense of calm. He could think about the incident objectively, as if an alter ego were sitting with him in the front seat and dispassionately gazing and studying him.

Ed parked the car in the hospital lot and got out, not looking back at the damaged car. For the moment it was of no consequence. He pushed the entrance door open. The surgical resident and O.R. nurse had their heads together, talking in low tones. They turned at his approach. Ed explained without slowing his gait, "I had a bit of an accident—held up for a few minutes—have they called for the patient yet?"

He disappeared into the surgeons' dressing room. He felt their eyes trained on his back for a few moments.

The patient was a very old little lady. Her lips had fallen inward, due to the absence of her dentures. She was well sedated. Ed asked, "How are you feeling, Mrs. Linch? Are you having much pain?"

Her response was slow.

"You will feel much better in a few minutes, Sadie." He gestured to Dr. Ullrich to start the anesthesia.

Ed forgot the mishap on the parkway. The only reality was the operating room. Fractured hips were commonplace and this one did not prove to be a problem. With the operation completed, he changed back into civvies and, after once more checking out the old lady, left the hospital.

The afternoon office hours were filled with the usual run of aches, pains, limps and bumps. After the last patient, his secretary came in and fussed around the office, checking out the electrical appliances, and generally tidying up the office for the night. He said good night and went home.

Stacy greeted him with a kiss on the cheek. After a resume of the day's happenings, including her activities in the ladies' hospital auxiliary, they sat down to a satisfying dinner. Ed did not mention the morning.

With his practice burgeoning, Ed began to nurture the habit of a cognac in a snifter after dinner. He insisted that the day was not complete without it. Stacy preferred something less strong. He mixed a little Grand Marnier with the cognac to make it more palatable for her. "Cognac is not for everyone," he used to say when she grimaced at the powerful fumes from the snifter. "You have to place it on the tip of your tongue—just a sip—and then allow the delicate bouquet of the brandy to trickle backwards on the tongue where it can be really savored. Some cognacs are good; many are mediocre."

This evening he was having some Henessey X.O. when a little tremor began in his hand. It started in the fingers and gradually migrated up the arm. When he placed the glass to his lips, it rattled against his teeth as if he had suddenly been affected with the palsy. He shifted the snifter over to his right hand, only to witness the same phenomenon. His knees began to shake and his body twitched.

Stacy looked across to Ed. His complacency was tottering precariously. A terrifying vision of the crazy skidding of the car appeared before him. He could hear the crash of the splintering fence. He jumped up, spilling the cognac. He shouted, "My God, Stacy, I had a horrible near-fatal accident this morning. Come here and help me lie downon the couch. I hardly have the strength to stand. The mere recollection of it is enough to give me the shakes. Let me tell you about it—"

◆◆◆

CONVERSATIONS OF SILENCE
64

Whenever Ed thought back to that day, he speculated on the conditioning that must go into what finally produced a surgeon. It was not only the mastering of techniques; it was also a discipline of the mind. The finished, skillful doctor had to be more than a fine technician. Much more. Without this discipline he was like a healthy, vigorous body without the spirit.

Given a chain of reverses or distractions—or intrusions into his personal daily living—the doctor experiences the same anguish and frustrations everyone does. He may bring these feelings with him into the hospital, but when the patient is wheeled into the operating room, all extrinsic problems must be left behind. As the operative area is draped and prepped, his attention focuses exclusively on the area exposed under the bright light.

Ed assumed that this same conditioning must have come into play at the time of the crash. It permitted him to go ahead and do the surgery. It carried him along through the rest of the day. It deserted him when he no longer needed it.

He described his feelings about the incident one night in his diary:

Reaction apparently can be caged, but eventually it will break loose, with all its pristine violence and depth.

The years pass quickly for a busy surgeon, not so quickly for the doctor's wife; not unless she can throw her pent-up energy into hobbies, other activities or enterprises. Stacy became involved with the Hospital Ladies' Auxiliary. They raised money for the hospital through luncheons, the Charity Ball, fashion shows and the gift shop. Stacy became chairwoman of the gift shop committee, a post which she was to hold for over ten years. She found that she had less and less time to do her painting and sketching. Ed early realized the importance of sharing his life with his wife as much as possible. Although he could ill-afford the time away from his work, he made it a point for them to get away at regular intervals. They took trips and occasional cruises together. Through their joint effort it became feasible to take trips or cruises together every three to four months. Each vacation turned into a fresh honeymoon. Stacy was content; she could observe what happened to idle doctors' wives with much time on their hands.

His practice was well established. He moved his office to a new professional building. Surgery was scheduled for mornings, office hours filled afternoons. He gave one day a week to surgery at the University Hospital where he also held a teaching appointment and made rounds with the resident staff.

It constantly surprised Ed that most people believed an orthopedic surgeon was a doctor "who treated broken bones." The public was unaware of the versatility of the orthopedic surgeon. This branch of surgery included conditions involving practically all areas of the body except the head and abdomen. All diseases, infections, injuries and deformities. Also many conditions and disabilities arising from disasters to the nervous system. Ed was becoming increasingly occupied with back and spinal problems. It was a difficult field, not well understood, a challenge. He practically threw himself into the further study and surgical treatment of this refractory problem. Later on in life this was to become the most successful and extensive part of his specialized practice. Of course, there were the "broken bones," but these constituted only a small percentage of Ed's cases. The percentage, however, becomes immeasurably greater when nations become engulfed in wholesale destruction. The orthopedic surgeon becomes indispensable during war. WAR!

Dispirited and broken Chamberlain, Prime Minister of England, announced over America's radios one early morning, "England is now at a state of war with Germany." Millions heard the fatigue, disillusionment, and futility in his voice. They sensed that this evil thing was creeping perceptibly closer to America.

All Americans were talking about the war. Then, on a bright Sunday morning of 7 December, 1941, the Japanese bombed Pearl Harbor. The news flashed across the country. America was stunned. Edward Rankin and Stacy were among those who heard the news. They looked at each other, knowing what it meant. There would be a great change in their lives. How great, neither one could guess. A vague apprehension crept through Stacy. It enveloped her, isolated her from everything around her; even from Ed. She felt small, alone, in the creeping misery which was taking hold.

Ed was angry. He realized the implication of the news. He knew that he would eventually have to leave Stacy and his practice. He remembered the trip (he always called it his "pilgrimage"), several months earlier to Washington, to acquire a classification in the Reserve Medical Corps. In view of what had transpired then, Ed had no illusions about being called up. No illusions. And soon.

Throughout the previous summer the entire atmosphere was charged with rumors about an impending clash with Japan. One day, on rounds at the hospital, Ed heard a voice in the background saying, "With my years in the Reserves, I am sure I'll get a commission of—" The other voice answered, "I am attached to—Reserve Unit. I know my rank will be Captain—"

The talk disturbed him. Coming from another country he held no reserve rank in any service unit. He was unattached.

When he got home that evening and discussed it with Stacy, she agreed, "At least you should know where you stand if—if—something should happen."

Ed spoke to his chief at the university a few days later. The chief had the idea to call a Dr. Leadbetter in Washington. The doctor, in turn, suggested that Ed come to Washington; he would give Ed a note of introduction to the Commanding Colonel at the Walter Reed Hospital.

There was nothing special to remember about the trip, except that when they reached Maryland, Stacy remarked that they were getting into what was considered part of the South. Was it his imagination or did she think she was "feeling warmer" when she took off her light jacket? After all, they were in the South!

The Colonel met Ed in his office at Walter Reed. Ed gave the Colonel the letter of introduction. He read it and placed it on his desk.

"What can I do for you, *son?*"

"Well, I hear everyone talking about their reserve units. They all seem to know just where they stand in case of hostilities—"

"What hostilities?" he asked, a military crispness creeping into his voice.

"Well, they are all talking about Japan. If anything happens, I want to be sure that I will be assigned to an Orthopedic Service. I hear some strange stories about the Medical Corps."

"What stories, son?" He smiled by pulling the corners of his mouth down--a deprecating smile. Ed did not know what he had said to amuse the Colonel.

"I hear that medical men are assigned to unrelated surgical units, that such as I could be assigned to an ear, nose and throat unit, for instance. Colonel, I am no good at anything except as an orthopedic surgeon. Since I have no Reserve status, I was worried about where I would stand."

The Colonel thought for awhile. He got up from behind his desk, came around it to Ed. He was a relatively short man but every inch military.

"Son," he said, "as it stands now, there are no—no hostilities, as you say. Not being in the Reserve, you would probably not be called for some time. Why do you want to go now?"

Ed answered, "Mostly because I want to make sure about myself. Besides, Chamberlain—we all know it is only a question of time."

The Colonel took Ed's address and recorded some additional data. "Son, I have all the information I need. We can give you a commission, a Lieutenancy, when you are called."

Ed knew little about Army rank. Imagine, he thought, an officer right away! An officer! Especially since he had no Reserve status! It sounded good to him.

When he and Stacy returned home, he discussed the trip with his colleagues. He informed them that he was assured of a commission even though he was not in the Reserves. They all looked at him, astonished. "You mean that you will be only a Lieutenant? Is that all he promised you, you idiot? You deserve at least a Captaincy, with your Boards and all." They could see the expression slowly change on Ed's face. Thoughts of doubt and suspicion, changing to disenchantment filled his mind.

"You mean he—was pulling my leg or—he won't do anything about my visit to him?"

No one answered. Their silence was more than a corroboration. Ed sighed. If he had minded his own business and not dashed off to Washington, he would have been better off.

◆◆◆

CONVERSATIONS OF SILENCE

After Pearl Harbor, Ed was among the first to be called up. Even ahead of many of the Reserve men. This is what came, he was told, of "volunteering." "Never volunteer," he was advised. He was inclined to agree, he thought ruefully. However, his orders read: "To the Orthopedic Service, Station Hospital, Fort Sam Houston, Texas." This made a difference to Ed. It meant exactly what he hoped it would. The Colonel had not forgotten! He might have been amused by Ed's naivete, called him "son," smiled in that curiously downturned way, but he also must have been in dead earnest when he gave his promise. And Ed was going in as Captain.

Tripler's in New York was the place to go for military uniforms. The salesman helped Ed select the articles he needed. When he stood in front of the mirror completely outfitted, the reflected image made little impact on him other than he saw a man who looked uncomfortable and strangely out of place. Immense changes would come into his life; an unknown future lay ahead. His reaction was vague and unformed. He was in a state of apprehension and confusion which dulled his senses.

Ed was leaving the next day.

Stacy and Ed talked far into the night—a sober discussion about mundane matters such as household arrangements, insurance, taxes, admonitions, interspersed with lovemaking which had a melancholy sweetness all its own, perhaps a touch of desperation.

They finally slept. Both awoke at the same time to greet the last day they would be together for a long time to come. Ed donned his uniform, his first day as a Medical Officer. At breakfast, seeing him for the first time in full uniform brought tears and quivering lips to Stacy. Her husband was already a different man. It seemed as if Ed had left some time before and a stranger was sitting in his place.

Most of the country's railroad system was rapidly pressed into service for the transportation of armed services personnel. Ed had to board a train at Harmon. It would have been more convenient to go to Grand Central, but his orders read otherwise. It was an early evening in August. A large crowd was gathered on the station platform. Young brides cried softly and were gently, albeit awkwardly, comforted by their young husbands. Some had been married just a few days before. There were men from army reserve units and had said their goodbyes at home. Tearful, public leavetakings were not for them. They wore their uniforms comfortably, unlike the new recruits.

Ed and Stacy were part of a separate silent group. Their arms were around each other's waists. They were all talked out. There was nothing more to say. After a long silence, Stacy spoke in a remote, somewhat absentminded tone. "Today is my birthday. The tenth of August."

Ed remembered it with a start. Neither one had thought about it. He found it difficult to wish her a happy birthday.

"I'm sorry, Stacy," he said in an apologetic whisper, "it slipped ;my mind." He lapsed into silence.

The sound of the approaching train alerted the crowd as they all turned their heads in its direction. After a moment of indecision, people started to pick up bags and coats. The station platform resounded with disorganized noise and bedlam. There were final shouts and admonitions mingled with assurances of undying love and nervous goodbyes.

There followed much banging of doors. Soon afterward, the train slowly started, rapidly accelerated, and was gone.

Those left on the platform followed it silently with their eyes. Each person wrapped in a separate cocoon of thought. A depressed silence hovered over them as they began to disperse into the gathering dusk. It was the beginning of a long vigil for the return of their loved ones. Much would happen "over there." Many changes would take place in the lives of those left "here." It would never be the same again.

Stacy first felt the deep, poignant loss when the caboose of the train disappeared in the distance. "He's gone," she thought. "He's really gone away and not coming back. Tonight . . . or any time . . . soon. He's gone and I am left alone." Tears blurred her eyes.

On her way home, she thought of the children at the railroad station and she envied their mothers. She wished she could have had children. They would wrap their little arms around her neck and cling to her. She would hug and kiss them and they would comfort and cheer each other.

CONVERSATIONS OF SILENCE

At home she poured herself a drink and carried it into the room where Ed kept his clinical books and did his paper work. She sat down at his desk and sank into thought. The diary which he always kept was gone, of course. He would be using it. Pens and pencils were neatly placed in a tray beside the memo pad on the right side of the desk blotter. She retrieved a pen from the tray and placed it alongside the pad ready for him to use when he came in. It was still unreal, his not coming home. She wondered how long it would take for her to shed the daily expectation of his return.

The nights proved particularly bad. She missed his warmth and closeness. She continued to sleep on her side of the bed, often stroking Ed's pillow before turning out the lights. She gradually developed the habit of reading for long hours in bed before falling asleep. There were occasions when her loneliness and her desire for Ed became overwhelming; she would impulsively hug Ed's pillow and at last fall asleep with it tucked between her legs. As the months dragged by, she hoped that her sexual longings would become less intense and less frequent.

The Army Medical Corps was rapidly built up around the nucleus of a relatively small regular Army Medical Corps. Hardly a week passed without more doctors being called up and ordered to various Service Commands in the country. Practically all of the younger doctors, except those exempted for physical reasons, were eventually called up. Soon there developed a community of doctors' wives whose husbands were in service. They arranged group activities to raise money for the war effort and for the hospital, as well as for their own social activities and entertainment. Stacy began to paint in earnest again, mostly landscapes and scenes of nature.

She developed a closer friendship with Dotty, whose husband Clyde, markedly overweight, was declared unfit for overseas duty, but whose professional training had earned him a commission attached to the Adjutant General's office. Theirs was a friendship which would last.

One day Dotty dropped by and found Stacy absorbed in a relatively large canvas. She stood behind her watching the colors Stacy used. There were slate-gray and dark blue cumulus clouds masses alternating with shadows of brooding black. Emerging from the clouds was a partially obscured cold, pale full moon shedding its anemic light upon a long abandoned clapboard house. The house was done in gloomy shades of blues and grays. Part of a shingled roof of the adjoining lean-to had fallen in.

It was a scene of abandonment and neglect. It was a picture of devastation made more depressing by the subtle impression of a comfortless cold night.

Dotty studied it in silence as Stacy painted, her eyes glued to the canvas. Dotty shivered involuntarily. "Is there really such a place?" she asked. "Don't you always paint from sketches?"

Stacy stopped painting. She slowly put her brushes down. Without warning her shoulders began to shake as she sank her head into her hands. Her pent-up feelings broke through with a succession of deep, uncontrollable sobs which shook her body. She turned to Dotty and wept on her shoulder. Dotty held her and patted her comfortingly. "I know, my dear Stacy. I know how you feel." She continued to whisper consoling words. She knew that the devastation on the canvas was a reflection of what she was going through without Ed. Stacy finally cried herself out; all that remained were a few sniffles. Finally, the quietness of exhaustion. She remained seated while Dotty went to prepare some tea. When she returned, she found her sitting listlessly with her hands resting limply in her lap. In a voice thick from crying, she said, "I miss Ed very much, Dotty. I don't know how I'll manage without him. It seems such a long time. I need my man."

They silently drank the tea and ate Stacy's special brownies. Dotty thought about Stacy's last words. She wondered.

The months turned into years. Stacy discovered many beautiful landscapes in the Westchester and Fairfield Country areas to sketch and paint. Dotty was a frequent visitor. They confided many personal things. But Stacy would not confide her innermost desires and longings to anyone, not even to Dotty.

She painted many canvases and donated most of them to the Ladies' Hospital Auxiliary for their annual benefit fund-raising. She possessed real artistic talent and most of her paintings were sold each year, realizing a tidy sum for the hospital. She threw herself into other hospital projects including the Blood Bank and Transportation for the sick and the elderly. She was able to achieve a measure of contentment and quiet optimism from feeling useful and helpful. Except on her birthday. Every August 10th she would relive the anguish of the leave-taking on the railway platform.

Still, she was settled into a routine and a life style not unlike that of a single woman. Her days were filled.

This is, until she met Dwight. But that was later.

CHAPTER XIV

Ed decided to catch up with his diary which he had neglected for quite some time!

> *It was all very new to me, strange, foreign, the Medical Corps. I even had trouble pinning the insignia on the shoulder of my "blouse" just right. I wondered why it was called a "blouse" when it is obviously a jacket.*
>
> *Far away from Stacy and home I feel an emptiness which will not leave me. The other doctors around me must feel the same way, I suppose. They come from all parts of the country. Like myself, they present a calm exterior to the others.*
>
> *The Regular Army doctors are a different lot. They are pleasant enough but seem to shy away from forming personal relationships and invite no confidences. I feel sure that, after I get to know them better, I will not perceive them as a phlegmatic bunch. They apparently avoid contentious subjects but lean, like flowers turning toward the sun, toward those happenings which carry the quality of humor and cheer.*

What started as a trickle of casualties gradually swelled into large convoys as the war dragged on. Ed did much salvage work. The army installation was so extensive that it took the better part of a day to do the regular ward rounds. The average age for the Surgical Chiefs of Service was in the early thirties, younger for the Junior officers. The entire Medical Corps rested in the hands of these young men, except for the older consultants and Commanding Officers.

During his first year as Chief, Ed retained much of his civilian friendliness and comradeship. He liked listening to the Junior officers with their personal stories; where they came from, what their hopes were, particularly from the newly married officers. Many showed him snapshots of their young children and their beautiful wives. He still found it pleasant to share, with them, their happy recollections of home, hope with them that, after it was all over, their plans would come to fruition. Later, much later, Ed wrote in his diary:

> *Two Millennia ago Cicero wrote, "Let the soldier yield to the civilian." Today it is the other way around. The civilian is again the soldier. It is just . . . it has to be! For now.*

CHAPTER XV

The months dragged into years. At regular intervals he would meet with the hospital Commanding Officer to learn of new orders for the transfer of Junior doctors to forward stations. It was always with a dull and heavy wrenching that Ed recognized familiar names on the list. He remembered their hopes--their family snapshots, and it always threw him into a depression. It was usually in the early morning hours when the doubts and guilt feelings nudged him out of sleep into full wakefulness, staring wide-eyed into the darkness.

After a few such trying experiences, he began to build up a form of self-insulation. Except for conversations concerning technical business at hand and discussions at conferences, Ed tended to appear infrequently among his junior men. It was not that he felt so deeply about these men themselves. He could not escape the laughing, smiling faces in those snapshots.

Only one recourse lay open to him. To protect his sensitivities, he gradually developed a resilient outer emotional integument, inside which he would isolate himself. He assumed a firmer, calculated, dispassionate attitude. He often wondered if he himself was becoming "Regular Army." He was understanding the character of army doctors better, much better, ruminating on his own changes. He began to notice something else. Occasionally, humor could be extracted from what was previously considered humorless. Sad events were mentally skirted. Good news, on the other hand, was jealously nurtured—like blowing on a spark to keep it glowing—into great happenings, a cause for celebration, a reason "they should all have a drink." If work was long and the day dreary—there was always a drink or two after duty. It was a good idea to keep a bottle under the bunk, where hands in the dark could reach. A few good gulps always helped to chase away those— things. Strange, he never became an alcoholic. The ingredients for becoming one were all there—the events, the fatigue, the loneliness, and a good whiskey supply.

CHAPTER XVI

Ed had spent a number of years overseas before he decided to use up some of his accrued leave. Pretty soon he would lose it if he let the time pass without using it.

The trains were overtaxed because of the war. There were delays and stopovers, but Ed finally reached his destination, a coastal town in France. He dropped into the Officers' Club and was directed by the kind lady at the desk to accommodations elsewhere. After getting settled, he stepped out into the street and headed for where the pedestrians were most dense. He wanted to mingle with them, get lost in the crowd. A cool breeze blew in from the sea. The sun was shining. The town was small, but very pleasant. An ideal place for rest and recreation. It was also over-crowded. Mostly American uniforms . . . plenty of girls in town. The cabarets and bistros were already making inroads into the American Foreign Exchange and balance of payments.

He sat down at a small table at a sidewalk cafe and ordered a cassis. As he sat and sipped, he began to unbend. It was a strange feeling—this deceleration—letdown. It was pleasant. The introspective mood which had possessed him so tenaciously and for so long slipped away, although reluctantly. He ordered another cassis. It was mild as drinks go, but it went with his renascent mood. He noticed a sprinkling of British uniforms. Some had Polish shoulder insignia. Three British pilots walked by sporting jaunty handlebar mustachios. Ed thought that these mustaches were affectations, but later learned that only a special group of fliers was privileged to sport them.

A large group of uniformed laughing Americans went by. They

took up the greater width of the promenade and people around them good-naturedly gave way to let them pass. Their insignia indicated that they were from a medical group. This only mildly caught his attention; he had seen many such insignia and shoulder patches during the war years. As the meandering group parted, his gaze fell on a girl from the ANC. Her face seemed rather familiar. She turned at that moment and looked at him. They studied each other, puzzled. In another time and in another place, they would have instantly remembered. But out of context, memory can go through a refractory period. The light of recognition broke over their faces simultaneously. They moved toward each other.

"Peggy!"

"Eddy!"

From her jaunty cap down to her GI shoes, Peggy was slim and very pretty. She was not beautiful . . . not like Stacy.

They hugged each other with the universal greeting of people who meet far from home and completely by chance. At that moment, they both realized how lonely and homesick they had really been. This chance meeting opened the gates of submerged feeling. They broke into a sudden torrent of words which developed into a cloudburst, inundating them both.

"Peggy, it's so good to see you. You look marvelous. When did you get here? Where are you stationed? Sit down here and let me look at you. Garcon un cassis pour la demoiselle, ici, tout de suite."

"I'm with the—the General Hospital. Isn't it wonderful, Ed, our bumping into each other this way? Let me see, the last time we were together was before you were married." She paused, reminiscing. "About yourself, Eddy; how are you? You look thinner and . . . thoughtful. (Ed thought she almost said "sad.") Otherwise you look like the same old Eddy I used to know back home." She sipped her drink. "What do you call this drink? I like it."

"Cassis. Have you heard from anyone we know back home? How about Elmore? What's his first name? It slips my mind."

"Randy. Randolph. Our engagement did not last very long. He was too egocentric for my taste, although he did not seem that way at first. I never married. This drink creeps up on you, doesn't it?"

"I have an idea, Peggy. Let's celebrate our lucky meeting today. I am here on R and R for a few days. Please have dinner with me tonight,

Lieutenant. This is an order, please!" More than anything in the world he wanted her company that night. Without analyzing his feelings, he knew he was hungry . . . for her, for love, for the sheer enjoyment of what he had missed for such a long time.

"Okay, Major. I shall comply with your order." She saluted briskly, laughing. They both stood up. He walked with her toward her quarters. The thought struck him: had he left his table a few minutes earlier, he would have missed this happy turn of events.

"I know a little place, a boite, in walking distance. They serve delicious seafood and their wines are from the local area and are superb."

Thinking back to his affair with Peggy created the same stirrings in him he had then. The mere thought of her evoked a physical response which made him smile to himself. Peggy was always able to drive other thoughts from his mind, filling him with a deep sensual anticipation. Sweet Peggy, the modern Haitari.

Back in her quarters, Peggy thought of Ed. Her memory created a wonderful fantasy about her past affair with him, at least about specific happenings in bed. There had been others before, and afterward. But the lovemaking with Ed must have been good, or else she would not have remembered so vividly. She had felt terribly lonely and deprived and had gone much too long without love. She could not wait to see him, and have him again. What a piece of luck it was for them to meet each other this way!

Neither Peg or Ed realized just how much they had changed. The realities of war, the closeness of the wounded and the dying had spawned sober reflections. Dissimulation and affectation had no place. Camaraderie and openness were the human qualities which sustained them all. Also, a facile sense of humor.

When they met later, they linked arms and, with a spring to their step, set out for the night spot. The evening was beautiful.

The cafe was not overcrowded like most other places. A man played a guitar and a buxom woman sang in a typically throaty Gallic voice. Peggy and Ed paid little attention to anything . . . except to each other. They drank a white wine which the proprietor assured them was "as good as any Burgundy." A haze of smoke hung everywhere. His eyes were bright, hers—languorous. They were both becoming slightly intoxicated. It was an evening of closeness and easy confidences. They talked a lot about back home and about themselves. They were together; it was all that mattered. The war did things to people. Small, happy things mattered. Little isolated enclaves of cheer and love were enough to satisfy—for the time being. Peggy and Ed were enjoying each other in such an enclave. But the evening passed quickly and she had to return to her Unit. When they finally stopped in front of her place, he whispered, "Peggy, we have found each other. We were close once. Try to get a few days leave and come with me. We'll go up the coast a little way. I know a little `pension.'"

"Yes, Ed, yes—I feel like you do my dear. Let us not lose the moment. I hope I will be able to get away. I'll try to soften up the Adjutant first." There was desire in her trembling voice. "Ed, this time I must not let you go. I have thought about you so often. I thought we were in love; really in love."

Ed did not answer.

CHAPTER XVII

"Three days; three full days." Peggy laughed and hugged him as she announced the news jubilantly. Ed had managed to obtain a vehicle from the Motor Pool. She wore a dark plain skirt and a tight wool sweater which accentuated her beautiful figure. A saucy little beret at a ridiculous angle completed the bewitching picture. With her happy smile and gay chatter, she was a vivacious, seductive enchantress. They climbed into the jeep.

Ed again felt the stirring of desire which had long been dormant. Anticipated pleasure suffused his being. Peggy's mood matched his. They were both determined that nothing should change it. Peggy's heart pounded at the thought. She looked at Ed at her side. He had a thoughtful smile as he drove along the winding road.

They arrived at the pension. Ed drew the car up on the bluff overlooking the ocean. A winding path led to the rocks below. The dull roar of the ocean reached them, carried on a gentle northwesterly breeze.

Peggy climbed out of the car and walked toward the edge of the bluff. She pulled off her beret and let the wind blow through her hair. Except for the sounds of the ocean below, there was a peaceful silence. She breathed in deeply to drink in the peace so much in contrast with her inner turbulence.

CONVERSATIONS OF SILENCE
78

Ed walked toward the Auberge du Cygne. The door opened and Raoul, the owner, wiping his hands on his apron, hastened out to greet him with a characteristically French embrace. "Edouard, mon ami, it is a long time, n'est-ce-pas? Not many friends are here anymore. My Adrienne is not also here to greet you. She is—gone, my Adrienne." The old man's eyes filled with tears. "When Etienne went away—Adrienne could not . . ." He finished with the typical Gallic gesture of a shrug of the shoulders and the pursing of the lips. He let his hands fall to his side. Wiping his eyes he remarked, "Now that you have come, my friend, I rejoice. It will make me happy for you and your . . . amoureuse . . . to stay as long as you wish." There was the look of a lost love in his aging eyes, as he turned his head toward Peggy; her gaze was still fixed on the sea's horizon.

The trio climbed the inn's stairs, the old man leading the way. He gave them a large, bright, corner room, the best in the inn. One dormer window faced the ocean; the other faced south.

Raoul informed them that it was difficult to obtain many foods, so would they be pleased if he prepared a salmon for dinner. He promised to make a sauce "you will forever remember in your dreams, once you have tasted it."

"That will be fine, Raoul. Since you do not have other guests, let us know "a l'heure du souper."

Raoul bustled off.

Peggy and Ed were alone for the first time. They turned to each other. She quickly came into his arms. He kissed her lightly on her eyes, her face, the tip of her chin and the tip of her nose. Finally, the lips. They clung together hungrily, merging themselves into one. There was a roaring in their ears and a pounding in their hearts. Their desire became unbearable. They finally separated, breathless. Peggy's knees would not support her. Ed picked her up and gently carried her to the bed.

Their lovemaking was like an unquenchable thirst. Peggy beckoned; Ed responded. He remembered how they had been not so very long ago. She was so totally abandoned in those days, making little hoarse sounds, constantly and breathlessly desiring everything. Her whole body was consumed in the act of love. She wanted his caresses and kisses everywhere, begging him to linger in the more erotic parts. She was no longer the little slip of a girl, looking quietly out to sea.

What possessed her was a primal force of such intensity that it took over completely, changing her into a creature of the earth itself. Nothing else seemed to matter. Only this.

They lay side by side, spent. He looked at her face and gently wiped the drops of perspiration from her brow and upper lip. She did not open her eyes but smiled gently as he dabbed at her face. Her expression was of complete release.

Ed rolled over on his back and looked up at the beams of the low ceiling. His thoughts and feelings were mixed. He was thinking of Stacy. He tried not to disturb Peggy as he slipped quietly out of bed. The sea had turned slate gray and a blustery wind rattled the windows. He rummaged in his valpak for a fresh pack of cigarettes. Peggy opened her eyes and looked at him. He lit two cigarettes and brought one over to her. She took it wordlessly and pulled herself into a sitting position. She was at peace, Ed thought-but for how long? He remembered her restlessness in "those other days." His lovemaking always left her the way she was now. It usually left him depleted, but the feeling of total release was mixed with an indefinable, vague stirring which he had never understood. It was deeper than any sex drive. It happened only with her. He sensed a wildness in her which he could not satisfy for long. He never felt that way with Stacy. He stood close to her side of the bed, looking down at her. Peggy studied him as he stood there. She ran her fingers over his thighs. His chest was hairless, his body lithe and trim. After the immediate urgency of her desire had been requited she could think soberly about "the other days" when they had been lovers. Then, it was so completely good for both of them. Like it had been just now. To think about it made her feel a warmth all over again. What went wrong? Why did he leave her for this other woman? She sighed, tamped out the cigarette and swung over the side of the bed. Her feet did not quite touch the floor. She was nude. She looked at Ed for a moment and spread her arms toward him, smiling. As if driven by an invisible force, he came to her. He knelt before her and pressed his lips to her abdomen.

When they came down to dinner they were both ravenous. Raoul was sitting over in a corner conversing with an old friend who had dropped by. Only the old men and women were left to do what they could to keep things going.

When Raoul saw them he came forward and showed them to their

CONVERSATIONS OF SILENCE

table, which he had decorated with a vase of flowers. Peggy was pleased by this little gesture and wondered where he had found the flowers. He proudly displayed napkins which were of fine old linen. They obviously were used only on special occasions such as christenings or marriages, and had belonged in the family for generations. Now that Adrienne and Etienne were gone, he was celebrating the return of an old friend. Peggy wondered about Ed's other visits. With whom?

The sauce imparted a delicate flavor to the salmon which almost melted in their mouths. The wine had a bouquet born from the local soil. It was different from the other vintages but somehow blended just right with the fish. They ate with zest, and a happy, languid glow suffused their faces, induced in part by the wine. There was quiet laughter and much spontaneous chuckling, some of it for no apparent reason. They were with each other. There was always love to come. It was enough.

After dinner, Ed thanked Raoul for being such a considerate host, which made the old man very happy. If only Adrienne had been here, he sighed.

Peggy and Ed decided to go out for some fresh sea air. "Prenez-garde mon ami," warned Raoul. "It is dark and please remember where you are, up here. Do you have a lampe de poche—a—a torchlight? Please stay close. While you stay outdoors, I shall have fear for you."

They put on their topcoats and went outdoors. The flashlight threw only a weak beam so they stayed close to the inn. They huddled next to each other, their nostrils flaring, breathing in the salt air. The breeze was chilling and soon their cheeks began to burn and a strong wind blew tears horizontally from their eyes. They soon decided that they had had enough of the penetrating breeze, but they felt refreshed. The wine fumes were completely dissipated.

After removing their topcoats they sat down in front of the fireplace and stared into the flames, each steeped in private thoughts. They remained there for a long time. As if by telepathic thought, they stood up and, hand in hand, walked over to the staircase and up to their room.

Ed came out of the bathroom first and was thumbing through a dog-eared magazine published by an Association of Wine Growers. The publication was almost four years old.

When Peggy came out she wore a gossamer shift that revealed

everything. It was the only thing, she later confessed, that she had brought with her from back home. She looked almost shy as she came slowly toward him. He caught his breath and gazed at her.

She stood before him. He reached up and loosened a little bow around her neck. The shift fell around her feet in a gossamer ring. He could smell her femaleness. The familiar rushing in his ears began. His vision seemed to blur. In a moment he was standing, pushing his body firmly into hers. She responded and a long sigh escaped her lips.

CHAPTER XVIII

Ed was up early. He had already shaved. Peg was sprawled sleepily over the bed. He tiptoed around the room and tried to be as quiet as possible. His thoughts returned to last night; soon they would have to go back. Ed had a little more time left, but Peg had heard scuttlebutts that her unit might go to Italy, or maybe to Paris, where they would form a permanent installation.

They wished without expressing it in words, that the little time left to them should be enjoyed as fully as possible. Last night it was a gentle and tender lovemaking; feeling and touching each other with a sweetness neither suspected was possible. They wanted it to last, and murmured the soft words of love that go back to the beginning of time when the first man and woman met and made love.

Last night the tears just came. It was a release of all her deep feelings. In the past she had cried often enough for joy. This time she wept for the future—a future without Ed, whom she had lost once and would soon lose again. She knew.

Ed studied her sensuous curves as she lay breathing softly in sleep. She finally stirred. Stretching her arms in that attitude of abandon that only a female can perform, she yawned and looked around. When her gaze fell on Ed, she smiled and made a comical little grimace by momentarily squeezing both eyes closed and wrinkling her nose. Ed looked at her; he felt a mixture of joy and sadness. It seemed that these emotions had to go together. There was no such state as unalloyed joy. Sadness always had to intrude. Playfully, he bent over, slapped her bottom gently, then kissed it.

"Lieutenant Peggy," he crisply ordered, "out of bed and early breakfast for you. You and I are going for a climb down the bluff. Be sure to bring something to cover your head and put on warm clothes. I know what the spray is like down there." Again Peg wondered how many times had he been at the inn before.

She pouted for a moment, then deciding on another tactic, beckoned, like a siren, crooking her index finger for Ed to come. With her other hand she patted the bed beside her. No reaction from Ed. She stood up and sulkily, like a spoiled child, began to dawdle toward the bathroom. Ed, grinning broadly, gave her a quick harmless slap across her bottom. She scampered, squealing, into the bathroom without any further delay.

"Here, Peg, give me your hand," Ed cautioned. He caught her, as she jumped from the boulder, to keep from slipping. They rested on a spot sheltered from the constant wind by an overhang. They sat huddled together. Their eyes sparkled and their cheeks reddened as the brisk sea air buffeted them.

Ed pulled a carefully wrapped package out of the tote bag he brought along. It contained Brie and crackers. With a legerdemain flourish, he also produced a bottle of very dry wine. They munched on the crackers and cheese and passed the bottle between them, with a camaraderie born of deep knowledge of each other. There was no affectation or pretense between them. Just two people together in a vast island of loneliness, seeking comfort and solace and joy in each other. Seize it! Hold the moment! Don't let it pass! They prayed silently for their few split-seconds in the history of time.

Ed reflected on how he and Peg had become so close. He was practical enough to know that, in another time and under different circumstances, this visit to the Auberge would not have happened. When loneliness and hunger for physical and emotional needs creep into one's very bones . . . He knew how unendurable it had become for him . . . it must also have been for her. Ever since they first met a few years ago, he sensed the undercurrent of abandon and wildness in her. Instinctively he knew that her thirst for life and love would never be requited. He realized that no man would hold her love indefinitely.

Raoul decided to prepare a stew with all the vegetables he could find. He was sad, because "when the enfants go tomorrow, there will remain only echoes in the Auberge—only echoes. This war—will it never end!"

The smell of the stew permeated the entire inn. Raoul was going "to put in my secret ingredients so that they will remember my stew wherever they go in this world. They will eat other stew, but they will always shake their heads very sadly, and say, 'Yes it is good; but never like the stew we tasted at Raoul's 'Auberge du Cygne.' That is what they will say after I serve it tonight."

That night was their last together. With the war dragging on, and the units being moved, they both knew that they might not see each other again after tomorrow. Ed was lying on the bed with his hands clasped behind his head, looking off into a horizon known only to himself.

She sat in front of the mirror pensively brushing her hair, occasionally casting a glance at Ed. The faraway look of abstraction revealed her own contemplation of their going . . . back. Her brush stopped in midair. A few more strokes and she put the brush down.

Ed sensed the change in her mood and turned his head toward her as she slowly moved to him. Her sensual walk began to stir him. He moved to his side of the bed to allow her to lie next to him. She touched him; he responded. She slowly slid over and straddled his hips. As she felt the deep penetration, a long gasping sigh escaped her. They looked at each other and she began to slowly move with the rhythm of love.

Afterward they talked about many things. Mostly, they talked about themselves. They did not talk about Stacy.

Later, like someone preparing for a long deprivation of love, Peggy once again felt herself being carried along a wave of passion which would not spend itself. Her hands gently stroked his thighs. Her fingers fluttered over his abdomen as softly as a butterfly. Ed could again feel the pulsating surge of passion diffusing through his whole being, sweeping over him. Ever so slowly, as in a trance, he turned over to her. He passed his lips over her thighs and abdomen. She began to beckon and whisper. His lips and mouth came to rest where she beckoned most.

The following morning, strong gusts of wind blew over the edge of the bluff. The roar of the ocean was muted by a thick swirling fog. Peggy walked to the edge of the bluff and looked out to sea, holding onto her cap. The winds buffeted her body and her spirit was one with the restless ocean.

Raoul had tears in his eyes as he helped load the vehicle. When Peggy came back to the car, he took her hand, kissed it, and held it for a long moment. "Goodbye, my child." He wiped his eyes. "If only my Adrienne were here—" Raoul was a lonely old man.

"Edouard, mon ami, mon fils. I pray for you and your amoureuse for giving me back a little remembrance of my own youth. It is too much to hope that we meet again? Maybe? Who knows? Now then, we say au revoir, only." The old man blew his nose very hard.

Neither Ed nor Peggy spoke on the way back. They were lost in their thoughts. Peg finally broke the silence. "Ed, you called me Stacy last night." She lit a cigarette and blew a cloud of smoke. "You still love her, Ed, don't you?" Ed started to speak. "No, don't say anything," she interrupted. "I guess I knew it all along, but . . . it has been wonderful, us being together . . . like old times." She lapsed into silence.

When they arrived, there was a message from the Adjutant's office waiting for her. The General Hospital was moving to Paris where it would become a permanent installation. Transportation had to be arranged, further assignments clarified and defined. Several new medical officers were to be met and introduced. There were many small details that had to be attended to. Peg was suddenly busy. She decided she felt better for it. At least it kept her mind off other matters.

Ed spent two more days, literally "with his hands in pockets," sauntering around and window shopping. He bought several small gifts for back home, and a little gold ornament for Peggy.

The night before Peggy's unit pulled out, they sat at a sidewalk cafe until they were the last ones, talking about those many personal things a man and a woman find so important. When Peg reached her quarters, Ed pulled out the little gift he had bought for her. She opened it and found a tiny gold swan—like the one on the sign that hung over the door of Raoul's little Auberge. Her eyes filled with tears.

Ed whispered, "Once in a while, try to remember how it was, dear, dear Peggy."

They looked at each other a long time. Finally, they embraced each other tightly, as if they would never part again. Peggy rested her cheek on his shoulder. Then, one more deep, clinging kiss, and she was gone.

A moment later, Ed turned and walked away, slowly at first; his gait quickened to a decisive, brisk step. He had finally relinquished Peggy and their rich, happy moments. He was walking toward whatever lay ahead.

"Hello."

"Is that you, Major? Where the hell have you been? You were to report in yesterday, the 17th. There's a convoy coming in and we'll all be busy. By the way, how was your R and R? Just a moment, it says here—well, I'm sorry Ed, it does say here that you are to be back on the 18th. My mistake, sorry. How was your R and R? Or did I ask you that already? I don't remember you answering, though. Did you meet up with any good stuff; you know what I mean. Don't tell me that you went off with that long face of yours and came back the same way. Wouldn't surprise me, though."

Ed finally answered. "It was okay. I had a good rest. Give me half an hour, will you. I'll jeep over in a little while. Do we have a full complement, or have some of the men shipped out since I left? Never mind, hold it until I get over to you."

Major Edward Rankin hung up.

Lieutenant Colonel Granstaff hung up at the other end.

CHAPTER XIX

TRIAGE

Triage is a word curiously absent from some of the more prestigious unabridged dictionaries. It is always found in medical texts. It comes into play following catastrophes of nature—such as floods or earthquakes. It is intimately and inevitably part of man-made catastrophes—such as war.

Triage is the task that falls to a group of medical men stationed in the forward areas of combat during and following an action. When casualties begin to pour in, a grim sorting-out begins.

It becomes the mind-dulling work of the triage team to decide who is dead; who will inevitably die due to the extent and location of the wounds; which casualties stand the chance of being salvaged; who can be ambulatory and who must be stretcher-borne. The triage team further screens the salvage cases, to decide where to transfer the casualty for the best medical help. All casualties are ticketed (including the dead) and cleared out of the combat area as soon as possible.

Diary:

   A convoy of casualties arrived shortly after my conversation with Lt. Colonel Granstaff. It immediately plunged every member of the staff into action; the Orthopedic Service labored continuously for many hours. Some rested while others worked. I moved about constantly, checking each operating area, as well as putting in many hours of surgery myself. The workers are all young men and in good physical condition. It is not an unendurable hardship for them. They worked silently.
   The less they spoke, the more they wanted to say.
   Occasionally, someone would burst into animated swearing or loud carping, but I knew it was only a cover-up, an attempt to conceal deeper feelings which remained unsaid. Occasionally, there came a penetrating silence when a young man breathed out his life on the operating table. There was no time to commiserate or moralize, no deceleration of effort. With a bleak expression on their faces, the operating team prepared for the next candidate. Another man waiting. Waiting to be restored to what he was a few short hours before. Restored? Never. The scars always remain.
   Our teams worked as if there were no end. Hour after hour passed. The dull feeling that we would be doing this for the rest of our lives grew upon me. Our men and women come from all parts of America. I can almost believe that the inexorable guiding hand of Fate has somehow shepherded them gently together so that they should play out their roles together in this one place. They were chosen, long ago, for this special event—a cast of characters acting out their destined parts on an eternal stage, imprisoned in this pocket of time; a plot with no ending, to labor interminably without a finale.
   The unbidden specter of Shiva often enters my mind during such engagements. Shiva, the destroyer. There would appear the

image of the giant Hindu god swinging a battleaxe as big as a house, as he stomps indiscriminately, crushing the human ants which are contending and struggling against each other below. With wide sweeps, Shiva cuts huge swaths through metal and soil and flesh and bone, exploding them and the very earth beneath, into a fiery fragmented destruction, hurtling the toy war machines, tanks and guns, and pebble-like boulders into space—all of it settling back in slow motion, like so much macabre confetti-debris of blood and metal and mud. The smell. Then, Shiva lumbers off, the ground trembling with each tread only to reappear over the next horizon when the thunder and the roaring return.

Every conceivable injury to limb and spine came under our attention. As fatigue and weariness creeps in, the entire scene loses its bright colors and takes on a chiaroscuro of dimness and light. There is a dull, almost automated determination to continue. A sense of desperate futility seizes some of our workers, like Sisyphus condemned to roll the stone uphill only to have it go crashing down, compelling him to toil uphill again and again.

By early sunrise, most of the serious, complicated cases were attended to. By daybreak a feeling that the major effort now lay behind us gradually spread throughout the unit. Finally, I could look forward to some finite end to this particular emergency.

I made a final tour of the entire Orthopedic unit. I was thankful and grateful for the heroic work done by our forward medical units. Their preliminary work made our efforts easier. These units function close to combat areas. They are the first link in the chain along which the casualties are evacuated to the base hospital.

They are the unsung heroes.

Toward early morning we finished up. It has been a long haul, as arduous as any I have encountered. Nevertheless, I was mildly surprised and gratified by an unexpected feeling I was at peace with myself. As a matter of fact, I decided I never felt physically better. I was not conscious of fatigue, my hands were steady and I walked with a firm tread. My voice showed no sign of weariness. This peaceful feeling of control usually stays with me for some time *following these periods of activity.* The "putting-together" of these broken men is what rewards me most. I remember one particular phenomenon I experienced a few hours before. It was a curious heightening of all my physical senses. A dropped instrument created an odd tinkle-echo. A slight sneeze or cough was thunderous to my ears. The sound breathing occasionally crescendoed into hissing noises. Even the silence, when it happened, had a "sound" of its own. There was no blunting of perception, no loss of muscular coordination or surgical dexterity. So I thought. I felt a quickening, a sharply-honed receptivity to stimuli from my surroundings.

It did not occur to me that it was an emptiness of feeling—a depletion of my ability to react to the horror around me—that gave me this pseudo-peace. Physical and emotional responses to unremitting exposure, to a backdrop of death and destruction, ultimately changed from initial fear and revulsion to perceptual bankruptcy. I suspect most of the hospital personnel were enveloped in this same aura of nonfeeling toward the end of their work at the base. However, it seems to serve a purpose. It permitted them to carry on, to bounce away the constant bombardment of traumatic stimuli. Those who cannot accomplish this eventually have to go to other areas. Their leaving is not a sign of weak spirit.

I got into my vehicle and drove along the road which was marked out with a faint white line. I noticed, abstractedly, that the car was weaving slightly from side to side across the line. Grasping the wheel firmly I made a determined effort to concentrate on the road. Inexorably, as if it had a will of its own, the car continued to weave. Somehow it struck me as humorous that no amount of effort on my part could control the car. The weaving continued. Up to that moment, no one could have convinced me that I was functioning below my optimum capacity, but the perverse behavior of the vehicle was objective proof which could not be refuted. The truth was that I was "out on my feet—or seat." It brought a slight smile to my face as I thought about it in a disembodied sort of way. The situation had a quality of humor—this revelation—this contrast between the way I felt and my actual condition. Like a tree bereft of its leaves, I was measurably bereft of my emotional and physical ability to react.

I would not have otherwise suspected what was undeniably proven to me. I was "out" although I never "felt better."

Since then I have wondered about this war—and the history-making strategists—the generals and the statesmen. Fatigue and mental exhaustion have many faces.

Among the decision-makers and leaders, were there men who "never felt better" and who could not be convinced that they were otherwise, when indeed they were "out on their feet?"

They were willing to stake their lives as well as those of the fighting men, on their convictions.

The answer is buried in history.

As time passed, Ed was to repeat the experience periodically. He had learned to accept these occult limitations. He was cheered by the fact, however, that being "out" did not keep him from being "in" when the convoys came.

"Throw it, Kruger! Throw it, you stupid son-of-a-bitch!" Kruger looked yellow and wide-eyed with fear. He had already pulled the pin and was ready to lob it, when something made him freeze. His arm remained in midair holding the grenade. There was no time left. Jansen, all 225 pounds of him, made a flying tackle and caught Kruger around the hips. The momentum threw Kruger forward and jolted the grenade out of his hand. It bobbled along the ground for a few feet before it detonated with a loud explosion followed by a ballooning of dust that would not settle. Kruger was not hurt but he messed in his pants. Jansen lay on the ground moaning, holding his right thigh. He was doubled up with the pain. There was surprisingly little blood.

The other soldiers who had been receiving training in grenade-throwing, came out cautiously from behind the barricade in twos and threes.

Without wasting any time, the buck sergeant backup for Jansen got in touch with the hospital medics. Soon, Master Sergeant Jansen, regular Army for 22 years, was splinted, placed on a stretcher, and on his way to the base hospital.

The men crowded around Kruger. "What the hell happened to you, Kruger?" "You had the god-damn thing in your hands; why didn't you throw it?" "What the hell were you thinking of?" "We could've gotten killed!"

Kruger stuttered so badly he could hardly make sense. He kept saying, "It was m-m-meant to kill. I couldn't throw it. I couldn't kill—so help me. I-I looked at the damn thing and I said to m-y-myself if you throw this, you will kill someone. I c-couldn't do it. I d-didn't think anymore. I d-d-don't even remember pulling the p-pin."

The buck sergeant took charge. "All right, you men, fall in. You too, McCloskey. Why the hell are you always the last. Move your fuckin' ass and fall in like I ordered." They marched down the road in close order where the army truck waited, and climbed in.

The truck disappeared in a cloud of dust. Soon, the hubbub faded, leaving the training area silent and deserted, except for the dust devils that swirled around in a crazy ballet.

Ed and Captain Salter had finished going over Sergeant Jansen. "He has no dorsalis pedis pulse in his right foot. The posterior tibial artery is not palpable. The foot is cold and pale. I'm afraid that Jansen has a poor prognosis," said Captain Salter. "He'll probably need a mid-thigh. Will you take a look, Ed? We'll have to decide soon."

The point of entry of the grenade fragment was in the upper popliteal area of his right knee. It followed an oblique course, rupturing the popliteal artery, a vital structure responsible for practically all blood supply to the leg below the knee. The point of exit was in front and at a much higher level. Nothing unusual about such a course of the missile through the soft tissues. The only dismal fact was that it had caught the artery along the way.

Ed straightened up. "Did you notice the smell? Rather faint I'll admit, but it's there."

"Yes, I did. I'm afraid he is developing gas gangrene. The deep tract is a perfect nidus for it. We took a smear and found a few spores. His thigh is as large as a tree trunk, from the swelling. Will you amputate?"

"No. You do it, Julius. Or get Captain Singer. Jansen will need a guillotine type, of course."

"It's the only way, Ed. We'll set him up for a soon as possible if he does not improve in the next few hours."

Captain Ralph Singer was whispering to Julius. "The last time Rankin did one was over four months ago. You know, Julius, I think he is shying away from them. Do you supposed he has had it up to here.'" Captain Singer passed the edge of his hand across this throat in a familiar gesture.

Staff Sergeant Jansen was told the bad news. The leg had to come off. It was gas gangrene. X-rays showed the bubbles traveling up along the muscle planes. It would kill him if the leg was not removed. Jansen was regular Army. He knew how to take orders and he instinctively recognized "a situation" when it presented itself. Ed dropped by to check on Jansen.

"Where will it have to come off, Major?" he asked. He looked haggard. His eyes were sunken and his breathing was rapid due to the high fever and the poisonous toxins coursing through his body.

"Probably mid-thigh. About here." Ed placed the edge of his hand at the mid-thigh level. "Any lower and we won't be able to contain the gangrene. We want to do it today, Sergeant." Ed sounded weary.

"All right. I guess we'll have to go ahead with it." After catching his breath, "If it hadn't been for that little yellow bastard—" After another moment, "Promise me you'll do it yourself, Major. That is all I ask." He looked up at Ed with his haggard eyes, breathless from the mere exertion of talking. He felt very weak.

Ed did not answer directly. He seemed deep in thought. He finally answered with another question. "Why me in particular, Jansen? Both Captain Salter and Captain Singer are excellent surgeons of fine judgment. They are perfectly capable. You can depend on them. I—er— have not been doing any amputations recently. I'll see that one of these good men is assigned to your case. Is that okay, Jansen?"

"No, Major, it is not okay. I want you to do it. I've known you much longer than them and I have faith in you. I never went around kissing anybody's ass or saying `please' but this once, Major, this bloody once, will you please do it yourself, for me?" He was gasping.

CONVERSATIONS OF SILENCE

His deep sunken eyes were becoming bright.

The silence which followed seemed to never end. Finally, Ed said, "Okay, Jansen. I'll do it myself. Tonight. We can't wait any longer."

Later, Jansen was brought into the operating room. The smell was all pervasive. Ed was hoping that it would not happen to him this time. Please God, not this time.

It first happened with a young private infantry man, approximately four months ago when he had to amputate what remained of both legs below the knees. It was one of the countless cases resulting from land mines. The boy was prepared in the usual manner and the amputation started.

Without warning, he tasted salt in his mouth; before he realized, he was biting his own lower lip. The scalpel in his hand slowly turned into a meat cleaver. He was so horrified, he let the meat cleaver drop from his grasp. He gazed at the scalpel on the floor.

Sergeant St. John saw Ed's pallor and the sweat on his forehead. "Major, you all right? I saw it slip from your hands. You okay?"

It took a few moments for Ed to recover some of his poise. "Yes—yes, I'm okay. Sorry. Thank you, St. John." He took another scalpel. He completed the remainder of the procedure without any problems. By the end, Ed had recovered sufficiently to feel and look quite normal.

Later, Ed's hand trembled as he wrote in his diary:

> But it <u>was</u> a bloody meat cleaver I saw in my hands! All I could think of was that I was going to bring that meat cleaver down on the legs of this boy, hack them off like a butcher. I saw it clearly! God it was awful! In the name of heaven what is happening to me? What happened was so horrible I cannot trust my sanity to a repetition of the horror. I will not do another amputation. I'll contrive it somehow. I'll use any avenue to escape.

The meat cleaver with its bloody edge poised and dangling in midair doing a death dance, invaded his dreams, awakened him to jump up with a cry and the taste of bile in his mouth. As the weeks passed, the night terrors finally left him. Ed knew that he would never do another amputation.

As Chief of Service, he managed to assign the amputations to Captains Singer and Salter. For the past few months his troubled spirit was at peace ... until now ... and he had promised Jansen.

The operation started; he worked fast in order to get it over with. It usually took about seven to nine minutes, but Jansen's thigh had swollen to the dimensions of a small tree trunk which slowed Ed down a little.

The meat cleaver did not appear in his hands, but his mouth filled with something vile. There came a rushing and a shouting in his head. It was as if the voices of all those whose limbs he had removed over the years combined into a great swelling chorus—all shouting accusations at him. The shouts crescendoed until Ed felt his head would burst. His conditioned reactions sustained him until he was through. The amputation stump was left completely open; dressings were applied. He could hardly wait to get outdoors. When he reached the outside, he breathed in the air in deep gulps. Finally, he regained his composure and left.

◆◆◆

Ed was sitting opposite Major David Morland of the N.P. Service.

"David, it was very real. I held it in my hands, as if I were going to bring the cleaver down on the boy's legs. I was someone else. Someone brutal and sadistic. It dropped out of my hands. Sergeant St. John must have noticed more than he admits, but I'm not sure about that. I have kept it to myself, hoping that it would pass as long as I stayed away from amputations. I thought I was going to lick it until Jansen's case turned up. I tried to assign it to one of the other men, but Jansen wouldn't have it that way. He wouldn't have it any other way. I promised. So I did it—" Ed paused before continuing, "—no meat cleaver, but something just as bad. I know as well as you what is probably the underlying reason. This has been building up inside me, this rebellion against any more amputations. You know, David, the philosophy of an orthopedic surgeon is to reconstruct—to restore. He mends broken bones; he restores faulty joints; he repairs severed soft tissues; he braces weakened limbs. His work is one of returning the impaired, the damaged, the infirm, to a state of normal function as much as possible. It is true that amputations are as necessary as the removal of other parts, when indicated. But in my case, David . . . in *my* case, it has gone contrary to my concepts, and I cannot do it anymore. Amputations are so . . . so totally irrevocable that what was at first a simple reluctance has grown into a rebellion—a revulsion that has become so overwhelming it has pervaded my body and my mind. The truth is, David, I don't want to do another amputation as long as I live. Even if it means disobeying orders from higher up. I just cannot do another one. As a matter of fact, if I cannot reconstruct, I won't do an operation at all."

Major Morland listened attentively. He was the head of Neuropsychiatry. The problem before him was not obscure. How to treat it was something else. This was the salient concern. He doubted that anything could be done. It was paradoxical, that Major Rankin's irrational hallucinations and psychosomatic phenomena were spawned by rational happenings—the Major was fed up, ad nauseam, with destroying. That was what amputations had come to mean to him.

The simple remedy was to avoid all further amputations. Morland decided he would explain the problem to Ed's commanding officer. Colonel Rowan was a reasonable man. After all, he was a doctor, though regular Army had him doing only administrative work for the past number of years. He arranged an appointment and dropped by. Colonel Rowan was having a cup of tea and asked Morland if he would have one. Morland politely declined.

"Now, Major, I understand you want to speak to me about Rankin. Frankly, I was surprised to find that his problem lay in your field. He always struck me as being very stable. He has built up an Orthopedic Service which has been commended on several occasions. I hope I am not going to lose him on N-P grounds."

"No, Colonel, nothing like that." Morland told Colonel Rowan the story, sparing no detail. The Colonel tilted his chair back, swiveled around to gaze out the window and drummed his fingers on the desk. He twisted his head back toward Morland. "And your recommendation, Major?"

"That he be spared from doing any more amputations. After all, there is a full complement of surgeons who—"

"I am very well aware of the condition of our T.O.," the Colonel interrupted a little testily. He picked up a paper on his desk and studied it for a few moments. Then he tossed it to Morland. "Here, read this. I received it just yesterday."

It was a letter from the Colonel in Command Headquarters, ordering Rankin to General Hospital. He was being appointed Chief of the Amputation Center. It would carry a Lieutenant Colonelcy with it.

The Center was becoming well known for the orthopedic development of prostheses (artificial limbs). Soon all major amputations would be funneled from the various theaters of operations into the Amputation Center. The extremities would be "tailored" to fit the new prosthetic devices which the Surgeon General ordered to be tried out. It was another example of something good being born through the convulsive labor pains of war.

Colonel Rowan had recommended Rankin for the appointment when Headquarters first communicated with him.

"What do you think of that?" the Colonel asked.

Morland shrugged his shoulders. "Colonel, I am sure he will not accept it, even though it means a promotion. He as much as told me that."

"I'll have to hear it from him personally, because I must send headquarters a detailed report. I wish I had known about this earlier. According to this letter, he is already under orders to go. I'll have the Adjutant set up an appointment with Rankin today."

Rankin entered, saluted and remained standing until the Colonel requested him to sit down.

"Edward, I have had a long talk with Major Morland. He has told me all about your . . . your difficulty. Here, read this letter which I received from Headquarters about your transfer and appointment to General Hospital."

Ed read it twice. The General Hospital was where Peggy was stationed. It would mean more amputations with more sophisticated techniques; but amputations, nevertheless. He had heard that an entire three-fifths of the General Hospital was now earmarked for an "Amputation Center" and he would be Chief in charge of it. Much new equipment was being moved in and there would be a great increase in paramedical personnel.

He returned the letter silently to the Colonel. "May I speak freely,

Colonel?"

"Yes. That is what I expect you to do. I have these confounded orders. An argument will have to be pretty strong to convince Headquarters to get someone else. Remember, this also means a promotion for you, so what's it going to be?"

"I cannot do it. I do not want it, Colonel. Last year it would have been all right, I guess, but not now. If necessary, I would rather be admitted into the N-P Service than comply with these orders. I'm sorry."

"I see . . ." Colonel Rowan said simply. "Carry on here same as usual, Major. No amputations for you. Most of them seem to be going to the Amputation Center, anyway. Sorry you could not have complied. It would have been a good promotion for you."

Jansen was the last amputation Edward Rankin ever did in his life. The ghost that had haunted him was finally exorcised.

He was content.

CHAPTER XX

In the early years of the war, Stacy counted the days and nights. She often dreamed of Ed and their early courtship. It was not so long ago. She would lose herself in a fantasy world full of amorous mysteries and delightful surprises only to awaken to a reality of emptiness and unsated longing. She would clasp the pillow and talk to Ed.

With the gas rationing and enforced inactivity, she tended to gain weight and it became a constant battle of calories and weight watching. She did, however, find much more time for sketching and painting, a godsend in helping her to pass the hours. It did not assuage the longing in her young body. She had an art showing, of sorts, at the annual Ladies' Auxiliary and sold several paintings, turning the proceeds over to the hospital fund. Thereafter, the "show" became an annual feature.

At one of the annual bazaars, over three years after Ed left, one of the senior officers of the bank which handled the hospital's financial affairs, was present at the invitation of the Administrator. Dwight Everett was not a handsome man, but he possessed a quiet, magnetic elegance of speech and dress. Gray hair at his temples enhanced his general appearance. He was about fifteen years older than Stacy.

"Mrs. Rankin," he said pleasantly, "I am Dwight Everett. I handle the hospital's financial matters."

"It was nice of you to come," Stacy answered genially.

"I like your painting of the grove of birch trees with the dark background of pines. I should like to buy it. Does it represent a scene near here?"

"As a matter of fact it does," Stacy replied eagerly. "It is in the northwest area of the county. I discovered it some time ago and decided to paint it when I could find the time." She was thoughtful for a moment. "Time is all I seem to have nowadays," she continued wistfully. Resuming an air of lightheartedness, she said, "Let me wrap this up and put a piece of string around it, Mr. Everett. There-that does it."

After Dwight Everett had the painting snugly under his arm, he turned to go, paused, and turned back to Stacy. "Mrs. Everett and I are having open house at our Connecticut lodge and are inviting several doctors and their wives. We know that Dr. Rankin is overseas, but we would be very happy to have you come—"

Stacy started to decline, but before she could do so, Everett hastily added, "If it is a question of transportation, I can arrange for someone to pick you up. Please say you will come."

"I shall love to come," Stacy answered.

"Good," Everett answered. "I'll have Mrs. Everett call you," he replied, looking pleased.

When Stacy arrived, she discovered that the "lodge" was a spacious, beautiful summer home. The living room was large with a vaulted cathedral ceiling. A spiral staircase led up to a balustraded circular landing which opened into the guest rooms.

Although it was cool outdoors, the room was warm due to the large gathering. Several of the casement windows were wide open. The large swimming pool was still empty at that time of year. Acres of untouched woodland extended away from the house on all sides.

It was a cheerful gathering. The waiters seemed to be everywhere with trays of cocktails and hors d'oeuvres. Stacy was feeling slightly light-headed from the unaccustomed strong drink, but she was happier than she had been in a long time. It felt good to see new, eager faces and to converse about topics other than hospital matters.

Dwight Everett appeared by her side unobtrusively. He was wearing a navy blue blazer with the crest of a well-known yachtsman's club over the breast pocket. Conservative gray flannel trousers and a very light blue shirt finished off with a navy blue tie with a regimental stripe design imparted an air of quiet elegance.

Stacy was drawn to the man. He exuded success and accomplishment. The difference in their ages made him all the more attractive to her.

"Are you enjoying yourself, Mrs. Rankin?" he asked solicitously. They were standing in a corner near a tall bay window. To one side extended a short hallway into a smaller room. It was curtained off by a beautiful silk hanging drape of oriental design.

"Yes, I am, Mr. Everett," she answered cheerily. "It was kind of you and Mrs. Everett to invite me. With Ed away it has been dull and quite lonely at times."

He chose not to answer. Changing the subject, he asked, "Would you like to see some of the grounds? It is getting a little stuffy in here."

Stacy answered hesitatingly, "I would like that very much, but..."

"But what?" he asked softly.

"... but Mrs. Everett might—well, you are the host—and she might perhaps want you to stay with your guests," she finished lamely.

Everett's expression remained benign. "You need not worry about that, my dear. Harriet is busy keeping our guests happy." He nodded in the direction of the hanging drapes. He lifted it aside just enough so Stacy could look in. Beautiful, blonde Harriet was in a tight embrace, sharing hungry kisses with a man who was obviously much younger. They were oblivious to their surroundings with their bodies pressed together. Dwight dropped the drape. His expression remained bland. It was obviously, to him, a not infrequent scene. If it had ever devastated him in the past, it must have been long ago. Dwight could just as well have shown Stacy his prize hunter, probably with greater feeling. It was quite clear to Stacy that Everett wanted her to see that little tableau. She would soon understand why.

Harriet's behavior was a source of much discreet gossip in the elite circles of her world. Especially her preference for the younger stallions. Her drinking had not yet marred her striking beauty.

She was the sole heiress of a recently deceased, well-known United States senator who had been a widower for many years. In Washington, the duties of the hostess at her father's political gatherings devolved on Harriet. She was a sparkling and beautiful woman. Many men on the Washington scene were attracted to her. She was friendly to all of them. It was there that she and Dwight met and later married. It was a posh wedding. Her father started imbibing long before the ceremony, and when it came to giving the bride away, the senator had to be helped to stand up. Dwight soon discovered that Washington living carried a pattern of behavior not unlike ancient sybaritic Rome in many respects. Moving to Westchester did not alter matters as far as Harriet was concerned.

Stacy studied the bottom of her glass, in embarrassment, when Dwight turned to her. Gently taking her by the elbow, he escorted her out of the noisy room into the hallway. The heat of the room and the cocktails gave her cheeks a high flush.

"Here," Dwight said softly, "put this scarf around your neck and put this on." He had reached into a closet and brought out a hip-length mink jacket. She put her arms through it. The jacket held a delicate, exotic scent which she could not identify. Dwight studied her for a moment. "It is one of Harriet's coats. She won't mind. As a matter of fact, she will not even notice."

They followed a path through a gate which opened some distance from the service entrance. The scent from the coat and the slight intoxication mingled with her light mood to give her a sense of freedom and abandon. She began to feel an unformed desire to enjoy it to the full. She felt hot and flushed and trembled at Dwight's closeness.

"Watch your head as you come under this heavy branch," he cautioned. As she came out from under, her foot caught in a root and she stumbled forward. Dwight caught her. As she straightened up a little breathlessly, laughing, she found herself in his arms. A languid feeling of warmth came over her. It was such a long time, she thought, since she had been held by a strong pair of arms. Too long . . . for years. She was suddenly hungry for the fulfillment of her fantasized dreams. Her young, vigorous body craved love. She wanted love instead of loneliness and emptiness. She was ready for such a man as Dwight. They kissed each other hungrily, silently. He placed his lips softly on her earlobe and kissed it while whispering, "Stacy, it is the first time I have called you that, but I have known of you and have watched you even before I bought that painting. I want to see you again soon—alone. I know that it is what you want—as much as I. It must be soon, my darling Stacy."

She felt breathless, almost suffocated. "Everything is happening too fast—" she stopped and tried to think more calmly. Was this the dutiful, faithful wife who had been waiting patiently for the return of her husband? Yes, she thought, she was the same loving wife. She loved Ed with her very being. In another time and another place, she would not be doing what she was about to do. This was something quite apart from the world of Ed and Stacy.

What she was doing now belonged in an unnatural world which had imposed restrictions and prohibitions beyond any human endurance. As if she had acquainted Dwight with her thoughts, she murmured, "Oh, how I have waited—and waited. But I don't want to wait any longer." She began to tremble again with the emotional drive she had kept in check until this meeting. Now she was ready—she was ready. Dwight led her back to the house.

They met a few days later in New York. Stacy was only mildly surprised to learn that Dwight kept the apartment year round. She had no illusions that she was his only inamorata. She came across intimate female articles. Somehow it did not disturb her. She was not in love with Dwight. She admired him and was fond of him. She needed him as a lover and she was sure he needed her in the same way.

As they undressed, a nervousness seized her. She felt as if it were the first time for her. It had been so long. When Dwight touched her closely for the first time, there was an explosive climactic response. She thought about this while she let him continue. She slowly built up to a second time, but Dwight had finished. If he suspected what had happened, he did not show it. A little later they made love again. This time it was a shattering response from Stacy, Dwight whispered little words of love.

When Stacy could observe him nude, she noticed a beginning paunch. She also saw that Dwight, without his expensively tailored clothes, was not quite so elegant. But she felt better—almost cheerful. She was still in bed when he leaned over, fully clothed, and kissed her. "Darling, I have to get back to the bank. Be sure to straighten things out before you leave." When he reached the door he turned and added, "You were wonderful, Stacy. Be sure to take the key when you go."

Although it was not love, she needed him. He was reaching middle age. They had an assured privacy in affluent surroundings, all in very good taste. Better this than to satisfy her sexual needs with some man her age. An affair with a young stud could destroy her future with Ed.

How strange, she thought, that she should be going through lovemaking with Dwight, all the time thinking of Ed, her husband, as her lover. She felt a deep understanding for all the wives whose husbands were away from home for much too long a time. She finally bestirred herself, took a bath, applied her makeup and, after tidying up the bed, left. She pocketed the key and caught the next train to Westchester.

Stacy and Dwight met each other at least once, and occasionally twice a week. Their lovemaking improved as they became better acquainted with each other's needs. Her needs were always greater than his, yet he always left her satisfied. Their liaison continued for almost a year.

She refused to accept gifts of money from Dwight. To do so would demean the whole affair—copulation for a fee or price, she reasoned.

In a vicarious psychological compromise and self-reconciliation, she succeeded in adjusting to the changes in her attitude. She considered the clandestine meetings therapeutic, proved by the improvement in her general appearance. There was a glow to her cheeks and a brightness in her eyes. She was down to her former figure. She was almost narcissistic in her self-appraisal as she turned in front of the mirror studying her shapely nude body. Her thoughts went back to yesterday with Dwight. She would have to be more careful, she decided, not to cry out Ed's name at the height of her passion. She had done that on one other occasion as far as she knew. Dwight did not seem to notice, but there were many things he chose not to see or notice . . . like his wife's increasingly open affairs with her younger male escorts. Her drinking was becoming an open scandal. Stacy wondered what Harriet's side of the story would be, if anyone could ever really know. She did not have to wait long.

◆◆◆

One afternoon there was a letter waiting in Stacy's mailbox. It was not the usual A.P.O. letter that Ed was able to send at times. It was scented and on expensive, engraved stationery. It was from Harriet Everett. Could they meet soon to have luncheon together, she asked. "Since we first met in our lodge, I have not had the opportunity to have a real chat . . ." There was a phone number at the bottom of the carefully written note. It was in a fine, delicate handwriting—reflecting Harriet's personality?

Stacy tapped the letter against her chin meditatively. She had mixed feelings about the invitation—more like a request which could not be ignored. The picture of Harriet in the sensual embrace of the young man rose before her. She called the number and was surprised to hear Harriet's voice, as if she had been sitting by the phone waiting for the call. "Hello, Mrs. Everett." She tired to keep her voice light and agreeable. "This is Stacy Rankin. I received your note and . . ."

"Oh, yes, Stacy," Harriet interrupted, "I am so glad you called; and please call me Harriet. After all, we do have much in common," she laughed easily. "We must get together soon, don't you think so?" As if to reassure her, she sounded sincere when she said, "I really like you, Stacy, and do want to get to know you much better. Agreed?"

Stacy was so nonplussed by the direction of the conversation, she was without words.

"Stacy, are you there? Hello—"

"Yes, Mrs. Everett—uh—Harriet, I am here. I was thinking about when we could—or where would you—"

"Get together?" she helped Stacy. "Why, I can send the chauffeur by to pick you up around twelve-fifteen, shall we say—tomorrow? He can drive you out to the lodge. Does that suit you, Stacy? We have no problem with gas rationing."

"Yes, Harriet," she answered calmly, "that will be fine."

"—I hope," Stacy said to herself after she hung up. She began to have a feeling that she was drifting beyond her depth.

The house looked more beautiful in the sunlight as the limousine approached. A maid escorted Stacy to a bright sunporch. A tea service had been set up, with a small buffet. Harriet was sitting when Stacy entered. She rose and came forward to greet her. She was wearing a form-fitting sweater and matching tweed skirt. She was ravishingly beautiful. She held both of Stacy's hands and kissed her cheek as a token of welcome. It was the first real opportunity for Stacy to study her face; she found it difficult to reconcile what she heard and knew with the beautiful woman standing before her, smiling so graciously and candidly. She realized with a shock that Harriet and she were probably the same age.

The luncheon was cheerful and the time passed with much small talk about the war, charitable activities, and the difficulty in obtaining things.

"A little more tea, Stacy?" Harriet asked, smiling. Without any preamble or change of expression, Harriet continued, "Then let us talk about Dwight." She looked steadily at Stacy. Stacy waited, hoping that she did not show the loss of composure she felt.

Harriet continued genially enough, "Oh, yes—Dwight has been telling me about you. He has spared no detail, including your behavior in bed." Stacy cold feel her face flush, and her heart begin to pound. ". . . from your very first meeting in New York . . ." Stacy began to feel something shameful and dirty coming over her. "—You see, Dwight and I understand each other very well. Too well, perhaps . . ." A cloud momentarily passed over her face. "It is his way of goading and tormenting me for doing—what I do. We have been going our separate ways for some time now. We remain married—" she looked pointedly at Stacy, "because divorce is something we do not consider in our family. Surely, you had no plan to take Dwight from me, did you?" Her manner was almost mocking. Her face had hardened and Stacy could see the woman Harriet would become in a few more years.

She felt naked and despoiled, as if she were having sexual intercourse in Harriet's presence. Dwight had done this to her . . . and to Harriet. With her small fists clenched, she jumped up and spoke in whispered fury, glaring down at Harriet. "Since you know all the details, as you say, then you must also know that Dwight was nothing more to me than a bed-mate, a male whom I have used—do you hear? —whom I have used as a male! He has been the only man—I thought he was at least honorable—besides Edward, my husband. I chose Dwight because of his elegance and . . . character. I am not a whore like you who sleeps around with younger men. I am a healthy young woman with normal sexual drives who has had to be without her husband for years. He is over there fighting a war and I have been over here wishing that it had never been necessary for me to . . . Dwight is not half the man my husband, my Edward, is. Does that surprise you? because you must also know—if he spared you no detail—or did his ego prevent him from telling you—that many times during my . . . during . . . I have cried out to Ed—my only love . . . *not* to Dwight."

Harriet listened, a sardonic smile frozen on her face. What manner of woman hides behind that beautiful face? Stacy asked herself. "Goodbye, Mrs. Everett. Will you please see that I get back home. After all, you and Dwight do not have to worry about such things as gas rationing. The war has not really touched you people has it? No, do not bother. I'll show myself out."

Stacy turned, hurried out through the front entrance and waited under the portico. A few minutes later the limousine drew up.

She tried to sink back as deeply as possible into the seat of the car. She wanted to hide. How did all this come about, she asked herself. She, Stacy, the wife of her absent beloved husband. How did she let herself be carried into this alliance? How had it become increasingly easier to be with Dwight at each successive meeting? She never believed that the affair would carry the potential of a triangle mess. It was all terribly beyond her and she felt very vulnerable. But did she really feel remorse about her self-gratification? She was not sure . . . but she did not think so. It was just the sordid and humiliating ramifications that made her feel so miserable and apprehensive.

The following days were dark ones for Stacy. When she thought of Dwight it was with a feeling of revulsion. But no self-flagellation for her, she decided.

She continued to engage in the usual social and hospital activities. Her friend, Dotty, occasionally had a questioning look in her eyes. Did she suspect or know? Stacy thought not—she had been discreet.

The war news during the ensuing months gradually improved. Conjecture about the war's termination began to appear in the newspapers. A subtle change came over Stacy. She was quite patient now to wait for her homecoming lover. They had been married for so short a period of time before he had to go away. She stifled the memories of the past months. The difficulty of living backwards, in the present, was too confusing and disturbing. She had the power of self-will to do it—she thrust the past deep into a dark recess of her mind where she hoped it would be forever buried.

She was waiting like an expectant bride for the homecoming of her man, the one whom she had always loved. No one else really mattered. It would be that way for the rest of her life—dear God, yes!—forgive me, Ed, for what I have done. I hope you will never know. I needed to do what . . . had to be done, but it has left me feeling soiled. I'll make it up to you, darling, dear God—yes. I am coming back into our world again. Yours and mine.

Ed was not in the best of humor. He was not given to swearing unless driven to a frustrating impasse by people and events. To him, swearing meant a descent into grossness. But this was one of those days. Some special instruments he had requisitioned months before finally did arrive and turned out to be not much better than army surplus—World War I surplus from the looks of them. They were carefully oiled and packaged with the proper item number and the proper designated name—but they were the wrong instruments. It was only one SNAFU of many that had plagued him over the war years and which he had to tolerate and compromise with—always after an explosive barrage of oaths of varying degree and sulphurous words of anathema heaped on the "stupid bastards who shipped them."

So, when Lieutenant Clinton Antrim's arrival coincided with the unwanted instruments, it was not a propitious time for the lieutenant, especially since his presence was going to involve Ed personally.

Major Forester, of the Medical Administrative Corps, had called a few minutes before and said, "You're getting a new anesthetist, Ed. He is coming over now." Ed had lost two of his best experienced anesthetists when they were transferred to General Hospital installations. The commanding officer assured Ed that replacements would be arriving in a day or so. Ed was always skeptical about such men and was particularly dubious of the clinical background and experience of these hasty replacements. They always worked out, however, because what they lacked in expertise, they soon made up by the sheer volume of experience which was quickly thrust upon them. Ed and the staff always managed to make out.

But this case was different. About two months before, the major part of Ed's outfit was stricken by a severe attack of dysentery. Most of the personnel had to be hospitalized, including Major Rankin. The vomiting and diarrhea were so severe and frequent that some of the hapless men resembled whirling dervishes as they constantly turned to satisfy the involved portions of their anatomy as one or the other end demanded. Soon they were all receiving intravenous administration of fluids and also sedatives. It was only after everyone was provided with an additional basin of one sort or another that some order was restored to the stricken men. In about forty-eight hours most of the men had recovered sufficiently to return to their quarters. Ed felt wan and weak —and empty. However, it was not over for him. He knew the signs. Being an orthopedic surgeon did not exclude him from a good general knowledge of surgical problems.

Four weeks later he was talking to Lieutenant Colonel Granstaff about it.

"Let's take a look. Let your pants down," he said, talking with a cigar butt in the corner of his mouth.

"Here, in the office?" Ed asked.

"Sure. Why not. Your ass is no better than anyone else's. What do you want, a private showing?"

Ed studied Granstaff's bland expression. For some obscure reason, Granstaff decided to smile with the cigar butt still in his mouth, clamped between his teeth. The result was an exaggerated leer.

"Well, alright," agreed Ed reluctantly, looking at the cigar butt suspiciously. "But take that damn thing out of your mouth before you examine me. I don't want a hole burnt in my tail, or getting cauterized. For God's sake, do you sleep with it in your mouth?"

Without answering, Granstaff got up and pulled on a rubber surgical glove. He told Ed to place his hands on the edge of the desk and bend over. Before complying, Ed pointed an accusing finger at the cigar.

"Awright, awright! For chrissake."

The Colonel placed the butt carefully on an ashtray on his desk. He was loath to part with it.

Granstaff was surprisingly gentle. His gruffness and his New Yorkese were all external wrappings to an underlying gentle and altruistic nature.

"It's a fistula, alright," he gruffed. He already had the butt back in his mouth. Ed began to suspect that it was the man's pacifier. Why not, he thought.

"So what do we do now?" Ed asked.

Granstaff answered, "It has to be laid open and allowed to granulate in. You know that as well as I do." After a pause, he added, "–under general anesthesia," looking at Ed with his head cocked sideways.

Ed hesitated. "This damn thing is a bloody nuisance," he answered wryly, "in many ways, including my personal hygiene. When do you plan to do it, Granny?"

Granstaff's eyebrows went up in surprise. Ed very rarely addressed him by his nickname.

"We can use Borden right away. Too bad we lost our best anesthetists. If it is alright, I can–"

"No, you don't," answered Ed, "not Borden. When he puts you to sleep, you wake up a day later–and groggy as hell. Oh, no, not Borden." Ed thought about it a moment longer. "Can't you do it under local? Why not local?"

"Local is no damn good. The Novocaine is too rapidly absorbed into the extremely cellular perianal and perineal tissues. It doesn't last. How about a caudal block? Maybe–"

"No caudal blocks for me, thank you. Nobody is going to poke one of those long needles into me. Damn it, Granny, you can use local–and I have a high threshold for pain. How long would it take you, anyway?"

"Not too long–a matter of minutes if I work fast." Granny looked at a message on his desk. "Tell you what," he continued, "let's wait a few days: I understand that a 'crackerjack' anesthetist is coming in. You can look him over and then you can decide. How's that suit you?"

So it was decided to wait until the hotshot anesthetist arrived.

And now Lt. Antrim of the U.S. Army Medical Corps was standing before him. Ed looked him over. If Antrim could have known what was going through Ed's mind and what mood he was in, he would have stayed away a day or two. He could have found some excuse–like a broken leg or something.

"I understand that you have had a lot of experience in anesthesia, Lt. Antrim. What was your outfit?"

"Oh, no, sir. I actually have had no experience in anesthesia."

"You have had none at all, you say?" A thundercloud began to form over Ed's head. "No experience?" Keeping his rising anger in check, he remarked, "They have you down as an anesthetists and we need at least one badly. How do you explain that?"

"Oh, I can explain that, sir. You see, I recently finished my internship and when I went down to Whitehall for my physical, they asked me if I was interested in any special branch of medicine and I told them I planned to go into anesthesia, and the captain down there said to me, 'Okay, you are an anesthetist.' He was a real pleasant officer. He smiled when he said it. So-soon after I was given my first assignment, I got fresh orders and was shipped out. Here I am."

"I see," said Ed.

The lieutenant said brightly, "But I am willing to learn, sir, and—"

"Not on me, you won't," Ed growled. In some way he felt sorry for the young lad.

"What's that, sir?" the lieutenant asked.

"Nothing," answered Ed. "Did Major Forester, the Adjutant, inform you about your B.O.Q.—your quarters?"

"Yes he has, sir."

"Well, I'll see you at conference," Ed remarked. His tone was one of dismissal and the lieutenant left, not knowing what to do—to salute--or what?

"It's okay with me if that's what you want, but don't come bellyaching to me afterward. You are a damn fool and it will serve you right if you feel your rear end—or your head—coming off." Granny's cigar was puffing like a locomotive pulling uphill. It was a fresh one. Ed had begun to believe that all Granny ever had was a box full of butts.

Ed's look was of stubborn refusal--refusal to take anything but a local anesthetic. His eyes wandered everywhere, but never rested on Granny. "I'll take my chance," he said. "Nobody is going to get me with nerve blocks or general anesthetic. That lieutenant kid would kill me for sure, and anyone poking those long needles—oh, no, I'll take my chances." Poking a rigid index finger in Granny's direction, he said firmly, "You are going to do it under local. Why the hell should that be so bad, I ask you? Can you or can't you do the job?"

"Aw, go to hell. What's the use of arguing with you. Get yourself prepared. Get Sgt. St. John to get you prepared. No breakfast and get your stupid carcass on the table for eight in the morning." He did not wait for an answer but reached for his cap. Ed hurriedly did the same and they both headed for the Officer's Club.

"Here, swallow this." Granny gave Ed a couple of pills, something to sedate him a half-hour before surgery time. Ed hopped up on the table. He wore only a short hospital jacket. He lay prone on his abdomen and rested his head on a small pillow which he hugged with both arms. He was covered with a sheet which kept him from seeing what went on in the operating room. Sgt. St. John sat on a stool at the head of the table, facing Ed. Even with local anesthesia, occasional adverse systemic reactions can arise and must be watched.

Granny was speaking in monotones. Then, "Ed, I'm going to give you the first needle, so don't jump when you feel the needle prick." That done, he infiltrated the entire area with Novocaine. By then the barbiturate effect of the pills was catching hold; Ed was beginning to feel drowsy and about to drift into sleep when—a sudden tearing pain made him jerk his head up with surprise. St. John steadied his head and shoulders. A profuse sweat broke out on Ed's face and forehead. Sgt. St. John wiped it away with a gauze pad.

> *I'm feeling the whole bloody thing. I wonder if that bastard used anything at all, just to teach me a lesson. He must have used water instead. He must have pretended to use the Novocaine. God almighty! There it goes again–the bloody vivisectionist is cutting me up alive! I'll get him for this if it is the last thing I do.*

"Ed's head and body were hidden from the operative field by the anesthesia shield over his head. Only St. John could see his face clearly. He could see him soundlessly grimacing and wincing through a wide-open mouth. He kept on wiping Ed's face and forehead with a towel.

Granny had to use a ligature suture or two—which he had to pass through the tissues so they would not tear out. They felt, to Ed, like long, slender corkscrews. With his last shred of objectivity, he was surprised to learn that what appeared to the naked eye as a perfectly smooth suture had a "spiral" sensation when passed through the tissues. All he could think of was a barber pole. He began to drum his fingers impatiently on the table above his head, and with as much calm as he could muster, he asked from beneath the sheets, "How're you making out? (He avoided saying Granny.) Think you'll be through soon? How does it look?

With maddening slowness, Granny replied, "Looks okay. It's wide open and the sinus tract excised. What's your hurry, Ed? Feeling any pain? You don't want me to hurry and do a sloppy job, do you?" All the time his hands moved nimbly and expertly.

"No-o," Ed managed to say. "No-no pain. I was just asking." He clenched his teeth. His eyes squeezed tight as he grimaced with each sharp pain. His shoulders hunched up. St. John was the only witness to what Ed was actually suffering. He continued to wipe his face.

> *The goddam sadist. I'm going to poke one of those cigars he's always smoking up his own asshole with the thing lit. Ow! If I ever get over this. Maybe I should have been a little more tolerant with Antrim. Almost anything is better than this.*

He was reaching the limit of his silent endurance when he heard Granny growl—music to Ed's ears. "All done. I've got some packing in there, so stay on liquids only for the next day or so. Did you hear that, Ed?"

"Yes," said Ed feebly, "I hear you."

"Now, that wasn't too bad, was it, Ed? Better than I expected."

Did Granny sound sympathetic? Impossible, swore Ed. But he replied, "No-not too bad." He wanted to sound cheerful, and now that there was no longer any pain, he was thankful.

Granny finished the dressing and on his way out patted Ed's shoulder several times. The gesture of kindness worked a minor miracle on Ed. Gone were all the silent dire threats of retribution and all the pejorative thoughts about Granny.

"Uh-er-Granstaff," Ed called. He caught him just as he was passing through the swinging door. Granny stopped and turned around. "Yes?" he said.

"Thanks," Ed said. "Good job. Didn't feel a thing."

St. John looked squarely into Ed's eyes. They exchanged unblinking stares.

"'S'allright," said Granny and he was gone.

It was a few weeks later. Ed was talking to St. John about changes in sterilizing techniques. After the matter in hand was settled, St. John loitered instead of leaving promptly, which was his usual custom. He had something on his mind.

"Is there something else, Sergeant?" asked Ed.

St. John was not given to much talk, at least not to Ed. "Major—about your operation a few weeks back—" he hesitated.

"Yes," Ed prompted, waiting for him to continue.

"You felt the whole thing, Major. You and I know it."

"Yes," Ed said, a trifle impatiently.

"But you told Colonel Granstaff that you felt nothing—?"

"That's right," agreed Ed with a smile of reminiscence. "It is a long story, St. John. Why do you mention it now?"

"Well, sir, we enlisted men say that an officer should never order his men to do anything that he could not—or would not—do himself. I thought you would like to know that." He wanted to say more but changed his mind. He saluted and left.

"I see," said Ed. But he truly did not see.

CHAPTER XXI

HOMECOMING

Lieutenant-Colonel Edward Rankin was on his way home. Not to a fireside, a hearth, or a refuge. Not to a particular place, but—to Stacy. Many times he imagined her open arms and sweet, welcoming smile. He could almost feel her warmth spread through his own body. Ed, like so many others, sustained himself with the magic of such imaginings!

Stacy was the only constant finite thought in Ed's mind. All Else was a melange of reflections, expectations, fantasies. Many thought-images crowded his brain. They all pushed and shoved through one narrow turnstile of his mind; no single crystallized thought fighting free through the frenetic bottleneck. Compounding his confusion was an apathy, an unwillingness to bestir himself to restore orderliness in his thoughts and aspirations. Ed was content to drift awhile in this mental inertia. He recognized it as a "coasting" period—a defense mechanism submerging his instinctual drives. Soon enough, his mind would police the traffic through the jammed mental turnstile and restore it to orderly dimensions. He was content to wait.

He realized that four and one-half years of tumult and casualties had inevitably dictated the present trend of his thoughts and actions, subordinated his own feelings and drives. In the early army days he was still perceptive enough to distinguish between his civilian and army personality. His perceptions gradually dimmed until he eventually became the Medical Corps, the convoys, the surgery. These were the only realities. All else was pushed into a dim alcove, pigeonholed for the duration.

Now that he was coming home to Stacy, he could not wipe away the war years like a thin coat of veneer. War had become a permanent integral part of him. The dormant civilian was finding it hard to surface; had been in hibernation for too long a time. He was still encased in an outer shell which he himself had created. Ed knew the man returning to Stacy could never be quite the same man who had left.

Stacy—warm-blooded, warm-hearted, vital, lovely. How had she fared? Would he find her very different? Her letters were warm and expressed great love. Still—it had been a long time for both of them. He had had Peggy for awhile . . . and Stacy? He dispelled the thought from his mind. Oh, how he ached to feel the warmth of his wife . . .

Dottie drove Stacy down to the port. The noise from cheering and shouting and laughter was almost unbearable. Everyone was friendly. Arms waved.

Stacy caught a glimpse of Ed. Without clearly seeing his features. She knew. She followed the slow progress of the strange yet familiar figure. She nervously nudged Dottie and pointed him out to her. Dottie craned her neck to catch a glimpse. He seemed serious and unsmiling, and allowed himself to be jostled with a patience that Stacy observed from where she stood. Finally, he was off the ramp. He began to look around slowly. At last his eyes met hers. Like a man in the desert who has espied an oasis, an eager longing lighted his eyes. He focused on Stacy from that moment on, as he moved slowly with the crowd toward where she stood waiting. When they were a few feet apart, eh put down his bag and looked at her, silently drinking her in. Tears streamed down her face. They stepped toward each other, hesitated for a split-second, fell wordlessly into each other's arms. She buried her face in Ed's shoulder and murmured over and over, "It has been such a long time—such a long time, my darling." She broke into convulsive sobs. Ed stood holding her, wordlessly comforting her, kissing her hair and her cheek. He had nothing to say. That would come later . . . when he could bring himself to talk. For now, all that mattered—was this.

Stacy finally stopped weeping. Dottie came over to Ed; they kissed. "How is Clyde?" he asked.

Stacy blew her nose, feeling more composed. She gazed at Ed's face. "You are so thin, my darling. Didn't they feed you over there?" At last Ed smiled. And so did Stacy.

Ed picked up his bag. The two women directed him toward the parked car. Stacy hung onto Ed's free arm. The women looked like two solicitous mother hens.

It was Ed's homecoming.

Max Bloom carried the watercolors to the shop's front window in order to study them better in the full daylight. He squinted at them through thick lenses, studied them at arm's length, one at a time. Stacy and Ed stood behind him. Without taking his eyes off the paintings, he asked in a high-pitched, squeaky voice, "Where did you get these, Dr. Rankin, might I ask?"

Ed replied blandly, "Funny thing, Mr. Bloom. I forgot about them until I was clearing out my foot locker. They were lying flat on the bottom. What do you think of them?"

Bloom's voice grew squeakier. He sounded like someone with a case of permanent laryngitis. "Just take a look at the name, Dr. Rankin, and—oh, excuse me—you, too, Mrs. Rankin. It says 'Waltner,* Wien.'

Does that mean anything to either one of you?" He quickly added, "—might I ask?" He was polite that way. Almost subservient.

Ed turned to Stacy. "Darling, you are the artist in the family. Have you ever heard of this man? He was an Austrian prisoner-of-war. I reconstructed his thumbs. That was before the War Department issued orders to discontinue rehabilitative surgery on prisoners slated for early repatriation."

Stacy puckered her pretty face, in deep concentration. After much pursing of the lips, she answered, "I'm afraid I do not. I am more at home with oils and with the old masters." She turned to Bloom. "You seem to know more about him, Mr. Bloom. You sound as if he were someone important. Will you please tell us."

"Of course, Mrs. Rankin. I shall be glad to do so. But do me a favor, please—call me Max. Well—to begin with, I am surprised that he was in the Austrian German army. He could not have been such a young man even then. Excuse me . . ." He stopped and blew his nose violently. Then, cleaning his glasses carefully and replacing them on his nose, he continued, "Maybe he was taken in to be a war artist or illustrator. The Nazis had many such artists on all the fronts—to illustrate the military 'glories' of the Third Reich. After the 'Anschluss'—you remember that even? It was in 1938—the Austrians were put into German uniforms and were told to 'go march.'" At this, he surprisingly straightened up quickly and, Prussian-like, extended a rigid arm toward a vague horizon in a Bismarckian order to "Go march." He wilted quickly into his former nondescript posture, like a collapsed souffle, and was silent for a time. "Where was I? Forgive me, I was wandering a little—oh, yes, the Anschluss—but the Austrians did not like so much to 'go march,' at least, not most of them. Waltner was probably in Vienna at that time, and his landscapes were popular everywhere. Such beautiful paintings! They were even copied on postcards—mostly of the Alps and the small villages. Such colorful pastoral scenes!" max again lost himself in thought. Stacy and Ed, understanding his mood, waited for him to resume his narrative. Max wagged his head from side to side in silent reminiscence. He seemed to be a man not used to smiling. He looked up, a kindly smile flitting

---

*Not his real name

across his deep-lined face. "And you, Dr. Rankin—you reconstructed his thumbs, you say? For an artist like Waltner! Imagine that! What is your pleasure? Do you perhaps wish to sell these pictures?"

Stacy took the initiative. "No, Max, we plan to keep them and would like to have them framed. What would you suggest? I think a simple black frame that does not detract from the beauty of the paintings should be appropriate."

Max and Stacy went into a huddle about the frames. Ed was temporarily left out of the conversation. He studied his wife's animated face. It had changed subtly during his absence. It showed a mixture of thoughtful introspection with a whimsical smile which played constantly around the corners of her mouth. Her eyes expressed a depth which seemed to change even while he looked at her. He could not penetrate those deep pools of her mind--her thoughts, her silences. Oh, if they could ever again be . . . one--as they had been in the past. Perhaps Stacy was but a reflection of himself. He knew he had not been overly communicative since his return. He was morose at times, preoccupied with the present while trying to shed the past. The shadows were still very much alive. They resisted relegation into the dark pigeonholes of memory. So much of the past was still so real; the present was yet strange.

There were both changed. It was inevitable . . . over a span of five years. How much had he changed in her eyes, he wondered. His wife was prettier than he last remembered her. The contrast between the Stacy he had known and the wife he had returned to, had become more perceptible with the passage of time. She had acquired a patina, an early veneer, that life had delicately laid upon her. He found it puzzling, disquieting, that she should always appear pleasantly contented. She seemed almost too agreeable and when desire arose within them, she became sensuous and almost wantonly demanding. Although their gratification was complete and joyful, Ed had a sense of unanswered questions after a particularly abandoned love-making. Long ago he had learned that answers eventually came with patience and compromise. He could not push; force. He must wait.

He was plucked back to the present as Max and Stacy finally settled on simple walnut frames. When they left the shop, Stacy was in a jovial mood. She turned toward Ed coaxingly. "Ed, darling, I know you haven't talked much about your experiences and I understand. I have avoided asking you. But the story about the artist sounds so interesting, I am dying with curiosity. Could you tell me about him? That is, if you want to." Encouraged by the smile on Ed's face, she pressed his arm affectionately against her breast and, like a child, wheedled, "Let's drop by Hubbard's for coffee and you can tell me all about it, good husband mine." She looked at him searchingly. "I—I want to start sharing your experiences, dear one, so that . . ." she hesitated, " . . . so that I—we—should get to know, feel for, each other. To try to find each other somewhere in the lost years."

The words told Ed something of her inner conflict. Ed turned to her without slackening his pace. "And you, Stacy," he said lightly, "you, my dear will do the same. Will you share your experiences with me?" Before she could answer, Ed continued, "It is a rather unusual story. I am sure it will intrigue you. One proviso, though . . ."

"What is that, O great medicine man?"

"That you let me have a big fat slice of the torte I saw in Hubbard's window to go with the coffee, and that you, my slim little darling, will not look at me as though I have fallen from everlasting grace with this calorie lapse."

Stacy playfully rolled and fluttered her eyes dramatically. "Yes! I promise, I promise." They both burst into refreshing, unrestrained laughter and set out at a fast pace toward Hubbard's.

It was a cheerful place. They found a table toward the back. As he guided Stacy between the chairs, Ed noticed there were only two other male patrons. A constant hum of chattering and nattering pervaded the pastry shop. The women seemed to talk all at once. Ed wondered how they could tell who was saying what to whom. He passed one group of six women, all leaning forward and apparently talking simultaneously across the table. Somehow, he decided, they had to be turned in on identical (auditory) wavelengths to preserve their words from being chewed up in the hopper-melange of their conversational crossfires. He must ask Stacy, he reminded himself, if that was how she managed to communicate at bridge parties with her friends.

They were served coffee, and Ed had his torte. Stacy did not press Ed further, but simply waited. He began, "You will remember that after I was transferred back to the U.S., I had orders to go to the hospital from which I would be finally separated. Due to some snafu in the records, the separation was delayed for a few weeks. I was, in effect, assigned to their surgical staff. Here, hand surgery was becoming a specialty. Many of us had considerable experience in hand injuries and early skin graft dressings, but this was a center for hand rehabilitative surgery. Dr. Sterling Bunnell and other great pioneers in hand surgery taught the younger men. In later years these young men will become well known as the new generation of hand surgeons, having learned the precepts laid down by their teachers who were the pioneers in this field. Anyway, this man Waltner, although a prisoner-of-war, was a prime candidate for hand rehabilitation. Both thumbs were missing except for small bone stumps. Considering his age and portly build, it was a surprise to all of us that he could have kept up with the troops.

Waltner was a genial, friendly person. None of the arrogance that we encountered in the younger Nazi-inspired prisoners. How he got his first box of watercolor paints was a mystery to me. Probably the Grey Ladies down in the Eighth Service Command, kindly women who couldn't feel malice toward anyone.

Waltner started painting on the backs of corrugated paper cartons--on anything, Stacy, for a painting surface. Purely from memory he painted different scenes of his village—the towering Alps, the huts, the sheep and cattle grazing in the foothills, the wayside chapels, the young man wearing lederhosen and his liebchen, grand vistas of sky and craggy precipices, deep ravines of perpetual snow, and mountain streams and waterfalls. So realistic, so beautiful, you could almost hear the thunder of the falls' raging torrents spawned from the depths of the massive glaciers. All in rich sepia tones, as well as greens and blues and whites. But I am getting ahead of my story.

"One day his case was presented. After examination and x-ray studies, it was decided that large pedicle skin flaps could be fashioned from his abdominal wall and attached to the stumps of his thumbs. Since there was some bone left at the base of each thumb, it was decided that a bone graft inserted into the completed and attached skin flap would contribute additional length to his thumbs to provide his hands with sufficient prehensile power and allow him to swing his thumb over toward his little finger. Luckily, the method worked out quite satisfactorily. It gave Waltner enough of what he needed as an artist. I wish now I had taken more time to get to know his background, but, in all honesty, I thought he was just another artist of no great distinction."

"Somehow he obtained a supply of paints and large sheets of paper. With his improved hands he turned out a veritable avalanche of paintings which he prodigally gave to the nurses, the corps men, the officers and—a few to me. In exchange he received cigarettes or other small articles. But above all, more paints and more paper.

He was repatriated some time after I left and I really did not think much about him until this afternoon with Max Bloom. Stacy, Waltner showed no outward signs of great emotional upheaval or despair at his loss. What greater deprivation can an artist suffer than the loss of his thumbs, particularly a man like Waltner whose very life depended on his ability to paint? Without that ability, life must have held little meaning for him."

"So now you know, my love. You must have found the story interesting—you have absentmindedly been nibbling away at my torte. By the way, I am now the only man in this whole coffee shop. I feel outflanked, at a strategic disadvantage. The best plan is to retreat before encirclement." He made a motion to get up, but Stacy remained seated. Ed sank beside her.

"It was a thrilling story, Ed. Do you suppose Waltner is still alive?"

"I don't see why not. Why do you ask?"

"Oh, I just thought that an artist like Waltner—you might write to him some day now that we are at peace, and find out about him. It would be beautiful to know that he is back in his beloved mountains—and painting—with contentment in his heart." She paused. "I remember that wonderful first day we really got to know each other—the day you found me painting in the museum." She looked at Ed. Unalloyed joy was reflected in her face. Ed drank it in greedily. How long, he wondered, will it be for them to know each other again? They were starting a new life. Soon he would be back into full practice. Soon he would start forgetting those other things. Soon he and Stacy . . . soon, he prayed.

CHAPTER XXII

ONE YEAR LESS TO LIVE

Before a year had passed, Ed was so busy in his practice that it was as if he had never been away. His diary had been neglected since his return. He had neither the time nor the inclination.

This day was different . . . he sat deep in thought, almost motionless, staring for a long time at the empty page. Heaving a deep sigh, he dropped the pen and stood up impatiently. He walked over to the radio, turned it on, listened for a few moments, abruptly turned it off. He stared moodily through the window, with his hands in his pockets. Finally, he turned back to his desk, sat down and began to write:

> *I have given it considerable thought. It is hard to put into words. A persistent reluctance, to write this, tugs at my coat-tails. Perhaps, in doing so, it will help me to achieve some objectivity. Evangelism is not my line and miracles—well they are something else again. I do not know what to think—how to think—about what happened.*
>
> *I was foolish to make such a bargain though I had the highest of motives. I was younger then. All young people think lifetime is forever. It is only some time later that we begin to harbor the thought that life is actually a rather abbreviated existence and its abridgment a real possibility.*
>
> *The more I think about it, the more the entire matter strikes me as bizarre if it were not for the fact that I am living through it. I hope that after I have written it down, "purged" myself, I shall be able to look at it more objectively.*
>
> *It all began some time before my army days when Molly Kyland came to me with a painful impaired hip joint from an injury she had suffered years before. Surgery was not quite the same, in many respects, as it is today. New techniques, special metals, bone cement, implanted spare metal parts and joints in those days were not even thought of. But one operation which enjoyed a fair degree of success was available to Molly. It involved a medial-shift osteotomy of the upper femur. The femur would form a buttress, for better weight-bearing and eliminate a good deal of the pain and stress on her hip. I recommended the procedure. Molly agreed. The day for the surgery came.*

Ed sat back in reflection, reliving the desperation he felt in the operating room. He resumed writing:

> When I exposed the hip joint, I discovered that much of the neck of the bone had absorbed at its end and what had appeared as adequate bone by preoperative x-rays turned out to be a mere shell, something that I could not use. I was filled with desperation. I felt that nothing, absolutely nothing, was going to help that hip.
>
> I pushed the bone over; what remained of the calcar support was only a large spicule of bone. Although we had not been using casts for quite some time, I had to apply one on Molly Kyland. That was the only support she had.

Again he stopped, thinking back to that episode of years ago. He resumed writing:

> When I left the operating room, I was never so depressed, disgusted and desperate in my whole life. I felt that Molly did not have a chance. Here I was, just starting out in practice, with this failure staring me in the face; it could ruin my reputation before I even had one.

Ed hesitated again. He continued slowly:

> I was alone in the hospital library. The words just came out. "Lord, in your great love, answer me. Help Molly Kyland in a way I could not have helped. I gladly offer one year of my life, if Molly Kyland recovers and can walk again."

Ed stopped writing. He sat so motionless that he barely seemed to be breathing. He felt the prickling of his scalp and the sides of his face as he remembered—an eerie, frightful sensation. What a foolhardy pact to make! For Molly Kyland!

He stood up and poured himself a cognac. Swirling the liquid around in the snifter, his mind drifted into another world. He could think only of that other awful pact—made by Dr. Faustus. But Faustus had bargained for years to be <u>added</u> to his life, for hedonistic pleasures. This was different. Ed looked around the study. He could not shake the feeling that there was something powerful and turbulent in the room—an overwhelming, shrieking silence. He resisted the urge to leave.

He finally returned to his diary:

> *The war years came along. I had forgotten Molly Kyland by the time I was separated from service. There were so many other things to remember, or to forget. I was in Bloomingdale's a few days ago, picking out a scarf for Stacy, when someone tapped me on the shoulder. The man looked familiar but I could not place him. "Doctor," he said, "you probably don't remember me. I am Robert Kyland, Molly's husband. You did a hip operation on her."*
>
> *I asked Mr. Kyland how Molly was. He said she was "doing fine—just fine." I asked if I could see her and Robert agreed that it would be a good idea. He would also bring some x-rays take in San Francisco about a year ago. "These were the final ones," he said.*
>
> *I saw Molly Kyland today.*

Ed wrote furiously. It was pouring out of him. He remembered "today" in great detail, every moment deeply imprinted in his memory. Findings from x-rays Robert Kyland brought and his examination was astounding. Healing and union had taken place. There was only minimal shortening. She was almost as good as new. He wrote:

> *I was so delighted about it all, until I happily said to Robert, "The x-rays look so good, so mighty good that it is almost like a—" I stopped right there. Until that moment I had completely forgotten my promise. The sudden recall left me stunned.*
>
> *I can write no more, not for now; not for a little while.*

He thought he heard the garage door rumbling open. Stacy was returning from her art class. He wondered if he would eventually tell her. Some day, perhaps, if he felt he could no longer keep the disturbing thought to himself. If he ever reached that point.

He came downstairs and into the kitchen where he found Stacy happily munching on a cracker and holding a glass of milk in her hand.

"I'm ravenous," she said.

She looked so sweet and home-like. Ed smiled.

Her cheerful, simple exuberance was a balm to his mood and his eyes lighted up with grateful tenderness which Stacy instantly sensed. She stopped chewing momentarily and offered her bulging cheek for him to kiss, then contentedly resumed her milk and crackers. Ed felt a vicarious sense of joy simply watching her in her apparent freedom from sadness or care.

If she was happy, he was.

It was several years after Ed's homecoming. Stacy settled into the life of a very busy surgeon's wife. She had never entertained any illusions about the heavy demands Ed's private practice would make on his time. There were days when she would see him at breakfast, if she arose early enough, and at dinner, if no emergency call came. She understood, but she was frequently alone. She read a lot and chatted on the phone a good deal with her friends.

It was curious that she did not paint as much as she used to in the past, particularly since she had more leisure time. She was always putting it off for one reason or another. Her days were filled mostly with her friends. There was a constant round of bridge, luncheons, fashion shows for charitable organizations. Also, the Ladies' Auxiliary for the hospital. Finally, there was always the most pleasant activity of all—shopping for anything that struck her fancy. Ed was generous that way.

Whenever she wore a new gown, Ed would gaze at her in admiration, and the look in his eyes told her all that she wanted to know. Occasionally, he would ask her to walk up and down the room, like a model, and to turn this way or that, just so he could feast his eyes on her.

She was trying on a new ensemble she had just unwrapped. As she studied herself in the mirror, he eyes took on a faraway look. She was remembering what Ed told her the night before. It troubled her, that for a long time he had harbored the belief that one year would be taken from his life! She shivered at the thought. It was all nonsense and she was not going to allow it to be blown out of proportion. Better to forget the entire matter. Besides, Dotty was coming over to help with dinner arrangements. Brownies! She promised Dotty she would bake some for her. Stacy quickly threw her new clothes on the bed, slipped into a housecoat and hurried downstairs to the kitchen.

"These are delicious, Stacy." Dotty said contentedly. "So moist."

"Ed likes them, too," Stacy replied. "Nice and chewy, but he abhors putting on weight and every time he has one, a sense of guilt plagues him. He is a bit vain about himself."

"I wish Clyde would do something about the pounds I can see developing," Dotty deprecated. "But, to get back to the dinner party–putting George next to Paula could be a DISASTER! All Paula talks about is her family and children. If you want my advice, I would–" Dotty could see that Stacy was only half listening. She obviously did not have her mind on the dinner arrangements. "Stacy," she cried, "If you are ever going to get your dinner arranged, you'd better–" Dotty did not finish the sentence.

In an absentminded way, Stacy turned to Dotty. "I have to tell you something, Dotty. You are my closest friend."

"Tell me what?" Dotty asked.

"I want to tell you what Ed confessed–no, disclosed–to me yesterday. It is disturbing me."

"You sound positively conspiratorial," Dotty whispered. She was always an attentive listener.

"Ed and I have discussed heaven on different occasions, Dotty. I see that surprises you, judging from your arch expression. Well, we do, Dotty. Ed calls heaven a 'going concern.' Did you ever hear of such a thing! Well, that is what he calls it and, you know, he has me practically convinced. Here, dear, have another brownie. You and your slim waist! I could positively kick you. Since you and I are so close, I am sure that it's all right to tell you. But first promise me that you will never, never repeat what I am going to tell you."

The suspense made Dotty squirm in her chair. Stacy finally cleared her throat. "You know," she began, "how sensitive Ed can be at times. Besides, what happened was when he was much younger. When you reach a certain age you begin, for the first time, to realize that life is really rather short."

Dotty fidgeted more than ever. Stacy hastily continued. "All right, Dotty," she admonished, "please be patient, I am getting to the point." dotty seemed pacified for the moment.

"It all began with a Molly someone-or-other. Ed operated on her hip. It seems that when he got in, he found a condition which made it practically impossible to get a good result and he had to do something other than what he had planned. He felt extremely despondent after the operation. So, what does that serious, sensitive husband of mine do? Listen to this—it gives me the shivers just to think about it—"

"Go on, go on," Dotty encouraged.

"So what does he do but promise the good Lord one year of his life—can you imagine that?—a year of his life if this Molly woman should have a successful result with her hip. But that is not the end of the story. ER—be a dear girl and pour me some more tea. You know, Dotty, I know a shop, not far from here, where they blend the tea to suit your taste. You can even take some home to try it. Afterward they name the blend after you and whenever you come by, they will prepare it for you while you wait. Isn't it delicious? It is expensive though. Where was I? Oh, yes—honestly, I will never, never understand why he did such a thing. Well-you know how the war years gouged a piece out of all our lives—"

Stacy paused and remained silent. Dotty gave her a sidelong glance and wondered if she was thinking about Dwight. Did Stacy think that she could make all those trips into the city without Dotty finding out about Dwight?

"—Where was I? Yes—the war years. When Ed came back he had completely forgotten about Molly. Until one day he runs into Molly's husband who tells Ed that Molly did very well. So Ed has them come to his office and he checks her. Well, you can guess, Dotty, what happened. Ed found everything so marvelous that he told Molly it was like a miracle. Then he remembered the promise he made years ago. So now he thinks he is going to die one year sooner. He said to me, 'So now you know, my love. That is the way it was.'"

"There was a long silence after that, Dotty. Ed was talked out and I did not know what to say. The dear, sensitive man. After awhile he got up and said, 'I am certainly not going to sit around on my butt wondering and thinking about it.'"

"So then what happened?"

"That's it, Dotty."

The two women remained strangely silent. Dotty finally stood up. "I had better be going, Stacy," she said. "Please call me tomorrow—about the dinner. Also, you promised me your special recipe for these delicious brownies."

CHAPTER XXIII

THE KEY

It was lying there in the top drawer under some things. She must have misplaced it, and forgotten it. She must have—she herself told me where to look for a breastpocket kerchief.

A key—to a suite in the finest hotel in the city, according to the attached tag. I held it in my hand. It was strange and sickening. Its outline became dim and blurred.

Stacy, my Stacy.

I hear her coming. I'll pocket the key. She will not miss something she has misplaced or forgotten.

Stacy, Stacy.

Could she have deliberately put it there—knowing I would find it, wanting me to know what she could not bring herself to tell me? I wish I knew. Somehow it would make a difference.

So—now it is up to me. Either I remain silent and pretend that nothing has changed, or—I speak. If I do, then what about Peggy? Do I tell Stacy about her? I must have time to think. Time—it always seems to bring the answer somehow. If she deliberately left the key for me to find, she will soon know that it is no longer there. My silence will be answer enough. Time and silence; silence and time.

Stacy, Stacy.

I feel tired and leaden and saddened unto death. As she stands in the doorway her face shows only sweetness. Can a face be so open and dissembling and still hide so much of what lies behind it.

He deliberately placed his pen parallel to the edge of the open

CONVERSATIONS OF SILENCE

diary, obeying an unnamed compulsion. He leaned back in the chair and stared at the wall.

"Are you busy? Doing anything special?" Stacy's voice was steady. She looked as if she waited for an invitation to enter, unusual for her. She never stood on ceremony.

"No, of course not, Stacy. I was just making a few notes in my diary." Ed closed the book. "Is there something you wanted to tell me?" he asked. He tried to sound noncommittal—too much so. Stacy stopped short.

> He is hiding something. My God, does he know? I have hoped the past was permanently buried. He suspects. How did he find out? He won't stop until he knows everything. He does not speak and his face is composed, but I see the hurt through the dull despair in his eyes. He knows. Be calm. My legs are trembling and my mouth is dry. I cannot speak. I just smile. My throat feels so tight I cannot breathe. I can hardly stand. I wish I could remove that false smile from his face. Make him speak; say something. I do not want it to end-in silence.

"Don't just stand there, Stacy. How did the art show go? What kind of day did you have?"

> I am sick unto death and I sit here asking her inane questions. The world is falling about my head and I exchange banalities. The key is not proof of anything. There may be another explanation. But she used it. And she kept it... why? I will have no real peace until I can tear this out of my mind. I cannot mention it now, cannot risk bringing this festering thing into the light without knowing the facts. Talking about it now will create a barrier which could never be torn down. So—I smile—and she smiles in return. How can I say what I really feel? I am torn. So—I smile, pretending that I do not suspect what is known to both of us. Pretend and SMILE.

"You look thoughtful, Stacy. Is there something wrong? Something bothering you?

She tried to walk nonchalantly over to an easy chair.

Will my shaking body and legs make it?

"As a matter of fact, darling, it was a rather disappointing day. There wasn't a single black and white that appealed to me. You know how long I have been looking for one—something that would be suitable in that spot over the floral arrangement. The only pleasant part was the luncheon. Dotty and I enjoyed that very much."

How long can I carry on this charade? I feel that I am floating in a gray purgatory, mouthing words involuntarily, the words themselves sounding far-off and without echo. It is closing in on me. Ed, my love, my love, you were always the only one. Even when I . . . when I . . . you were in my thoughts and you were the one I called out to. What is done is gone like a dream. It was a need that had to be met—for me.

"Can I get you a brandy, dear? A cognac? No, don't move, darling, I'll get it for you." She poured his favorite, brought it over to him, and sat down beside him. She desperately wished to dispel the tension, to restore things to the way they were. Shyly, she snuggled up to him and put her arm around his neck. Ed could feel her tremble. Instinctively, he put his arm around her. Stacy snuggled closer, placed her head on his shoulder and drew her legs up under her. Ed put down his drink and encircled her soft, yielding body with both arms. They spoke no words, were engrossed in separate thoughts. They clung to each other as if they feared losing a precious possession. Their marriage and their love would all be in jeopardy if their silence changed to accusations and denials. All they had cherished would disappear—like a house of cards before a hurricane. The silence was a comfort. Stacy's breathing became easier. Two large tears welled up and rolled down her cheeks. Ed pulled out his handkerchief and dabbed the tears away. He felt a deep compassion for her tears, a sadness, almost a bereavement. Someday, he hoped, their lives could be good again. But would they ever be without regret or recrimination?

As he sat there holding her, Ed reflected that he had never truly succeeded in fathoming Stacy's deeper feelings. His mind drifted to

Peggy. He remembered calling Peggy "Stacy" at the height of their lovemaking. He wondered what Stacy did when she was alone with this other man. It is unbearable to picture. Did she think of him at those times? When she was ... penetrated ... by this other man. Dear God, must I destroy myself with these thoughts? Help me blot it out. Dear Stacy, did you call out my name?

It hurt. It killed. It overwhelmed and destroyed his ego, his soul, and his spirit. It dragged him to a depth of crushing numbness. But he still wanted Stacy. He still needed her. He pulled her a little closer. She patted his hand.

They silently held each other, waiting for the silence itself to give rise to a healing. Twilight came, then the darkness closed upon them. The darkness became a haven of tender mutual solicitude and consummate kindness. It carried a quality of sensuality. In this rare moment there existed an unspoken deeper love and compassion than they had ever felt for each other. But it was a moment only. Neither could dispel a foreboding of what yet-unborn moments might bring.

Ed finally disengaged himself and turned on a light. Stacy also stood up. They slowly ascended the staircase to retire for the night.

CHAPTER XXIV

He buried himself in a busy schedule of operations. He lingered longer during his visits to his patients, spent more time in the hospital library. The evenings at home seemed to follow an even tempo. On the surface, nothing had changed, except their lovemaking. There was always a "good" reason why there should be none. Some evenings they went to a cinema—something they very rarely did in the past. It got them out of the house. When they returned, they were both "too tired." At other times Ed had emergency calls that kept him away until the early hours of the morning. So it went. The pretense and the play-acting went on.

Stacy did more painting than she had for some time. Except for volunteer hospital duties, she could usually be found in her upstairs studio. It was here Dotty visited one afternoon. Stacy cleared away a chair for her to sit on.

"Honestly, Stacy," Dotty chided, "you are behaving like those foreign artists who devote their lives to their art. I admit that you have great talent, but I don't think your paintings will wind up in the Metropolitan Museum of Art. This dedication is commendable, but you have deserted your circle of friends, and if I had not decided to drop by without warning, the greatest gaucherie, I would not be sitting here talking to you now."

"You were sweet to drop by, Dotty. Please forgive me. I should have called, or something. You see . . ." She did not finish but leaned back in her chair and squinted at the canvas in critical appraisal, deciding on the proper mixture of colors, then brushing it onto the canvas. The effect seemed to satisfy her. "—You see," she repeated, "I have neglected my work for so long that, when the 'spirit' moved me, I just had to get back to it. In my younger days, Dotty, I used to make copies of famous masters in the Metropolitan Museum; also in Europe."

Dear God, if she only knew what really is tearing me apart. I am "absorbed" in my work so I can be home most of the time, hoping and praying that Ed will come home at an odd hour and come to me. Oh, how I ache to fall into his arms. In the meantime, all I can do is paint my dreams and hopes onto these canvases.

Subterfuge was abhorrent to Ed. No matter what the justification, he felt less of a man—to do this behind Stacy's back. But if there was ever to be closeness again between them, he had to know. It was the doubt that harassed him mercilessly; even the truth would be more bearable. Occasionally, he was seized with an uncontrollable restlessness and would prowl back and forth like a caged animal. He had to do something about it. He sought out colleagues who played handball or indoor tennis. After an evening of such physical activity, he felt more comfortable—and very tired—when he came home.

◆◆◆

He dialed the hotel number with no precise plan in mind. The operator answered, "Hotel, may I help you?"

"Yes—will you please ring suite number 101-103."

Ed could hear the operator ringing the suite.

"Sorry, sir, they do not seem to answer. Do you care to leave a message, sir?"

"Yes, will you please leave a message for Mr.—er—er—"

"Mr. Dwight Everett, sir? He does not come in every day, sir. If it is an urgent message, I cannot say when he will get it—"

"Well," said Ed, "never mind. I have another number where I might contact him. I'll try there. Thank you."

So—it was Dwight Everett. The bank executive. Comptroller on the hospital board of governors. The man with the young wife. What was it he had heard about her?

A much older man. Very wealthy. At least, Ed thought, he was not some young handsome stud, some sexual athlete.

It was true, then. Just as true as it was about himself and Peggy.

Strange. Knowing it was Dwight Everett brought things into clearer focus. Some of his heaviness of spirit began to leave him. Without stopping to analyze why this information should be something he could live with, he felt his burden becoming lighter, though he knew he would never be completely free from it. Stacy could not have loved this man. She "used" him. It would have been no more than that. He remembered the loneliness he felt before he met Peggy in France.

At least he had discarded a burdensome doubt. He could handle the truth as he saw it now. He could not wait to drive home.

She was painting when Ed appeared at the door of her studio. She looked up and thought she was dreaming, but there he was with his arms invitingly open and a wide smile on his face. She smiled as she rose and went to him. It was a smile wet with tears. She fell into his arms. He held her and rocked her gently in his embrace. No words came. What was there to say? Silence had won out in the long run. The first murmured words came during their lovemaking—words intermingled with tears and tenderness, and sadness, and happiness, and joy, and moans, and a desperate clinging and holding and cleaving to each other.

Ed found he could not throw the key away. He kept it in a strong box in the lower right drawer of his desk.

On one of the inside pages of the City Reporter, a small item read, in part:

"Harriet Everett legally separated from Dwight Everett, who has for the past year been managing the bank's affairs on the west coast. Mrs. Everett is the daughter of the late Senator _____ and will be returning to her townhouse in Georgetown~"

The news item seemed to escape Stacy's and Ed's attention.

CHAPTER XXV

Stacy and Ed were settling into early middle age. They were members of a prestigious country club. They travelled extensively, crossed the Atlantic numerous times. Ed's practice encompassed patients from everywhere. Much of his time was being devoted to this "international" practice.

Through some perverseness within him, he was given to spells of depression and reminiscence. In spite of his success and the satisfying quality of his, and Stacy's lifestyle, which should have given him a sense of fulfillment, there recurred a sense of lack, a longing for something else, something more.

It was strange how he remembered Elena during these periods, and, from habit, "talked" to her, whose cheer and lightheartedness were a counterbalance to his moods. Stacy was a compatible, loving wife, a fact which induced a secret sense of disloyalty and guilt in Ed.

In his mind's eye he carried the picture of Elena as she was when they were together the last time in Canada. It remained a bright memory. He never stopped wondering why his letters were returned with no forwarding address and no word of explanation. He harbored a vague feeling that something more than her marriage was involved, that she was borne along on a wave of insurmountable events. They had loved each other with such a fullness of understanding and trust that an unkindness from either of them was inconceivable. She would never hurt him intentionally. It had to be something else—but he would never know the answer. Memories of that first youthful love still remained with him. The incandescence of hot passion of first love of youth usually burns itself out. His memories were not of that. Ed remembered Elena with a vague indefinable longing for the closeness which flowed so freely from their inner natures that they were truly one in his mind. Ed could still recall the quiet exultation of that time. That is what he truly missed and was lost to him.

His life with Stacy went on as usual. They were content. His practice made daily demands on him. Any extraneous emotional intrusions did not interfere with his work. He loved his wife.

Stacy was up early one morning and Ed, troubled by his thoughts of Elena, resolved to be particularly cheerful and thoughtful. When he kissed her before leaving, he did it with so much warmth that Stacy gazed thoughtfully at the door after it closed behind him.

Stacy was more socially-oriented than Ed. He was content to come home, have a cognac after dinner and read the papers. He periodically wrote in his personal diary which was fast approaching the dimensions of a journal. He also contributed scientific papers to medical journals and publications from time to time. He wrote a good deal of the latter.

They were popular members at the country club. Everybody knew the Rankins. In the earlier years they participated in all the club functions and social activities. More recently, their evenings at home assumed increasing priority. Occasionally, an evening trip into New York for dinner and opera. They were patrons.

One evening, Stacy looked across to Ed, who was reading the evening paper. She wondered if this was an opportune time to bring up the subject of a formal dinner. In her most guileless voice she started, "Ed, dear, it has really been quite a while since we gave a dinner party. Don't you think we ought to do something about it?"

He put the paper down and sipped his brandy; he looked at Stacy expectantly. She took the cue. "We have accepted so many invitations lately. Honestly, I am embarrassed to meet our friends again. We simply have to reciprocate. I was thinking of cocktails and dinner at the club. What do you suggest?"

The question was purely rhetorical, intended to make Ed believe that somehow it was his idea. If Ed saw through this transparent stratagem, he gave no inkling. "How many do you have in mind, Stacy?"

"About ten or twelve, I think." She actually had more in mind, but to get Ed to agree and to decide on the date was her principle consideration.

"It sounds all right, Stacy. Let me know when you have the menu. I'll call Richard to discuss the wines; and for captain we'll ask for Helmut—" He stopped. Funny how difficult it was to break a habit. One forgets . . .

◆◆◆

Helmut was the best dining room captain at the club. When Ed and Stacy first became members, they were advised to ask for him whenever they planned a dinner party.

When he escorted them to their table for their first dinner, they were impressed. He was tall and slim. He looked "aristocratic," Stacy thought.

Whenever they entered the dining room, he always accomplished his polite bow with just the correct degree of formality. The little flourish when he handed them the menu, the soft, solicitous voice when they discussed the choice of wine—all added up to a warm feeling of "Gemütlichkeit." Especially when he said "excellent" with such conviction that Ed and Stacy felt they had accomplished something much more important than ordering dinner. The brisk, imperious way he snapped his fingers for the waiter to clear their table between courses was elegant. He always made it a point to replenish their wine glasses himself. He would inquire if everything was to their satisfaction. Ed, of course, would answer in the affirmative.

"Excellent, excellent," Helmut would smilingly approve.

In the earlier years they entertained a good deal. Saturday nights were always black tie. The ladies wore evening gowns which changed with the seasons—from the summer décolleté to the winter décollectés! The female members had an eye on what each other was wearing. Ed was only mildly surprised when Stacy told him that women actually dressed more "for each other" than for the men. "Ask any man what a lady at dinner wore and he will do little more than stammer," she said. "His wife, on the other hand, will be able to describe in detail what she wore, down to the shade of her fingernail polish."

Helmut was at his best at these formal dinners. He seemed stimulated by soft lights, orchestral music, dancing figures on the terrace or on the ballroom floor, and the gay chatter. More than ever diners heard his "excellent" stamp of approval.

As the years went by a casualness crept into club functions. Only when the Autumn Chrysanthemum Ball took place did all the previous decor and the beautifully gowned ladies return.

Helmut's elegant formality remained the same. It was as if he were trying to hold back the change by his sheer refusal to alter his manner. In a way the older members appreciated it. He was a link with the past.

The various social events also changed with the seasons. Stacy and Ed always looked forward to the beach parties held on the club's private island on the Sound. The entire kitchen staff was transferred there for the evening. The buffets were sumptuous. They included every variety of seafood one could wish for. Also, roasts of all kinds. The buffet was arranged in the round—completely duplicated on each half-side so that the members did not have to stay in line very long to make their choices.

Nautical decorations, a small stage for the entertainment, a polished dance floor and a sense of belonging among friends, made everyone want to be invited to these parties. Here, too, an increasingly casual atmosphere prevailed.

It was during the beach season that rumors about Helmut leaving, circulated among the members. With the generous gratuities he had received over the years, he could have become "very well-off." Many of the best captains in various country clubs were able to retire comfortably. It seemed he owned a large farm where he raised cattle and grew grain.

Ed suspected that Helmut wanted to go for aesthetic reasons. He was brought up in the tradition of elegance and courtliness. While it lasted he was content and happy. Good taste and polish were his second nature. He could not conform to the less-than-elegant atmosphere. He was no longer happy—he wanted to leave.

Ed spoke to Helmut one night at the beach. Yes, it was true. Helmut's expression betrayed no inner feeling; he volunteered no explanation. Ed did not pursue it. They had the usual discussion of choice of wines. Helmut always deferred to Ed's knowledge of the ladies' tastes.

"Excellent," he agreed and went off to arrange things. Ed looked at his departing figure. He felt that an era was at an end.

The evening was beautiful and mild with a light ocean breeze. There were several hundred people attending the dinner, the summer's last. A beautifully arranged table overlooked the Sound. To the right was the Cove where many yachts rode lightly at their moorings. Harrison's yacht was there; it slept ten. Ed notice a flickering glimmer of light. It came from Harrison's yacht. The glimmer grew into a glare. Harrison's yacht was on fire! Soon, the diners watched the yacht being towed out into the open water where it would not endanger the other craft.

While the yacht was still burning, Helmut came by to refill the wine glasses. "Helmut, too bad about Harrison's yacht," lamented Ed. "It was a beauty."

Without a change of expression, and still pouring the wine, Helmut remarked, "Excellent," and continued around the table.

Ed and Stacy never saw Helmut again.

"See if we can get Enver as captain, Stacy. I have always found him—ah—excellent. I think I'll put a few words in my diary—about Helmut—"

"About Helmut?" Stacy asked absentmindedly.

CHAPTER XVI

Stacy instantly fell in love with the house when she and Dotty rode past it for the first time in late May. She begged Dotty to turn around and drive slowly by again so she could study it. The house stood on two acres of wooded land. It was built on a rise. Gable roof covered with slate shingles. A sweeping 400 foot drive up to the house with another drive leading around to a large garage. Beautiful rock gardens in front of the house, tiered so that the rows of flowering azalea bushes

CONVERSATIONS OF SILENCE

were a patchwork quilt of blazing color. Pink and white dogwoods in bloom. Along the main drive wild cherry trees. Like a shy interloper, a small silver maple growing among them. Trim boxwoods lining both sides of the flagstone walk-up to the door. The grove of dark pines in the southwest corner. A small discreet sign nailed on the split-log fence read: "For more information call Gordon Realities. 273-1000."

Stacy's eyes shone with the immediate dream of living in it. "How lovely," she murmured. "Dotty, I am going to call as soon as I get home." Dotty just smiled. Stacy, in her own quiet way, was a determined person when it came to house buying. This would be the second large house in the last ten years. Ed was too preoccupied with his patients to be of much help in these matters. He relied on her completely. Stacy bought their other home before Ed even saw it. She alone supervised the moving and subsequently commissioned the interior decorators. Dotty knew Stacy would be floating in a heavenly aura of planning and decorating. There were no financial hindrances, although Stacy never discussed money matters with her.

It was only a matter of few days when the real estate agent took Ed and Stacy through the house. Stacy's calculating eye noted the changes she would have to make.

Ed was a little discontented. Moving and changes irritated him to no end—but never for long. He had indulged Stacy all their married life.

There were more rooms than the two needed. One bedroom became Ed's study. A dormer would have to be sacrificed, in the maid's quarters, to be converted into a studio for Stacy, to get the proper light. "I want to live in this beautiful house, forever," she exclaimed happily.

It was their second winter in the new home. A Sunday morning.

Stacy was in a chiding mood. There was a slightly acerbic quality to her voice. Ed knew the signs—arms folded, lips lightly compressed, a look of determination, no vocal emission, her gaze fixed in his direction. Ed braced for the impending barrage and opening of "hostilities."

"I cannot see, I simply cannot," she chided, "what you can

possibly get out of reading the comics." It was a surprisingly mild frontal attack. He would require only light artillery for the counteroffensive. "Hmmmph," he responded. He looked up at Stacy for a moment, ruffled the papers and returned to the comic section—Li'l Abner. Didn't she understand that these people of Dogpatch were truly warm characters with the qualities and foibles of people everywhere? They were real. What's more, they made him laugh and smile—

"Only people with limited intelligence are interested in this childish stuff." She threw the barb at him, but in such an irresolute way that it was robbed of much of its effect. Ed again answered, "Hmmmph." Stacy must be getting low in her vitamin content, he mused. Her generalship was apparently slipping.

He wished he could point out to her that Dick Tracy had been in great difficulty in the last week's section; and now the wily detective had, at a critical moment, managed to extricate himself from an ominous and near-fatal brush with crime. Again triumphant over evil. It would have been gratifying to share this bit of good news with Stacy, that crime does not pay and that evil-doers are doomed to horrible ends. Bad cess to them!

Observing that she had not produced any visible discomfiture in Ed, Stacy decided her husband was beyond salvation (a verdict arrived at every Sunday).

She turned her gaze to the outdoor panoramic view. It was wintertime. The last night's snowfall was dazzling in the bright sun and cloudless winter day. The sun porch, glassed in with louvers and storm windows, proved to be a pleasant area of their home life. The Holly trees, the Arborvitae, the Floribunda, Mountain Laurel, and the Pines around the perimeter of their estate. A pheasant cock strutted into the clearing and unhurriedly approached the cracked corn she always left for him. She had hung several feeding stations and the winter birds were chattering and fluttering about. She loved birds. Stacy experienced a quiet happiness as she viewed the scene. She had to admit that closing in the sun porch was Ed's idea.

In a softer mood, she stepped over to Ed, and peered over his shoulder, studying the succession of vari-colored squares. With her hand on her hip and the other fluttering in emphasis she observed, "Take Orphan Annie right there. A homeless waif and her dog Sandy exposed to awful perils. She remains everlastingly a dear, brave child, with the ingenuous, scheming mind of an adult. If they would let her grow up, she would be going through menopause by now and taking Valium, or whatever the doctors give for such things."

"Hummph," Ed answered. He had just finished the comics.

"How about a nice cup of tea and a slice of fruitcake. The kind you like," she coaxed, giving up the fight until next Sunday.

He grinned. "Wonderful Stacy. Yes, let's." Putting his arm around her waist, he guided her into the den.

While he held her he was thinking that Stacy never failed to excite him, even after all the years of marriage. She possessed some priceless indefinable quality . . . femaleness. And she was amazingly unaware of it. Her closeness made him think of things other than tea.

"Sweetie, I was thinking that it would be the nicest thing if we could get into . . .?"

"Oh? So that's what's on your mind. Well . . ."

"Be a dear girl. We're home alone. Nobody is going to call. Tea and cake can wait. I am thinking of a much sweeter dessert—*you*, dear delightful little wife of mine."

Stacy had no affectations about sex. When she was desirous, she said so.

She was.

They always found great joy in lovemaking without planning. The passage of the years had brought an openness, a total knowledge of each other. Not the violent passion of the earlier years, but far more fulfilling—complete verbal and physical communication without reserve. They were as one.

Later, while they were having tea, Stacy observed, "I see the birds are still very hungry, with snow covering everything on the ground. I'll have to remember to pick up another hundred pound bag of food at Ferreira's."

Ed thought about her unfailing love of birds. To her they symbolized purity and spiritual goodness. Perhaps she was influenced by the depiction of the Holy Spirit descending as a white dove. She loved them to the point that she interpreted any adverse weather report in relation to the effect it would have on food for her birds. He felt the same about them, generally speaking, but not to her extent. Ed remembered nursing a sore shinbone long ago on account of one particular bird. "Do you remember that visit to Assisi?" he asked, "when you almost broke my leg?"

"Assisi? Yes. Oh, I remember, but you should not have had your long legs over to my side of the table. What was it you called the lump—a hematoma?"

He and Stacy were sitting on a wooden balcony near the church having a delicious thick soup—the only thing on the menu—and warm bread. He had a spoonful halfway to his mouth when he received a sudden violent kick to his leg.

"There it is. There it is," Stacy exclaimed. "Saint Francis answered my prayers." Somewhere, intermingled with her ejaculatory remarks, could be heard a loud "Ouch, why did you do that for goodness sakes?" from Ed. But it never reached her ears. Stacy was too excited and too loud.

He wiped the spilled soup off his tie and looked across the table to his spouse, who still seemed to be in some kind of spiritual ecstasy.

"Would you mind telling me what this is all about?" he asked. "I think you broke my leg." He massaged his leg under the table.

"My dear, you will never believe this," she jubilated, "but the most wonderful thing just happened to me."

"You almost broke my leg," he repeated as he grimaced and continued his massaging. "I'll probably need a plaster cast."

"Oh, don't be so—so frail. Besides, you know I didn't mean it."

"My God! What if you were serious about committing mayhem? I would probably wind up in the hospital. Now will you please condescend to explain this act of violence?"

Her eyes shone with sheer joy. "I was sitting here just looking out on the world while you were eating your soup." She said it as if his having soup during her "spiritual" exploration was a gluttonous, inexcusable self-indulgence. "I spoke—yes, I spoke—to Saint Francis. I said, 'Saint Francis, please show me a sign. If all they say about you and the birds is true, let a bird perch this very moment on that branch right there.' She pointed to the top of a tree close to where they sat. "And then it happened. Out of nowhere, mind you, this bird came and perched just where I pointed. My dear spouse" (she really was in a state of spirituality. He had never been called "spouse" as far as he could remember) "I am at a loss for words." She clasped her hands to her breast and her eyes were brimming and bright.

"Maybe the bird likes the crumbs from the bread we're having," Ed said grudgingly.

◆◆◆

Back to the present, Ed looked smilingly at Stacy. Her pensiveness could have been about anything from her painting, to a pair of shoes she saw in a shop window. Her mind was elsewhere.

"The cake is delicious. Now, don't preach to me about calories; I am going to have another piece," he insisted. He helped himself. "Want some more tea?" he asked. She nodded and he poured. It was a comfortable moment. They both were content.

"It is something to think about," she mused.

"Think about what?"

"I was thinking about heaven." So that explained the faraway look, Ed decided. St. Francis was responsible for that.

He looked at her, his mouth full of cake.

"We're getting older," she sighed and studied her fingernails. "Tell me, what do you think of heaven?"

"You sound like a little old lady, Stacy. I think it could be a wonderful place, but I would not want to abbreviate my stay on earth to get there."

"Be serious, dear. Do you think it could be there—somewhere? Waiting for us, like they say?"

From the Sunday comics to heaven, Ed thought. From ridiculous to the sublime.

Stacy appeared too serious for him to joke. It struck him that his life's companion had been harboring some secret soul-searching that he had not suspected. She often surprised him that way. He wondered why she, of all people, would not be certain of her final spiritual destination.

"Dearest, I assure you that heaven is a going concern. Of course it is there. It is there somewhere, everywhere. No question about it. You will have no trouble finding it." He spoke with authority of an oracle. "I have serious doubts about myself, however," he added.

This brought a smile to her face. "You call it a 'going concern' as if it were run like a corporation, a business."

"What a business it is! On a universal scale. I can imagine that

an encounter with the Guardian Angel would go something like this:
"I would say, 'And who are you?'"
"I am your Guardian Angel."
"You don't look like one. You look like me."
"That's the trouble. People have strange ideas about us."
"Why are you here?" I ask.
"Don't you know?"
"I am beginning to suspect. By the way, we're talking to each other, but our lips are not moving."
"It is not necessary. We can communicate without the physical apparatus. It is less tiring."
"We almost met before now, Ed. Do you remember that car accident on the Parkway years ago? I was there with you. But my instructions were 'not yet' so I nudged the car around a few degrees to make the rear strike the railing and you got off without a scratch. It was a neat bit of work, if I say so myself."
"I didn't know. I thought I was just lucky."
"There you go! *Miracles are happening all the time*, but do people appreciate them? Not often enough. They happen every day, but they go unnoticed or unrecognized. At a recent meeting of the C.O.G.A.—Congress of Guardian Angels—a resolution was passed decrying this strange paradox—'Paradox of Paradise,' if you will forgive the paraphrase."
"'Where are we going? What comes—next?' I ask."
"We go to the business office."
"The business office?"
"Well—there are so many people on earth, they all have to be recorded on our special computers. All this data processing has to be kept current. You never can tell. The staff angels are extremely overworked. They hardly find time for their own celestial enjoyment. The messages that come into, and go out from, the executive offices—you have no idea. We angels envy the 'Division of Saints.' They are assigned the more desirable heavenly duties. They do receive preferential treatment. However, they can be of definite help in special cases where a clear-cut decision concerning candidacy does not immediately present itself. Believe me, a stamp of approval from their department and you are "*in.*" You have to hand it to the Saints when it comes to experience." G.A. continues,

"You should make it a point to visit the Pediatric Department. It simply is a 'must' for all newcomers. All those beautiful babies and children! Another place of great interest is the Science laboratory."

"Science laboratory?"

"Yes. The greatest scientists and humanitarians of our—rather your—time, are still at work. After all, that is what heaven is to them. Their thoughts still live on earth. I can assure you that we have here a humming, active organization."

"About me—what happens to me? Do I ever get to see the—Head?" I ask.

"Our Music department is of the best. Here—let me tune you in."

"Immediately I hear restful, elevating music swelling around me. It is beautiful. It sounds familiar."

"It should be familiar to you; it's Handel's Messiah. I thought you might like it. You can hear anything you wish. Simply think it." "I think of Komenoi Ostrow and instantly I hear its sweetness."

G.A. cuts in and the music stops. "The composers and artists who have given so much pleasure to the people on earth are all here and they love to hear their music. All the hymns, antiphons, chorales, symphonies have ascended to us. Then they are ' piped in.' We have an inexhaustible library of music, you can understand."

"And all these writers, singers, and composers are here?" I ask.

"Most of them."

"But . . . about me—what happens to me?"

"How do you feel?"

"I feel nothing, actually. All in all, I feel fine."

G.A. puts a protective arm about my shoulders and says, "Let us get started for the business office, shall we?" . . .

Stacy listened, bemused. "You make it sound so real, so absolutely dependable."

"That's the way it is," he cheerfully answered. "Let's put our coats on and go for a brisk walk. Don't forget your high boots."

They tramped through the snow, holding onto each other. Stacy inspected the feeding stations and replenished those which needed it.

She also scattered more corn for the pheasant cock.

Ed was still thinking about their conversation.

"Stacy, what would you like heaven to be?"

"To begin with, I would love to meet my parents, and—"

"Would you like to see them as they were when they were young, or as you last saw them?"

"It would be nice to see them young again—"

"In that case, you would be older than your parents, when you meet, or, if you follow it through, you would have to be younger than a teenager. Is that what you want?"

"I didn't think of it that way. I really don't know what I would want. It is like wanting for nothing—but wanting everything—instant Everything."

"I think everyone has his own individual heaven. As for me, I would like to experience the Ultimate Revelation."

"Ultimate Revelation?"

"All my life I have been driven by a great curiosity. You know that, Stacy. We humans are each a dewdrop in the river of history which flows from the mountains and valleys of the past, through the cities and forests of the present, and into what is left of the future. We are a part, an inseparable part, of that stream of life. Without the accumulation of our individual dewdrops, the currents and course of that stream would be altered. I am as much concerned about the irrevocable past as I am about the unforeseeable future . . . although I can do nothing about what has been and very little about what is to come. But I have a consuming curiosity about these things, past and future."

"I don't understand what you are driving at. Oh! Look at that rabbit over there, up on its hind legs, eyeing us."

"That is what I am coming to. If I could have my wish fulfilled, I would consider it heaven if I were given the gift to look anywhere into the past and be able to say 'so *that* is the way it was'—or be able to do the same for the future and know how it was going to be. To slake the thirst of curiosity—the Ultimate Revelation—that is my idea of heaven. It really has nothing to do with music or singing or even joy, for that matter. Only the *truth*. A kaleidoscope spectacle of all three Time Dimensions. That is what ETERNITY really is, my dear." He turned to her; she looked confused.

"I think was should turn back. You nose has a little dewdrop on its tip, Stacy," he laughed softly, "but I doubt that particular drop will change the course of history.

CHAPTER XVII

SURROGATE WIFE

Stacy was enjoying a renewed interest in her art work. Not that she had ever given it up entirely. It was only that so many other things were always interfering. On more than on occasion she had resolved to go back to her sketches. She finally managed to break through the encirclement of activities and return to her paintbrushes. She realized she possessed real talent and it would have been a pity not to use it. Besides, she simply loved to paint and sketch. Her studio was arranged just the way she wanted, with the proper light. It was such a pleasant place that she wondered why she had stayed away so long.

Ed poked his head in. Stacy was absorbed in her work. From the look on her face, she was not satisfied with the color effect and was having difficulty achieving the right color mix. He looked around the room—her studio. Art materials were everywhere. It was a veritable atelier. Well, if she was happy—then he was also content. He did not disturb her. With the snifter in his hand, he went into his study. He sat and slowly drank his cognac. He was content.

Stacy decided to make a short visit to her only living relative—Aunt Ismelda Newcomb, the spinster sister of Stacy's late father.

"She is all the family I have left," she told Ed. "The poor soul has been 'ailing' all her life. It would be an act of charity to help her out. She has outlived all her old friends around her."

When she was ready to leave, she hugged Ed. "I'll be gone for about a week darling," she said finally. "I hope you will miss me terribly," she added cheerfully.

The day afterward he was already missing Stacy. The house was full of echoes. Ed hoped that the morrow would not be a "down day." He went to bed and finally fell asleep thinking of her.

The phone rang. It was Stacy. Her voice sounded wonderful to Ed. Just talking to her lifted his spirits. "Come home as soon as you can. I miss my lovely wife," he told her. Before she hung up, she threw him a kiss over the phone. She was catching a plane the next day.

CHAPTER XXVIII

Ed sat stunned in disbelief when the news broke. It could not have happened. Stacy was so vital, so warm—so alive when he spoke to her, when he kissed her goodbye over the phone just a few hours ago. He frantically turned the radio to other stations only to hear the announcer's emotionless voice repeat the same dreadful information—the airline flight and the city of departure. The report was sketchy, but they were sure of one thing. "No survivors," the newsman announced.

"Goddam you!" he shouted at the radio. "You are talking about Stacy, my wife, on that plane, not giving a weather forecast, you unfeeling bastards! You . . ." His voice cracked and he slumped back onto the couch and covered his face with his hands. "Oh, God. My Stacy. Oh, God!" he moaned. He became silent.

When the phone rang, he thought it was the airlines. Dear God, he thought, maybe they were going to deny it. It was another airline; the wrong flight number. It's all a mistake . . . It . . ."

Dotty's voice came over the phone.

"Yes," he said in a dead, flat voice.

"It's me, Dotty." Her voice was tearful, quivering, almost unintelligible.

"Who?" Ed asked.

"Ed, dear, listen to me. It's Dotty. Do you hear? It's Dotty, Ed. Are you there?"

"Yes, I'm here."

"Oh, Ed, Ed, this is terrible . . . horrible . . . unbelievable." Ed was vaguely aware of more weeping at her end of the phone. "Clyde is away somewhere and I can't reach him. He had probably heard by now. Oh, Ed—" A fresh burst of tears. Ed waited. He sat motionless, the receiver glued to his ear. He had all the time in the world. Stacy was gone. He could wait an eternity. Dotty's voice returned, calmer. "Ed, I am coming right over. You are all alone in that big house. Don't do anything until I get there." She hung up. Ed dully wondered what Dotty meant. "Don't do anything," he repeated. What was there to do? He did not feel alone. Stacy's presence filled the house around him. He could see her smile. He imagined a faint scent, the one she used the most. He could not believe that she would never again descend the spiral staircase or momentarily appear in the room. He began to cry inside. No sound came. He slumped back on the couch and sat dumbly waiting by the phone. Waiting for what? He already knew. He sat motionless, his hands limp by his sides. Unseeing eyes gazed at the floor. Waiting. He had time for that now.

Dotty was writing a letter and listening to WQXR's beautiful music when the sudden interruption of the program caught her notice. Even after the significance of what she heard filtered through her initial shock and disbelief, it still sounded like a scenario about unreal people in a mad dream. She knew that Stacy was booked on the flight that crashed. Maybe she was delayed or took another flight. It simply could not be. Not Stacy. Dotty turned to other stations. Nausea and gall rose in her throat as the news was repeated. "The passenger list will be completed before notifying the next of kin." They would all have to wait. Stacy, her dearest, closest friend . . . beautiful, smiling, still-young Stacy was in that flaming crash. The truth finally struck her like a physical blow. She could hardly breathe.

Her first impulse was to call Clyde. He was "still out in the field," and they could not say when he would call. Dotty left a message for him to call. Then she called Ed. On her way over, she again wished that Stacy and Ed had had a child or two. Stacy told her on several occasions that she had tried to conceive without success. Her gynecologist told her there was nothing wrong, that there seemed to be no reason she could not become pregnant. He also added that she could always think of adopting a child. Somehow, nothing came of it. For the first time, Dotty thought about her own childless state. It made her sad.

As she turned into the road of Ed's home, she was thinking that Ed was now alone in the big house, with no children clinging to him, no family group deriving comfort from each other. The poor man must be going mad. She hoped she could give Ed some comfort and solace since she was the closest remaining tie to Stacy. At least she would try, she resolved. She left the car in the driveway and hurried up to the door. She was surprised to find it locked. She thought Ed would have opened it after she called. She rang the bell.

Ed picked up the phone. Nothing but a hum. The bell rang again. It dawned on him that it was Dotty at the door. He had forgotten to unlock it. He opened it. Dotty fell into his arms and started wailing—something about Stacy . . . closest and dearest . . . devastating and unbearable. As she clung to him, he silently patted her back. He felt empty of faith or belief or hope. He could not shed a tear.

With arms around each other's waists, Dotty walked Ed toward the kitchen. A deeply embedded instinct told her that, in the time of tragedy or stress, the kitchen becomes a refuge. The kitchen or the liquor cabinet.

"Let me fix you a nice cup of tea. Or maybe coffee," she coaxed.

"Some coffee, I guess," was his indifferent answer. Then he changed his mind. "I think I'll have a drink instead." Without waiting for Dotty, he went into the den. Dotty followed and watched as Ed poured himself a stiff drink of Scotch, downed it in short order, and poured himself another one.

She thought, *Ed, poor dear. I must give him comfort and solace, if I can.*

Ed sat morosely drinking the whiskey. Dotty helped herself to the vodka and soda. She went over and turned the radio on.

"—the passenger list is complete before notification of nearest of kin—"

She switched it off. Ed did not seem to notice. She dialed Clyde's office and was told that he was delayed. If it proved too late, he would take a plane in the morning. They told her Clyde had tried to call, but got no answer at the house. Dotty knew Clyde would stay over—he did not like late night flights. She helped herself to another vodka. Ed silently stretched out his arm; the one holding an empty glass. She filled the glass. They sat side by side, drinking silently. It occurred to

CONVERSATIONS OF SILENCE

her that since she came over to give Ed comfort and solace, she was certainly derelict.

"You poor, poor dear," she said in her softest comforting tone. She put her arm around him and kissed him on the cheek. Ed felt numbly that he should return this kindness. He pulled her gently to him and returned the kiss. Ed was getting stoned but did not know or care. He pulled himself up from the couch and poured another drink. He brought one over to Dotty. She quickly downed her partly filled glass and accepted the proffered one. She longed to cheer him up.

Both Ed and Dotty were soon looped. The room was silent. No radio newscasters. No phone callers. Dotty began to weep softly and earnestly. Ed felt that he should comfort her. It somehow made him feel better. The heavy stone in the pit of his stomach was slowly dissolving. It had attached itself to him like a giant limpet. She he held Dotty and kissed her. Dotty held and kissed Ed in return. It seemed to work; they continued to give each other solace and comfort . . .

Dotty began to complain about the warmth. She said it was stifling and hot. Ed agreed. Each took off articles of clothing, an item at a time, feeling more comfortable as each one was discarded.

It would be the strangest lovemaking in their lives. Neither would remember much of what transpired that night. It was a night of—"comfort and solace."

Ed awoke in the den. The lights were still on. It took him a few minutes to collect his thoughts. The one thing he did remember was the telephone call in the middle of the night. "—the FAA are investigating the crash"—It made no difference what they said or how they said it—Stacy was on that flight and Stacy was no more. The smiles, the laughter, the silly little purchases, the warmth of her, the sounds and the perfume of her—Stacy was no more.

He stood up and instantly fell back onto the couch. Sweat broke out on him. He felt clammy and sick. He had to rest awhile before trying again. He needed coffee and made his way erratically to the kitchen. The coffee pot which Dotty had started the night before was still on the counter. He plugged it in. He realized he was naked, so he returned to the den, shaky and still in a cold sweat. He found his clothes in an untidy pile on the floor. His head developed an uncomfortable tremor and his teeth chattered. The need for a drink became overpowering. To hell with the coffee! The glass clattered against his teeth, but he controlled it by holding it with both hands. He tilted the glass too steeply and gulped his drink too fast. It made him choke. His face was distorted by a severe bout of coughing. It left him breathless, with tears running down his face. He wiped the spilled drink from his face with the back of his hand. Again he remembered he was naked, he shuffled over to the pile of clothes. He wiped his running nose with a swiping motion of his forearm. He managed to pull on his trousers, but the effort was so great that he fell back onto the couch, gasping for breath. He breathed hard with his mouth open, as if he had run a hard race. He lay completely exhausted, until his breathing returned to normal.

The horror returned to him in fully force. It skewered him. He was filled with fury and dread. He jumped to his feet. "Stacy," he shouted, expecting to hear her voice answer. "Stacy!" he roared, looking around like a man lost in a deep, dark forest. Bellowing, he staggered upstairs. He stopped short at the bedroom door. He fell silent and slowly stepped over the threshold. He walked over to Stacy's vanity. The cosmetics were in disarray—her lipsticks, powders, perfumes, cotton balls, and all the other feminine things that she used. They were waiting for her touch to bring them to life. He picked up a bottle of toilet water and put it close to his nostrils. It evoked such a strong compelling feeling of Stacy's presence that his longing and need for her overpowered him. He sucked in deep, hissing breaths through his clenched teeth. He stumbled out of the bedroom and wandered aimlessly through the house, touching mementos and pictures, occasionally picking up a piece of bric-a-brac that Stacy had liked and brought home.

He found himself outside her studio . . . her atelier, as he always called it. He stood in the open doorway. The room smelled of oil and turpentine. His eyes wandered over the sketches, her paintings, the unfinished watercolors. The pictures were alive with colors of open spaces and wide horizons. There were beautiful landscapes as well as drawings of her beloved birds. Stacy loved to paint bright, beautiful, cheerful scenes. For a moment he believed he could hear the songs of the birds and the rustling of the leaves in her landscapes.

He would not bring himself to enter the studio. The unfinished canvasses waited for her touch. He did not have the heart to enter among them and break the news that she would never return to smile at them and to stroke them lovingly with her brushes. Better to leave them alone to their expectancy. They can wait. After one final glance, he closed the door quietly.

He again found himself in the bedroom. He walked over to her wardrobe and pulled the doors apart. Impulsively, he buried his face in her clothes, breathed in her scent. The shouting and the roaring in him had left. He felt empty. He whispered softly, "Stacy—never again, my dear ... never again." He remained motionless with his face buried in her clothes for a long time.

Dotty awoke late in the morning. Her head was spinning violently. Her stomach was rebelling and she thought she was going blind. It took her some time to become oriented. She wondered how she made it home safely. When Clyde arrived, she woke up long enough to say she had a very restless night. "I have a headache that's killing me," she moaned. Clyde said, "poor girl" as he tiptoed out of the room and left for the office.

She finally got up and fixed her hair, holding it all together with a wide ribbon around her head. The effort was almost too much for her tired arms. She trudged downstairs and put on a pot of coffee. She thought of Stacy and tears once more filled her eyes. It was a quiet emotion. The hysteria of the day before was completely expended. She sat in the breakfast room looking down into her cup, deeply immersed in a confused mixture of hazy recollections and an unnamed doubt. After pouring her second cup of coffee, she swung around to the phone extension and dialed Clyde's office.

"How are you feeling, darling?" he asked breezily. "Would you like to come into town and have lunch with me?"

"You're sweet to ask me, dear, but I am really not up to it. I think I'll stay home and catch up with odds and ends I have to do." She got herself settled more comfortably before continuing. "I haven't had a chance to discuss Stacy." Her voice became tremulous. "But you must know all about it, Clyde. I'm sure you've heard about it and read the papers; they must be full of it this morning. I'm all cried out and I can hardly think." She paused. "The reason I called, Clyde, is that I want you to call Ed and talk to him. He's not thinking about it now, but you have been writing all the insurance for them both and something will have to be done sooner or later. At least give him a call and you will be able to tell how he is managing. Will you please do it as soon as I hang up? He needs us—he needs us both."

Clyde was a man of few words outside his insurance field. Perhaps it was because he found it necessary to do so much talking in his business.

"It was terrible, just terrible. Poor Stacy—poor Ed. I'll call him right away, dear. This is a very, very trying time for everyone. Yes, dear, I'll do it right away. See you tonight." He hung up, leaving Dotty with the phone in her hand.

The coffee had turned cold. She got up, poured it out and rinsed the cup. Back upstairs, she sat in front of the vanity mirror, absently brushing her hair. She stopped momentarily, looked at her image in the mirror and whispered, "Stacy would not have minded. I was the . . . surrogate wife. That is what it was . . . the surrogate wife."

There was an extensive investigation by the FAA and the papers were full of the tragedy for days.

Karen canceled all appointments and Ed could not be reached. She alone knew where he was. Ed felt a devastating loss. He took a leave of absence, turning all calls over to Deutermann.

He tried to get away. He always liked sailing—the smell of the salt sea air, the boom of the surf, and the walks on the beach. But no matter where he turned, Stacy's smiling face hauntingly appeared. His dream patterns began to change. He would find himself searching frantically for Stacy, never finding her. It could be at an airport, or in a large department store, or she would disappear after a party while he left to get the car he could never find; or it could be in a strange city where he could not remember the name or the telephone number of the hotel. The details changed endlessly, but the pattern remained the same. The stress and the agony and the sense of loss were always there. As the weeks went by, a subtle change in Stacy's face took place. It would strangely change to Elena's and back. He would see Stacy and call her Elena, or see Elena and call her Stacy. Confusion and indecision crept into his searchings. In desperation he climbed over high obstacles, or squeezed through tight places, or fled down blind alleys, not knowing how he came to be in these strange, unknown places.

Once he found Stacy. Only once. They were lying close together; she had her usual smile on her face. Due to numerous intrusions and interferences, they could not accomplish sexual union. Although he suffered in urgent desperation and effort, Stacy's smile never changed.

It was after such a maddening dream that he awoke in a sweat, muttering to himself. He swung over the side of the bed and sat, letting the inertia of drowsiness leave him before he turned on the light. The sudden brightness made him blink as he made his way over to the desk and opened a lower drawer. His mood was still heavy with the memory of its dream-induced frustrations. He reached down and pulled out a small strongbox.

The lid sprang open as he dialed the combination. It contained passports, some legal papers, a few rare stamps given to him by a grateful patient . . . and the hotel key. He turned it over in his palm and gazed at it intently, as if it would now reveal what went on behind its closed door. He had wanted to dispose of it. Once he got as far as the trash can, but found that he could not throw it away. He pocketed it, almost against his will, and returned it to the box. The reason for keeping it eluded him, since it always left him disconsolate and unhappy.

He looked at the key for one long final moment. He held it at arm's length directly over the wastepaper basket and released it from his fingers. The key fell vertically into the basket, hitting the bottom with a plop.

It was finally out of his life.

Later, while studying Stacy's face smiling at him from the picture frame, he knew the words had to be written. Thinking them was not enough.

He opened his diary and wrote,

> Stacy, I knew. I knew about you and Dwight. I understood. There was nothing to forgive. May your warm, tender, loving heart rest in peace.

◆◆◆

In California, Dwight Everett studied the list of the crash casualties in the local morning paper.

Stacy's name stood out.

Dwight had never tried to call her after her visit to his ex-wife.

He had had a sleepless night and looked tired and haggard. His eyes were dull, his face drawn. The buzzer on his desk startled him. A moment later his secretary's voice came over the intercom.

"Your first appointment is here, Mr. Everett."

"Have him come in, please."

He gently dropped the newspaper into the wastebasket and tidied up his desk. He reached into a drawer of his desk, took a hurried swig from a bottle, wiped his lips after the neat drink. He was ready.

CHAPTER XXIX

Dotty's visit to the doctor's office was for a Pap test. Vivian Boland, M.D., was her gynecologist, had been for a number of years. Dotty never looked forward to these periodic check-up examinations. They made her feel uncomfortable, an illogical sense of modesty. They were discussing something quite different.

"Your missed periods," the doctor was saying, "can be due to one of several conditions. Stress, nutritional changes, emotional disturbances, excessive exercise, to mention a few. Of course, there is also pregnancy to consider."

Dotty stared at the doctor, her mouth open. "Do you think pregnancy is a possibility, in my case?" Her voice shook a little. She was far from calm inwardly. She could not accept the possibility with equanimity.

"We'll have some blood work done, as well as a pregnancy test." Although she did not stress it, it was definitely in the doctor's mind, judging from what she found on examination. She studied Dotty speculatively. "You are still in the age group, where it must be ruled out." She wrote a few words on a slip of paper and tore it from the pad. "Take this down to the hospital laboratory. You know where it is. By the way, you didn't have breakfast, I hope."

"No. I came fasting, as usual, whenever I come here."

"Good. I'll call you as soon as I get the results."

CONVERSATIONS OF SILENCE

Dotty put the phone down slowly. She was stunned. When could it have happened. She and Clyde stopped taking precautions, after they finally gave up on her ever becoming pregnant. This was years ago. Now, this overwhelming news! Dr. Boland had reluctantly agreed to repeat the test, only at the urging of Dotty, although she was sure that the test was accurate.

Dotty had no one to turn to, for advice. It was like being lost in a cavernous building, where she had tarried too long. It was now deserted and silent. She kept plunging, panic-stricken, down never-ending stairways and against locked doors. She was the solitary soul left in its immensity, a terrified companion to echoes and whisperings.

Her life had lost much of its animation and vitality ever since the death of her closest friend. Her eyes filled with tears whenever she thought of Stacy. She missed her companionship and intimate confidences. Dotty's somber mood was understood by Clyde who accepted it as a phase which would eventually pass. She loved him all the more for his patience.

She tried to recall the few times she and Clyde had been together recently. The answer did not appear to lie there, unless she was completely off her dates.

It came to her with heart-stopping suddenness. Strange, she did not think of it sooner. It was the night of "*comfort and solace,*" when Ed seemed so utterly lost, the night of Stacy's tragic death. Much of that night's happenings would forever be a blank to her. The only certainty, her body told her the following morning, was the lovemaking. It was, as Ed's surrogate wife, she conceived. She did it for Stacy, her closest and dearest friend. Her spirit had guided Dotty into self-giving. That night she was STACY. Ed must have known that.

She barely made it to the bathroom. It felt like being on a violently-pitching ship, being buffeted about. There was no longer any doubt about her prospective motherhood. She remembered how her mother once was, before she miscarried. Considering how sick and miserable she now felt, she had strong misgivings about ever reaching full-term, herself.

Her dilemma was of an unsuspected kind, a surprise even to herself. She decided to keep the baby although she had not yet mentioned it to Clyde. He was solicitous and kind, suggesting all kinds of remedies for her "upset stomach, probably gastrointestinal flu." Dotty, in spite of her misery, could see the humor, the irony, of Clyde's attempts to rid her of her complaints. She thought back to the earlier days of her marriage, when desire for a child was exciting, and hoped for. Her lack of success made her thoughtful as time passed. The present knowledge that she could become pregnant gave her a vicarious feeling of contentment, a sense of fulfillment, of pride in her body. She was a woman, in the complete sense, as she was meant to be. If only the distressing nausea, vomiting, pounding in her head and trouble with her eyes, would let up.

She decided to call Dr. Boland who gave her an appointment for the following day. Dotty was surprised at the doctor's promptness and readiness to see her on such short notice. She wondered about it. She instinctively knew her visit to the doctor on the morrow, would be critical. Tears of frustration and self-pity flowed freely.

She thought about Clyde and his busy city office. She tried to envision him as the father, the companion to their child. It proved difficult to think of a single positive quality. She experienced deep self-guilt about burdening him with a child at this time in his life. Her dear, indulgent, loving husband.

"Your kidney problem worries me, Dotty. You are showing protein in the urine. There is a history of hypertension in your family. Your mother had a miscarriage with a subsequent pregnancy, after you were born, according to your family history. None of your systems are abating. Finally, you are not the young bride going through her first pregnancy." The doctor again looked at the reports. "You might possibly be in for a rough time if you carry it to term." She put the papers down and looked up at Dotty, expecting her to ask questions, but Dotty remained silent, deep in thought.

She asked, presently, "What do you recommend, doctor?"

"I'll carry you along, if you decide to keep the pregnancy, which

I know you do. It will require constant monitoring and regular check-up examinations. I'll do everything I can, to prevent a complication of toxemia. Whatever you plan to do, let me know soon, so that I can put you on a regular regimen. To begin with, I want to see you in about ten days, unless you have to see me SOONER. She emphasized the word. Dotty understood.

"You're going to be alright, Dotty," this from Dr. Boland, as she was bending over to check her blood pressure. She was in bed with legs elevated. Tubes led into her arm, while she received a blood transfusion. She was too weak to talk or move. She had lost much blood. In her twilight mind she knew that the pain was gone. The doctor was satisfied that the hemorrhage was under control. She studied the electronic monitors which showed satisfactory configurations. "I am sorry, Dotty," she said. "I know you wanted to carry it. At least, you did not have to decide, to choose. I think it was for the best." She was not sure Dotty heard her. She tiptoed out.

The night before, in the early hours, Dotty was awakened by severe cramp-like pains. Soon afterward, the bleeding started. She called out to Clyde who promptly called Dr. Boland's emergency number. The rest was like a dream. The car ride, the emergency room, the injections. She drifted into a cool dark forest where the sun's rays, through the branches, carpeted the ground with a bright dappled pattern. A gentle breeze ruffled her hair. She could fly by simply spreading her arms, like a bird. She floated close to the ground, then swooped up, to skim by the trees, banking and turning with ease, as she wished. There were sounds in the distance, like the tinkling of windchimes.

"I am grateful to you, doctor, for your prompt attention and for all that you have done for Dotty. I am extremely thankful that all went well. Believe me, I was scared out of my wits, when she cried out to me early this morning. Is she out of danger now? What was wrong with her? What caused all that loss of blood? She looks as white as a sheet."

"She was in the first trimester of pregnancy, Clyde. She lost it last night."

He winced at the news. "It's the last thing I would have expected. We tried for a long time, you know. I wonder why she did not tell me—"

"I don't blame you for being surprised. She and I suspected it only a short time ago. It was when she came to my office for a routine examination, that her condition became apparent. It took a few days more, before we were certain. Dotty was just as unprepared as you are. I am sure she was about to inform you the next day or so."

"The poor girl. I thought, all along, she was suffering from an upset stomach. Maybe an ulcer. By the way, I have some health insurance forms at the office. I'll be grateful if you will fill them out when you receive them. They cover mostly everything, including your fee. The poor girl. When can I see her? She is such a brave person." Tears were in his eyes, surprising him as well as the doctor.

Dotty studied herself in the tall mirror. A little more lipstick, she decided. She pushed back a stray wisp of hair. Turning one way and another, she looked at her figure in the new dress. She was satisfied. Clyde was waiting downstairs. They were going to a special dinner, in a special place. Just the two of them.

Ever since she came home from the hospital, Clyde had been hovering over her, dispensing love, laced with deep solicitude and tenderness. Dotty accepted his ministrations freely. She was living in an atmosphere of contentment, and unending gratitude to the good Lord, who decided for her, the events which followed. She was not sure she could have carried the burden of guilt and deception for the rest of her life, with impunity. She would never tell Ed. It would serve no purpose. Unless . . . he and she . . . the rest of her thought was strangely vague. There existed an ill-defined feeling, a sense, within herself, which had to remain ever-obscure, in her mind. It was better that way.

Earlier, Clyde had delegated many of his business responsibilities to others at the office, in order to be with her. He was president of his agency and could have done this at any time in the past, he realized. A closer relationship gradually grew up between them. He underwent subtle changes. Even in his voice. Dotty was constantly surprised at its authority, as he frequently talked to his office. It occurred to her, that her erstwhile monosyllabic husband was a product, in part, of her own dominance in their marital relationship. Clyde had indulged her to the extent that he was content to let her have her way in most things. It inevitably left little more for him to say. He loved her. It was all that mattered. Perversely, she missed the old Clyde, while discovering new depths to her husband. It filled her with a new understanding.

She came down the stairs, looking radiant, a smile lighting up her face. Clyde was waiting below, looking up at her, hand outstretched to hers.

CHAPTER XXX

With Stacy gone, living in the big house became intolerable for Ed. It was during this time that Dotty and Clyde proved to be such good friends. They frequently invited him to their home or to the club for dinner. When they were together, they talked about their friends' happenings and social activities. Occasionally, their conversation would run out of direction and drift into trivialities before lapsing into silence. As old friends, silences did not embarrass them. Dotty and Clyde knew Ed well enough to sense his occasional inattention and to understand the faraway look in his eyes.

Clyde and Dotty were doing what they believed Stacy would have wished. She had been very popular, cheerful and friendly to all who knew her; had moved easily and graciously among all her acquaintances. Although Ed was well-known in medical circles and in the community as a surgeon of note, his position in the social milieu was as the husband of the popular Mrs. Edward Rankin, the well known clubwoman and chairlady of various charities. Ed was content to have it that way. The environment in which he felt most comfortable was the surgical theater, the operating room. There, everything else was cast aside and his mind focused on the problem before him. The social scene held lukewarm attraction for him.

Dotty and Clyde lived in a comfortable home built in the old manor style. It boasted several wood-burning fireplaces.

One cold night the three friends were seated comfortably around the crackling fire in the den. Dotty was having her demitasse and Clyde was having another of several whiskeys. Ed, as usual, was having his cognac.

Dotty raised her eyes in Ed's direction. The shadows cast by the flames danced across his face, reflecting his mood of abstraction. She studied him speculatively before she spoke. "I was thinking, Ed," she began.

"Yes?" He turned his head toward her without otherwise moving.

"I was thinking, Ed," she repeated, "about your plans for the future. I know you are about to sell your house and live at the club. I think it is a good idea . . . at least until you are finally settled."

He looked at her thoughtfully. "But I *shall* be settled after I've taken up residence at the club. Were you thinking of something else?"

"Well–" Dotty felt uncomfortable about proceeding. "–you're still a young man and in good health." She placed too much emphasis on "good health." "Clyde and I . . ." Clyde raised his head in mild surprise and stared at Dotty. "Clyde and I were thinking that the time has come for you to begin cultivating female companionship again. We're the only friends you've been seeing since Stacy–what I want to say, Ed, is–don't you think that you have been out of circulation long enough? We understand, but your friends are beginning to think that you're becoming a recluse. It–it's positively unhealthy, I mean unnatural, to go on this way . . . Don't you agree, Clyde?"

The hapless man could emit only a guttural "h-u-m-m-ph," accompanied by a nondescript shrug of his shoulders, which Dotty accepted at total agreement.

Ed realized he had to say something. Dotty poured coffee into a shaking cup. He could not know that Dotty's discomfiture stemmed from a confused guilt feeling. It also had something to do with the great love and loyalty she held for Stacy's memory. So much so, that she felt as if she were actually suggesting to Ed to commit adultery.

Staring into the fireplace, Ed spoke barely above a whisper, in a reminiscent tone. "Although I might have had some doubt from time to time . . . my first love has always . . . been my work. To me it was a . . . vocation. I now realize that Stacy knew it and accepted it. She really had everything a wife could ask for–the kind of home she loved, anything that pleased her. We managed to get away on trips every few months. We were very close. Over the years she seemed happy enough– yes . . . I thought she was quite content–fulfilled. Still . . ." There was a long pause. He continued to gaze into the flames.

Dotty's pulse began to race. She wondered if Ed ever found out about Stacy and Dwight.

". . . Still, I could not have given her the one thing she most probably wanted—more time with her. How could I? My practice did not permit it . . . or it seemed that way. But Stacy never complained. She always had a sweet smile . . . a Mona Lisa . . . she smiled easily, Dotty."

He sipped his cognac for a moment. "You knew her better than anyone else, Dotty. Her painting and sketching; her club activities, her charitable organizations—her social activities seemed to fill her life as much as my work did mine." He stopped. He felt he had answered Dotty, but she wanted to hear more.

She looked at Ed for a few long moments before putting her cup down with a sigh. Ed would devote more time, if possible, to his work. What a waste. She sighed again. What a waste!

Ed looked into the flames and saw a young girl in a dirndl dress. Laughing eyes. She pirouetted and danced. Her full red lips parted in silent song. She sang of a love that was of long ago.

CHAPTER XXXI

Agnes Ballisteria and her husband, Dante, sat in Ed's consultation room waiting for final post-operative instructions before returning to their Michigan home.

As a young girl, Agnes, now in her forties, was thrown from her horse during a horse show. She struck the ground rather squarely on her buttocks in a jack-knife position. The doctor told the family she had sustained a fracture of the sacrum as well as the lowest lumbar vertebra of her spinal column. He said the fractures would heal without complications and no residual disability would remain. Agnes made a complete recovery, the doctor's prediction proved correct. She continued to compete in horse shows. It was at such an event that she met Dante Ballisteria and eventually married him. She bore him two daughters and a son over the ensuing years and was free from complaints or disability--until about four years before. She developed pain in the lower back with gradual radiation into the buttock and down into the right leg. The pain increased in severity until it kept her awake and she started to walk with a limp. After exhausting all the home remedies advised by her friends, she visited Dr. Graham, her family physician. The doctor recognized the problem to be of an orthopedic nature and referred her to Dr. Gordon Fraser.

She was admitted to the hospital and placed in traction. The doctors took a sizable number of x-rays, revealing the old injury. They made a tentative diagnosis of nerve root pressure and went to Agnes' room to tell her. Dr. Graham took up a position on one side of the bed while Dr. Fraser, the consultant, walked around to the opposite side. Agnes followed Dr. Fraser with questioning eyes.

Dr. Fraser cleared his throat. "Your pain is due to pressure on a root of the sciatic nerve. This has come about by a slow deterioration of the cushion, the disc, in your lower back. It was initiated by your fall from the horse many years ago."

From the other side of the bed, Dr. Graham interjected, "You see, Agnes, a condition such as yours can start many years earlier—sometimes so far back that even the patient can't remember. The deterioration sets in silently and painlessly. Only when it reaches an advanced stage does the nerve become pinched and the pain begin. This is your present situation."

Gordon Fraser quickly resumed, looking first at Graham and then directing his remarks to Agnes. "The only way to cure your condition, Mrs. Ballisteria, is to go in—that is, to operate—and remove the pressure on the nerve. But, first, I would like to do a myelogram. It could give us a more complete picture of what we're dealing with."

"A myelogram?" She looked at him wide-eyed and worried.

"Yes. It means introducing a special solution into the sac surrounding the nerve roots. The solution can be seen under the fluoroscope and any change in its contour due to pressure or some other obstacle to its normal flow becomes visible to the examiner. The test is usually done prior to surgery, Mrs. Ballisteria, and pinpoints the level of the trouble. All of which gives us additional important information. I recommend you agree to having it done."

"Please let me think it over. I am confused. I would like to discuss it with my husband. I—I'll let you know." Her voice shook.

"That's all right, Agnes," Dr. Graham soothed. "Let me know as soon as possible. Dr. fraser will have to set it up. He will take over when the time comes."

◆◆◆

Several weeks later Agnes was ecstatic. "He's a darling, Elena. So kind and considerate. And gentle—I hardly felt the stitches coming out. After all the horror stories I heard about this operation, I was petrified. I am much more comfortable than I expected to be. This morning I told—oh, here I go again gabbing about myself. Tell me, how are George and the boys?"

Elena sat in a comfortable, well-upholstered chair a short distance from the bed. "They're fine, Agnes. Just fine. But you just go ahead and talk about yourself as much as you wish. After all, you are the patient and we all want to spoil you with love and kindness. You have gone through a lot, dear girl. Your doctor sounds wonderful. I could kiss him for being so kind to you. Did he say when you could get out of bed? Or go home?"

◆◆◆

Two years passed. Agnes and Elena were lunching together. They both looked solemn. The years had been very kind to Elena.

"At first," Agnes said, "I tried not to pay attention to the pain. I was thinking that it was a twinge from that operation. You remember, Elena, I mentioned it to you a few months back? Well, it didn't go away. So I went back to Dr. Fraser and he took some fresh x-rays—" Her voice trailed off. Elena sipped her tea and waited for her best friend to continue. "—and now he tells me that the bones are settling! Whatever that means. So I asked him about the old operation and he said 'that part is okay! Tears started in her eyes, as she brought her coffee cup to her lips.

"What are you planning to do now my dear?" Elena asked softly. She was her closest friend.

Agnes put her cup down. She studied Elena's face intently as if she could find the answer there. "He says I need another operation-a bone graft. I'm so scared I can hardly think straight. Dante is no help at all. He keeps telling me I have to make up my own mind. But, Elena—another operation! I-I don't know. I just don't know. If this pain were a little less . . . but—tell me, what do you think? You're my best friend—like a sister. What do you think?"

Elena looked at her distraught friend, feeling great compassion. "Did you speak to Dr. Graham? What did he advise?" she asked gently.

"I talked to him. He has been looking after our family for so long that he has also become our confidant as well. He says I will probably have to go through with it. He has already discussed the case with Fraser. So...I told him Fraser was a kind, considerate man and helped me a lot-up to now-but I would like to get another opinion from someone who has had considerable experience with such cases. He mentioned a doctor in the East. Graham has referred cases to him from time to time. A Doctor Edward Rankin."

Elena stared at her friend. Agnes realized she had somehow struck a chord. "You don't happen to know of him, do you, Elena?"

Elena kept her voice steady, casual. "As a matter of fact, I do . . . or . . . rather . . . did. It was years ago." Changing the subject, she asked, "What have you finally decided to do? Is there anything I can do to help? This is awful news, your needing another operation." She reached across the table and gave Agnes' hand a gentle, reassuring squeeze.

"You're a dear sweet friend, Elena. I don't know what I would do without you," Agnes said gratefully. "Having someone like you to talk to has made it a lot easier. Well, Dante feels I should see Dr. Rankin anyway, before I do anything. We already made the appointment, and Dante, of course, if coming with me. He and I know no one in the city." There was a pause, "Elena, do you want me to mention you to Dr. Rankins?"

"Oh, I wouldn't' bother, Agnes. It is so . . . so long ago. He would probably not even remember." *Elena, Elena, you really do not believe that, do you? No more than you have forgotten him.* A blush crept into her cheeks. If Agnes noticed, she pretended not to notice. She added, "Dr. Rankin's secretary tells me it is possible I shall have to remain in the hospital there for some time after the surgery, and since we are leaving day after tomorrow I don't know when we'll see each other again." She stood up from the table and so did Elena. Agnes was lightly biting her lower lip and looked doleful as they walked out of the restaurant.

As Agnes and Dante Ballisteria waited patiently for Ed to

continue, he buzzed Karen to bring in the report. Agnes sat in a straight-backed chair, as ramrod as a West Point plebe. She wore a spinal brace. Except for some weight loss and a slight pallor, her appearance had not undergone any noticeable change. She had the relaxed, placid look of one who felt comfortable and was pain-free—a look that included gratitude for the doctor. Agnes was happy to have it all over with and behind her. To be free of pain—that was the greatest thing of all.

Karen entered and handed the report to Ed. He took it and nodded.

"—and this is a report in duplicate, Agnes, that you will give to Dr. Graham. He can give the extra copy to Dr. Fraser. It is a summary of your case history: what we found; what we did, and what I recommend should be done after you return home." He folded the report and inserted it into an envelope. He continued, "You have a substantial graft implanted. It will give you strong support after it finally consolidates and fuses. Until then, however, the graft must be protected; this is the reason for your brace. I am sure you will remember all the other instructions I have given you. Besides, your doctor in Grosse Pointe will keep an eye on you, so I feel that you are in good shape to leave for home." He stood up and leaned over to give the report to Agnes, but Dante jumped to his feet and reached for it, and placed it safely in his breast pocket. Ed escorted them to the door. He shook hands with Dante. Then, with a broad smile on his face and holding Agnes' hand in both of his, he remarked, "You were a wonderful patient, Agnes. It was a joy looking after you." This brought an equally broad smile to her face. She impulsively reached up and kissed him on the cheek. "Thank you, doctor," she murmured. "I think you're wonderful." Dante looked at her and smiled indulgently. They left for the airport.

Ed closed the door and returned to his desk feeling particularly cheerful and gratified. He whistled softly to himself. Karen looked in, grinned, and withdrew her head, slowly closing the door behind her.

Agnes and Dante had been airborne for about an hour. Agnes was lost in thought. She finally turned toward her husband. "I did not mention Elena to him." Dante looked at her, puzzled. "Should you have?" he asked. "Why Elena? What's this about telling Dr. Rankin?"

"She knew Dr. Rankin—years ago," she answered thoughtfully. Several times I was tempted to mention her." She paused. "But I decided not to." She lapsed back into her thoughts. Dante settled back to read a book when Agnes sighed. With a tone of finality she said, "—besides, he probably would not have remembered her." The remainder of the flight was uneventful.

Agnes did well and was permitted to discard her back brace six months later. She mentioned Dr. Rankin from time to time. Whenever she did, Elena listened with a gentle smile on her face ... and in her eyes. She asked no questions about him and Agnes did not pry. Since the birth of her second son, Elena had suffered intermittently from back problems. Agnes prayed that nothing would come of it.

CHAPTER XXXII

When George Waverly, Jr., was born, he weighed eight pounds eleven ounces. Elena suffered backache during the last months she carried him. Dr. Graham assured her it was not unusual to have backache, that it would disappear after her delivery. She was relieved, but the pain increased after the delivery and persisted. She saw Dr. Graham again.

"I think you ought to see a specialist," he commented after he examined her.

"Whom do you suggest?"

"Dr. Fraser has an excellent reputation. He has had the widest experience in such cases, Elena," he replied.

"Isn't he the one who operated on my friend, Agnes Ballisteria?" she questioned.

"Yes he was. As I remember, she had an injury to her back—a fall from a horse when she was a young girl. Yours is quite a different problem. Your x-rays show a congenital pedicle defect in one of your vertebrae. You were born with this. It means that a segment of bone is missing, leaving an architectural weakness in your spine. Later in life, this problem can be aggravated by a variety of causes—generally trauma, or, as in your case, by a pregnancy."

Elena sat lost in thought.

"Do you want me to set up an appointment for you, Elena?" Dr. Graham asked solicitously.

"Can I think about it for a few days, doctor?"

"Of course, of course. Just let me know what you decide."

When she reached home she thought about Agnes—and about Ed. If only Ed were near her now. She was tempted to ask for his help. But how could she explain to George that she wanted to go East—for a consultation. Besides, George had been in failing health and it would be an imposition on him—too much to ask. She had to remind herself how much older George was then she. She knew that he would intuitively see in her eyes what she could not hide. He had kept their secret well. She could not do this to the man who salvaged her life, who filled it with contentment and affection. She called Dr. Graham's office. The receptionist answered.

"Lucy, this is Mrs. Waverly. Will you please tell Dr. Graham to set up an appointment for me to see Dr. Rank—er—er-Dr. Fraser. I told him I would let him know."

She sat beside the phone and reminisced. *Ed, do you ever think of me? You cannot know that you have a son—our son. He looks very much like you. Do you ever talk to me like I sometimes talk to you?*

Karen escorted Mrs. George Waverly into the consulting room during the usual afternoon appointments.

Ed's practice and his reputation had grown considerably over the years. Patients from all parts, including foreign countries, came to him with their problems. Particularly patients who had previously undergone surgery elsewhere, but without success. A Mrs. Waverly, for instance, who had flown in from Michigan.

Ed rose from the chair. He came forward with a professional smile to shake her hand, while holding her medical record in his other hand. They exchanged some pleasantry about air travel and he politely asked her to take a seat by his desk. He did not look at her closely until he sat facing her.

A quiet, warm, affectionate smile played about her mouth. Her slightly graying hair was pulled back, accentuating her high cheekbones. Her lips were full.

Their eyes met.

His heart began to race and pound thunderously as he slowly rose from his chair and silently reached toward her with both hands. The years rolled away.

"Elena," he breathed barely above a whisper. It was the only word he could say.

She reached out to him with both hands. They simply looked at each other. She remained seated while he stood up and looked down at her, drinking her in.

The years had imposed a slight reserve on both of them. They did not kiss, and an awkwardness that can take hold of people who have been away from each other for a long time, prompted Ed to release Elena's hands although he did so reluctantly. As if he feared she might disappear if he did not hold her firmly. Was she real? Was it really Elena?

The words finally came. "Elena, my last letters to you were returned. But you have never been out of my mind. What happened to you? What have you been doing? Have you been happy? You look wonderful. It is hard for me to believe I am sitting here looking at you. Tell me all about yourself." Ed could not stop. Elena had to put up her hand in mild remonstrance.

"Ed, please," pleaded Elena. *This man before me has changed form the shy, reserved Edward I knew long ago.*

She related how she finally married George Waverly, an engineer who was very successful. He died three years ago. She had two children, both boys, who of course were now grown-up. She had been happy and content.

"I always knew where you were, Ed. You see, I followed your professional career. As a matter of fact, you operated on a friend of mine, a Mrs. Ballisteria, from Michigan, some time ago."

"You know Agnes Ballisteria? I wonder why she did not mention you to me."

Ed noticed she had never completely lost her accent. He found it difficult to realize that Elena, his first love, the passion of his youth, and whose memory he had always cherished, sat before him. As they looked at each other he thought of the numerous times he "talked" to her in the quieter moments of his mind and heart. He now recalled the devastation he felt when he lost her years ago. An overwhelming mixture of gladness and wonder came over him.

He realized he was unabashedly gazing at her, drinking in every feature. Elena understood and, gently smiling, waited for Ed to speak.

Ed extended his hand; she placed her hand in his. He said, "Surely there are very capable surgeons in your area, but you have come to me." It was in the form of a question. Elena's answer was straight forward.

"I am here, Ed, because I asked Dr. Winthrop to make this appointment. And please don't look so tragic." Her voice became matter-of-fact. "I am here because my problem falls into your specialty. Dr. Winthrop recommended you. So, here I am. I have already undergone one spinal operation. This time I want to make sure the chances for success will be greatly in my favor. I am selfish in my hope, and you, Dr. Rankin, must help me to realize that hope." A pleading look came into her eyes. "Now, doctor, look me over and tell me what I have and what has to be done. I want to be your patient."

Ed did not answer immediately. Strange, he thought, how the professional surgeon surfaced when confronted with the fact that he was to carry out an examination that required all the expertise he could muster. Ed became all doctor—Elena simply the patient. Elena felt it too and was grateful.

◆◆◆

Ed was thorough and gentle, whispering to her from time to time as the examination progressed. She studied his face for any clues his expression might reveal. She had brought a folder of x-rays which Ed arranged on the viewing stand and studied at length while she sat in her examining gown with legs dangling over the side of the table. He wanted her to delay dressing until he was sure there would be no need for further tests.

Some time later they were back in the consulting room. He leaned back in his chair and tented his fingers under his chin. Looking at her, he again found it difficult to be objective and professional. The flood of memories continued to wash over him, moments as clear as yesterday.

"Elena, your problem is amenable to treatment by surgery, I am happy to say. Your case is not an uncommon one."

Looking at him with mock tragic attention, she remarked, "I am impressed by your double negative, doctor."

He continued to study the record sent by Dr. Winthrop. "You show a disturbance in the fragility of your red cells. There is a tendency toward prolonged bleeding and altered coagulation—that is clot formation time. In an extensive surgical procedure the intraoperative and postoperative periods can carry an additional risk."

She looked at him and waited.

"I'll have you checked by our hematologist as well as our internist. They will, I am sure, have you in proper condition and ready for what I have to do."

"So you plan to operate. When will it be? Soon, I hope."

He was already in deep thought about what had to be done. "I'll have Karen, my secretary, call the hospital and check with the O.R. By the way, where are you staying?"

She mentioned a hotel in the city.

"I am glad you are staying there, Elena. It's an old hotel, but very gracious. The service is excellent and the food is good." He hesitated a moment. "Could we have dinner together tonight? Or have you made other arrangements? You mentioned your son; is he also staying in the city?"

"No. Lyle had to go back, but he made me promise to call him every night. I'm really quite alright. I have learned to manage very well by myself." She was pensive for awhile, and asked, "When do I have to enter the hospital and when will the surgery take place, Ed?"

"Karen will call you tomorrow. She will give you the exact time and date. It may take a few days, Elena. The O.R. schedule is always crowded, it seems." Ed continued, "Now about tonight, my dear—" Before he could complete the question, she answered, "It would be nice. Besides, it will give me an opportunity to meet your wife. You must bring her. We do have much in common." There was a twinkle in her eyes.

"Stacy, my wife—I lost her some time ago. It was very sudden. A plane accident."

"I'm sorry, Ed. I did not know." She placed a hand on his sleeve. "Of course I would love to see you this evening. Shall I expect you about seven?"

He saw her to the secretary's desk. "Karen, please arrange transportation for Mrs. Waverly. Just a moment—I have a better idea. Telephone the garage and tell Charlie to bring my car around. He'll take Mrs. Waverly wherever she wants to go."

Karen stared at Ed. He had never made such a request during all the years she had been with him. Her presence of mind concealed her surprise. "Very well, doctor," she said. She sneaked an occasional look toward Elena where she sat and waited for Charlie. She could see that Mr. Waverly was a very handsome woman; but many beautiful women had passed through the office doors. So—what else? At that moment Charlie buzzed. Karen addressed Elena, "Mrs. Waverly, the car is downstairs; be sure to press the lower level button, not the lobby. Charlie will be waiting for you as you step out of the elevator."

So—what else? Karen asked herself as her eyes followed Elena to the door.

Ed arrived at seven and rang Elena's room. She told him to come right up. She wasn't quite ready, but he could make himself comfortable. She was leaving he door unlocked. When he entered and closed the door, she called from the bedroom, "Help yourself to a drink, my doctor. I'll be out in a minute. You'll find everything on the cart."

It was a beautiful suite with good oil paintings hung on the walls. It occurred to Ed that Elena's late husband must have left her without financial worry. For some reason the thought piqued him a little, but he cast the feeling aside as absurd. He poured himself a drink and, with it in hand, moved around the large living room. He was too restless to sit. His shyness and reserve, which Elena always had the power to provoke, confused him. How much should he say and do concerning his feelings for her? Besides, he could not forget her surgical problem. He stopped at one of the large windows and looked down on the city traffic below. In spite of its grime and tawdriness, he reflected, the city always looked prettier at night, with its bright multicolored lights. Especially when seen from the air.

Elena entered the room. He turned around. His imagination tricked him into seeing the Elena he used to know. It was only momentary. Her warm smile rekindled all the old memories as she came toward him. Her eyes looked larger and more luminous. Her eye shadow had been expertly applied and there was a light blush to her high cheekbones. Her hair was combed severely back, as before. The entire effect was of expectancy, excitement. She wore a sheath-like, dark cocktail dress with a slit up one side, exposing her leg above the knee. She was devastating. Ed drank her in. Elena, remembering the reserved, often inarticulate man who had been her lover years ago, tilted her head saucily and did a pirouette before his admiring eyes.

The awkwardness which possessed them that afternoon was close to returning. Elena saved the situation. "Don't just stand there admiring me in worshipful silence," she quipped. "You will have to treat your patient with greater consideration. May I have a vodka and soda, please." Ed fell in with the change of mood and happily prepared the drink for her. After the second drink, they were well on their way, sharing memories.

At a point in their conversation they reached a hiatus of silence. Ed took the initiative. "Elena, about the operation. I know you are thinking about it although you have not mentioned it tonight. You must understand, my dear, that no surgery is foolproof; there is always the chance for what we call . . . the unknown and unpredictable factor . . . a risk inherent in any operation. This is why no reputable surgeon will guarantee, as it were, a successful result. This does not mean that you will not come through with flying colors. It is only . . . that you should know of this risk. I tell this to all my patients. They have the right to consider it. They must feel free to say `no'." It hurt Ed to have to sound so morbid about it, especially to beautiful and trusting Elena. He need not have worried.

"I know about the operation, Ed. Dr. Winthrop has already apprised me of much of the risk. But how can it be anything but successful, with you as my doctor."

"But, Elena . . ."

She put her hand over his mouth. He took it in his and kissed the fingertips. "Elena, I want to kiss you," he said.

"Alright, doctor. You may. But do not disturb my lipstick or make-up or eye-shadow. I can still remember your `inventory' kisses, and I suspect you have not changed."

He held her and whispered into her ear. "I wish it were different, that it need not be–this surgery I have to do."

The phone rang. It was a call from Grosse Pointe. When she hung up she said, "It was Lyle, my son." Then, looking steadily at Ed, she added, "Lyle Edward."

She stood there, motionless. Ed looked at her with the feeling that he was dreaming all this—this wonderful thing that was happening. He walked to her open arms. The glory and exultation of the moment overwhelmed them both. For so long they were lost to each other. And now this. It had to be a dream.

Ed telephoned the dining room to say that they were unavoidably detained and changed the reservation.

Ed was back in his apartment in the early hours of the morning. He was still in his dinner clothes as he sat writing at his desk:

> *Finding Elena was like a resurrection. As she sat in the office I was reluctant to release her hands for fear she would escape into my fantasy world where she has resided for so long. Now that she is real again she could leave me forever, simply by whispering ever-so-softy, "Good-bye."*
>
> *In a few days Elena will undergo surgery. She will be completely in my hands. I have never felt this way before, but in my great love for her will I also feel the silent agony of tissues recoiling under my scalpel? I must banish this thought from my mind.*
>
> *The past keeps sweeping in like a soft mist, carrying with it muted voices and vague forms; a shadowy kaleidoscope of images. So long ago! So very long ago!*
>
> *But I remember—so I write.*

CHAPTER XXXIII

CONVERSATIONS OF SILENCE

Elena was wheeled in asleep, deep under anesthesia. Standard operative skin preparation and draping were carried out. The patient was ready.

S. H. Nickerson

Dr. Philpott, the assistant resident, thought to himself:

My day to assist the chief. He's been getting these cases from everywhere—Amsterdam, Caracas, Chile, Tokyo—you name it. Salvage operations. Take this case from Michigan. Her disability is severe. The operation will be a long and tedious one. As far as I am concerned, after a number of hours of leaning over this table I know that my back will start to kick up. I wish the chief would converse a little more. His insistence on silence in the operating is a little too much. I'll have to admit, though, he points out all the important findings as we come to them; he is a good teacher. It is a bit officious of him, in my opinion, when, at the beginning of each operation he gives out with, "Now I want silence in the operating room. The only voice to be heard will be mine," I hope I'll be in good shape be tonight. For Cindy. Sweet, sweet Cindy.

Ed came through the door. Gown. Gloves. Adjust the overhead lights. There was silence except for the sounds of the O.R. equipment. Ed glanced up at Philpott, who nodded. He picked up the scalpel and began. To the left of Philpott was the scrub nurse, Thelma. She was thinking:

I know the chief likes my work. I like the chief. No lost motion, no confusion, no hesitation. He always follows the same routine. He always wants the same instruments in the same place and in the same order. I almost know in advance what he is going to want next. He should, about now, be asking for the interlaminar spreader but he's been talking about the "blooming adhesions." Whenever that happens, it can be tedious and long, and difficult to know. I hope it won't be as bad as Mrs. Baker's case. It took me the whole weekend to get over it. These new elastic stockings certainly are cooler than my last pair. Dr. Bernstein tells me they should be more comfortable. I hope so. Either this, he says, or get the veins stripped. I wish Dr. Philpott wouldn't crowd me. Who does he think he is?

The quick, precise clamping, cutting, stripping, and elevating of the tissues continued.

Philpott thought, *I have to hand it to the chief—no lost motion. Comes from long experience and hundreds of cases. Too bad you can't get experience except by growing older. You live long enough, you do enough cases—you get the experience. The chief looks worried.*

"How's the patient doing?" Ed asked, leaning over toward the anesthesiologist. "She's doing fine, Ed," George Kilpatrick reassured him. They were old friends and the chief trusted George implicitly.

Ed spoke aloud to no one in particular, "I'm not sure, from anything I read in Mrs. Waverly's history, if she actually had a mild deep infection, but with the history of a course of antibiotics, I'll have to cover her for the next few days at least." He looked up at his assistant. "Philpott, get a culture tube and swab here in this corner, if you will. She did have antibiotics before, for some reason. She possibly did not need them, but we'll play safe. Put her on tetracycline—maybe Keflex. You'll follow her case, of course."

Ed was alone with his thoughts. She was no longer his beloved Elena. She was the case and he was the surgeon. This circumstance created its own unique bond. Through the exposed square in the drape sheet he poured all the years of expertise and extensive experience. It was the arena of his concentrated skill and attention to detail.

Turning to his assistant, he muttered, "Look at these blasted adhesions, Philpott! I hope I won't have too much trouble when I get down to the dura. The nerve roots will have to be mobilized all the way out to their exit foramina. I'll also have to make sure to leave plenty of room around the bone to prevent any later compression of these roots. As you know, Philpott, I have always felt that here lies the crux of a successful operation."

Ed became silent. He had lapsed into a "conversation of silence" with his beloved Elena . . .

> *Elena, you are asleep and you will never realize how tedious this has been. You can't possibly know how anxious and concerned I feel. Believe me when I tell you that I pray, in my own way, that all will go well. I pray to the Architect that created us. There have been times during a particularly difficult case, with a history of previous operations, when I have reached an impasse—*

when I felt I could do no more—when the tissues were massively adherent and to continue could do more harm than good. This is when I prayed, Elena. Philpott, Deutermann, Thelma, or anyone else, do not know. Only you and I know. At times like this, I can almost imagine Someone behind me, gowned and gloved, like myself, and looking over my shoulder. I can also imagine a professional voice saying, "Now, Ed, let's see what we have here. Hm. I see. Why don't we just take that curlicue (my designation of a small delicate nondescript instrument that works in tight spots) and ease it around. Easy now. There, now it's freed up a little. Keep on, catch the free edge and work it outward and laterally. That's it. A little more laterally. See the edge of the nerve? Good. That wasn't so bad, was it?"

I tell you these things, Elena dear, because you and I are together in our hopes for you. We are closely bound by my great obligation to you as your surgeon. Medical school seems so far away now—we studied hard and for long hours. But it all seemed so wonderful, and how we loved each other, Elena. Those were the green years.

Stacy (you know about her, Elena) used to tell me I give too much of myself to this work and not enough to her, though we did try to be together as much as possible. She was probably right; I see examples of this all around me. Wherever a group of doctors and their beautiful wives gather socially, the doctors gravitate together, to the exclusion of their wives. Do you know what they talk about? Medicine! They are increasingly insulating themselves from things nonmedical, to the point where they no longer can carry on an interesting conversation about topics not related to their practice. "What a pity" Stacy used to say.

They are dedicated—to medicine. Make no mistake, Elena, about that, but their gradually increasing disinterest in things of aesthetic beauty—the arts, non-medical books, travel, the community needs—will convert many of these esteemed doctors into dull and boring men of narrow horizons.

My love, over the years, I have entered a niche in my mind where only you have resided. I have talked with you. You answered, in your silence. It was what I needed to hear. Today I have been talking to you as I always have, in silence.

CONVERSATIONS OF SILENCE

You are going to be alright, my love. I am satisfied. There. It is done.

Philpott looked over at Ed: *The chief has been very quiet this morning. I wonder if this case is troubling him more than he lets on. It looks good to me, except for the constant ooze, but it's completely under control, now.*

Ed began to hum a tune. It was always the same one and invariably meant the procedure was completed and he was preparing to turn it over to the assistant. He nodded to Thelma who was ready with the sutures he needed. Thelma passed the loaded needle holder to him.

Turning to Philpott he said, "On closing, we'll have to make sure to leave a completely drive field. The capillary oozing was troublesome all the way through. Put in a Hemovac suction for a few hours. That does it." He stepped away from the table, turned towards the exit door, and started to pull off his gloves.

Philpott was jubilant: *Good! Got through sooner than I expected. I've got to call Sharon. Tonight we'll stay at my place.*

Thelma was happy: *Good! Got through sooner than I expected. The chief did a good job as usual, and he always says thank you. He was sure quiet, though. Probably had something on his mind. I wonder whether I should have my veins stripped, like Dr. Bernstein says.*

Less than an hour later, Elena stirred. She grimaced with the sudden pain. She tried to cry out but her mouth was too dry to allow more than a slight groan. The recovery room nurse leaned over the guardrail and moistened her lips. "Try to lie still, Mrs. Waverly," she whispered. "The operation is over. Everything is just fine. I am going to give you an injection for your pain and you will soon feel more comfortable."

"Is Dr. Rankin here?"

"No—but we were to advise him when you reacted. I'll put a call through."

The injection took effect in a few minutes. They wheeled Elena down to her room and transferred her to her bed. When she opened her eyes, Ed was looking down at her.

"Try not to move too much by yourself, Elena," he instructed. "I want you to take some deep breaths. Good. Miss Bryson is your private duty nurse. She will help you turn from side to side and will give you something for pain whenever you need it."

"How did everything go?" Her voice was hoarse. Her throat felt irritated. An endotracheal tube had been inserted at the beginning of the anesthesia; she was "breathed" through it throughout the operation.

"I am satisfied," he answered soberly. "You should do very well. You were a very good listener," he added. Elena did not hear him. She was asleep. He turned to the nurse. "Be sure she does the breathing and leg exercises, Miss Bryson. You'd better get the Respiratory Care people to put her on IPPB three times daily. He looked once more at Elena. Then he left.

All had gone well. The surprising thing about the operation was that there had been no real surprises. The blood picture was stabilized and maintained normal values.

Ed visited Elena daily. Later, when she felt more comfortably, he dropped by in the evenings as well. It was remarkable, with these spinal operations, that there could be so much pain at first and so very little discomfort five short days later. Ed was always grateful for that.

On the seventh postoperative day, Elena was fitted with a brace, "harness" she called it. "For goodness sake, Ed, how long will I have to wear this? I never wore anything like this after the first operation." She looked dubious as she stood by the side of the bed and the last buckle was fastened.

"I know," answered Ed laconically. "What's more," he added, "you are never to sit up or stand without the brace, Elena. Never. That is, until I say you may." Elena noted the emphasis in Ed's voice. She knew that it was important for her to follow his advice.

The nursing personnel soon observed that a strict doctor-patient relationship was non-existent between Dr. Rankin and Mrs. Waverly. It was an occasional topic of whispered conversation, nothing more than that.

When she was permitted to be ambulatory with her brace, her

spirits rose with each passing day. One day she received a package from Michigan that she had asked her son to send. To Ed's amusement it turned out to be a package of mementoes and snapshots from their college days. It surprised him that after all the years she had kept them.

Ed and Elena knew that resurrecting their old fantasies could be enjoyed only by relegating them to the past, where they belonged.

Their bodies and minds had changed. No capricious dissembling could cloak their reminiscences in physical qualities to again be savored and experienced with their pristine joy. Dr. Faustus, at the cost of his soul, was the only one who was granted the gift of a second youth.

The present was a different time. The beautiful memories of passion and freshness woven into their youthful dreams would become illusory and stultified in middle age. Youthful vigor and fulfillment grew in abundance in the green years. The soil had changed its earlier nutriments with the passage of time. Although it had lost its earlier fecundity and fertility, it was now enriched and refined and was ready for a different harvest.

During the hours they spent together, they regained their deep feeling of mutual identification. Neither Elena nor Ed could define it. They only knew that when they were separated from each other, a part of each stayed with the other. It was a feeling which precluded words. It possessed them with a contentment and understanding that came from a certainty—an exultant awareness that they had somehow merged with each other and were as one. A gentle touching, a murmured word, a sweet questioning, a little secret humor that made them smile into each other's eyes, knowing full well that a fusion of their emotions and thoughts had somehow magically occurred. Elena had been gently lifted out of Ed's mental niche. She was very much alive, very much a vital part of him again. It was an inviolable union of spirit.

Their lovemaking would come later, when Elena was ready for it.

CHAPTER XXXIV

"Now, Edward Rankin, I know you have been staying here on

account of me." Elena pointed a scolding finger. "The nurses do talk, you know—enough for me to learn you should have gone on your planned vacation days ago. Your Dr. Deutermann has been coming in every day and is conversant with my case. It is only a question of time before I can go home. I know how tired you must feel."

Ed did not answer.

"If you do not go," she continued, "you will not have any vacation at all. I also know that you have a full operative schedule when you are supposed to return. Will you please go? For my sake? If you don't, I'll—I'll—have a relapse. That's what I'll have!" She made a grimace of mock defiance.

Ed agreed. "Okay, I'll go—for a few days."

Since Ed lost Stacy, preparations of any kind were a simple matter. He briefed Dr. Deutermann once again and cleared things up quite thoroughly. He had always possessed the happy faculty of "pulling down a mental window blind" when he finally turned his back on his practice. It helped him to leave his cares behind the moment he boarded the plane. Complications were comparatively infrequent, but inevitable in any extensive practice. They were dealt with, when they occurred. He did not anticipate any such mischance. There was no reason to expect it. He was at peace when he boarded the plane.

Ed routinely left standing orders from the office, that under no circumstances was he to receive calls from "back there" when he was at the beach house. This routine had worked well over the years; his vacations were never disturbed.

He was reclining in a deck chair, a cool drink in his hand, dreamily gazing out on an ocean dotted with sailing craft of all kinds. Near the shore the water was a fantastic aquamarine; one could see the bottom for a long distance out. The coral reef less than a mile away stretched in a gentle arc for several hundred yards. He was completely at peace, when the telephone rang. He disengaged himself from the chair, padded over to the phone and cut the insistent ring off as he picked up the receiver.

That was how it began. It was urgent, possibly grave. Elena Waverly was doing well when he left her. The wound was clean, the temperature flat, his beautiful Elena was cheerful. The day before, she had a chill and a rapidly rising fever with pain in her chest and difficulty in breathing. She was not quite conscious; she was not in coma. It looked very much like an embolus. Dr. Deutermann thought Ed should come back. Elena! The complication must have been brewing for two or three days. Elena! Deutermann had never called before.

His tranquility and peace of mind were shattered. He was dazed and confused.

The airline had a night flight he could make. A feeling of indecision spread over him. What could have happened? Could they have detected it earlier? Elena . . .

He threw a few things into a bag and called a cab. He could do nothing more for the present.

> *Elena, I should not have left you.*
> *I should have stayed. I should have stayed.*

By the time he reached the airport he was in a limbo of half feeling—mental inertia. He knew the body possessed a built-in mechanism which functions in the time of tragedy or loss. He guessed this was happening to him. Nature's opiate. It descends like a gray mantle; the senses become dulled; moving and walking are like a dream. It makes the immediate unbearable, bearable. Elena! He did not recall going to the counter, but he found the ticket and seat number in his hand. An accidental glimpse of himself, reflected in the glass, revealed a man who looked normal enough. He appeared self-composed; in control. Certainly nothing of what he felt was written on that man's face. What a fraud outward appearances can be!

His eyes traveled over the people jostling each other at the airport. Which ones among them were harboring the same leaden feeling; were drugged by the same apathy?

The tall man who wanted to look Texan, wearing a ten gallon hat and very expensive hand-tooled leather boots? The flight announcer with his laconic voice? There was a short, overdressed and overweight lady. She wore a miniskirt from which projected a good deal of her anatomy. Sheer black pantyhose. Feet shod with ridiculously high spike-heeled shoes. She looked like a madame taking time off from her stewardship at a bordello. She looked unconcerned. Was she full of despair and anguish?

None of their faces betrayed a deep ache or a crushing burden. The temptation to stop one of them and talk, to commiserate, to give solace, was overwhelming. Ed needed to talk to someone. Anything to lift this great pall in which he was enmeshed. It was already dark as he looked out on the tarmac. Planes were making their approach, while others were stacked overhead waiting to be called in from the tower. Their cruising lights sparkled like giant fireflies against the deepening velvet of the night sky.

He heard his seat number called and he passed through the door. He did not realize that he was airborne until the monotone voice of the pilot came over the P.A. system, "Good evening, ladies and gentlemen--cruising at 32,00 feet and . . . some tailwind . . . estimated arrival time—"

He had an aisle seat behind the bulkhead, for which he was grateful; more leg room and no disturbance to the passenger on his left if he wished to move about.

She was a young woman in her early thirties, he guessed. Fairly good looks. She wore a smartly tailored suit and a scent which was pleasing to his nostrils. He stole another covert glance. A professional woman, he decided, beautifully and expensively turned out. A slim attaché case rested in her lap. It was later tucked in by her side. There was something about her eyes, he thought—something distant and without focus, a certain fixity of gaze. That was it. Drugs or alcohol, he decided. She was trying hard to dissimulate with an exaggerated casualness. One vodka was soon followed by another in short order. Halfway through her second drink she began to drum her carefully manicured fingers on her handbag in cadence with some silent beat known to her alone.

Whatever the problems were that she was running from, Ed guessed, she was temporarily "in balance," the troublesome things pushed to the background. In his present mood he felt a solicitude almost a pity for the woman who obviously had the appearance of success and independence, but who carried within her the germinating seeds of something else.

When trays were prepared a little later, she slowly placed her glass aside. After rummaging about in her bag, she retrieved what looked like a small salt cellar. With exaggerated deliberation she removed its cap and shook some of its contents over the salad. He watched her, a puzzled expression on his face. Arresting her hand in mid-motion, she slowly turned her head toward Ed, like a mechanical mannequin, a vague smile on her lips. "Mustn't forget my vitamins, you know," she whispered conspiratorially. She then proceeded to forget Ed completely and returned to her salad. He had no idea what the powdery substance was.

He gradually drifted into sleep and was surprised when he was nudged by the flight attendant who instructed him to fasten his seat belt. They were beginning their descent. He puzzled over the fact that his sleep had been deep and untroubled. He had slept unhaunted by disturbing phantoms or images. He felt alert. Voices around him were clear. He found himself addressing the problem of Elena's complications and considering the options that lay open to him. He experienced a clarity and coolness of thought which, up to now, had deserted him.

Shortly after the plane's wheels touched the runway, the passengers were ready to disembark. As they filed past, Ed politely waited for the young lady to precede him. She acknowledged the gesture with a perceptible smile as she passed him. He remained a few feet behind her but walked on the opposite side of the long ramp which led to the exit.

At the far end, behind the barricade, stood a woman who started waving. She looked vaguely familiar to him. Although he was not quite sure, he was tempted to wave back, when at the same instant his erstwhile traveling companion began to wave and quicken her pace. In that split-second he recognized a frantically-waving Dotty. Clyde was not with her. Surprise and curiosity prompted Ed to move in her direction and by the time he reached them, the women were already hugging each other, as he came up behind them. As Dotty caught sight of Ed, her mouth dropped open in surprise as she disengaged herself long enough to exclaim, "Ed! Of all people! I thought you were down south basking in the sun. What a pleasant surprise." Putting her arm around her sister, looking first at her then at Ed, "Patti, I want you to meet Ed Rankin—Doctor Ed Rankin, a very good friend of ours. His wife, Stacy, was my dearest friend." She was positively bubbling. Turning to Ed and touching his arm she smilingly and proudly said, "Ed, meet my brilliant younger sister, Patti. She doesn't like to be called Patricia. She's our family's pride and joy. She's an attorney and has an office in Tallahassee. Isn't she terrific? You must have dinner with us soon so that you can both get to know each other better. Be a darling and say you will come."

Patti put on a charming professional smile showing all her brilliant white teeth. She said, "I think it is a wonderful idea, except it has to be soon since I am going back in a few days." She looked at him. A doctor? How much could he guess or know about me, she thought. Here I was sitting next to him during the entire flight as he was probably watching me take—and now this unbelievable coincidence of knowing Dotty and Clyde! I hope and pray he is someone who can keep a confidence; unless Dotty—

"That would be very nice." Ed tried to sound enthusiastic. "But will you please excuse me if I hurry along? I am in a bit of a hurry and have to go directly to the hospital."

"Ed, promise me you will call."

Ed was already hailing a taxi and waved back to them as he got in. Was that a look of relief he saw on Patti's face? What an unbelievable coincidence! Dotty's younger sister! Does Dotty know? After a few moments his mind reverted to Elena and banished all thought of Patti and everything else from his mind. He had returned from limbo. The self-discipline he had developed over the years eventually triggered an inbuilt instruction to marshal those resources he would have to draw on, for what lay ahead.

As he entered the hospital, he notified the telephone operator, "Please tell Dr. Deutermann I am here."

Mrs. Waverly was now in the Intensive Care Unit. He hurried to the elevator. As he stopped out on the I.C.U. floor he saw small family groups huddled together, whispering anxiously among themselves. In the I.C. Unit was a man with an acute coronary thrombosis; the wife and children outside waiting. An old man with an overwhelming stroke was breathing stertorously, his lips pulled in over his toothless gums. He was breathing his last. There was a postoperative patient, just arrived, following a long serious operation, and requiring several hours of careful monitored supervision. Another man was sitting high up in bed. He had had a pneumonectomy—a lung removed for cancer; a chain smoker. And there was Elena.

The nurse by her bedside was moistening her dry lips. She was semi-conscious. She moved her limbs spasmodically and rolled her head from side to side. A tracheotomy tube had been inserted to help her breathe. The tube, to Ed, looked like a violation of her beautiful white throat. No sounds came from her mouth due to the tracheotomy bypass, but periodic hissing through the tube could be heard whenever the nurse disconnected it for the suction apparatus. It was then reconnected to an oxygen outlet. The head of the bed was elevated.

Ed felt her pulse. It was full, rapid and bounding. Her respirations were very rapid. Her eyes were half-closed. She was critically ill. She was dying. He felt a heavy emptiness; a sense of an impending great loss.

with as much composure as he could muster he asked the nurse, "When did Dr. Deutermann last examine her?"

She answered, "He was in about an hour ago. You know, Doctor, I think she is reacting just a little better: her eyes—"

"Has the latest gas volume report come back?"

The nurse showed him the chart. The percentage ratios were all wrong. "I see there is a good output." He looked over to the intravenous tube in her arm and up to the bottles of fluid connected with it. "Will you tell Dr. Deutermann that I dropped by? Also tell the night nurses that I shall come by again in a short while."

He went up to the desk and studied the heart-monitoring unit to which Elena was hooked up. Her heart rate was very fast with a marked arrythmia. Ed looked over to Elena. Her face was as bloodless and white as the pillow on which her head was rolling.

He arrived at the club later in the evening and prepared for bed, but he was too keyed-up. It precluded any thought of sleep. He poured himself a generous brandy and sat back to think. Elena had suffered an extensive pulmonary embolism from some source. A fairly large portion of her lung had been rendered unavailable, leaving less lung tissue to breathe with. Her heart was laboring against this resistance. There was always the peril of further showers of emboli, or clots, to any part of her body. She remained in danger of dying—possibly instantly.

He knew the doctors had done all that was necessary. He simply had to wait and pray. Prayer was not a strange circumstance. Long ago he had promised a year of his life in a moment of dark despair. Life to him (and please God—to Elena) was too precious to be squandered. He prayed silently and long. Through sheer fatigue he fell asleep. The long-ago memories rushed through his tired mind. He and Elena were young again. She danced and sang and pirouetted and twirled.

These images faded, yet again he dreamed. He was standing in a meadow. There was a slight gentle rise upward to the right, where it met the sky. Through the meadow flowed a winding brook. The grass was tall and waved so that at times he saw the stream; at other times he could only hear it burbling along on an unseen course.

A quiet joy filled him. There was a singing and an elation in his being. It was almost too strong to contain. The sky became suffused with the orange-crimson of approaching twilight. It was the "betwixt and between" hour, when the day came to a close and the sun started to set, but twilight had not yet come. It was that melancholy fraction of the day when the earth and all else held its breath in suspended stillness.

He could smell the damp earth, and the earth-spirit enveloped him. He dreamed that he could "hear" the colors of the blue and red and fantastic orange as they kissed the crest of the hillock. It was like a song from heaven itself. He held his breath for fear of disturbing the fragility of his inner peace and joy. He closed his eyes.

She must have been there—although he did not see her at first. It was only a few moments later, when he opened his eyes. There, on the other side of the stream he saw a little girl. She was sitting in the grass looking pensively at a bouquet of white flowers she held loosely. In the tall grass he could only see her body from the waist up. She wore a white organdy dress with little puffed sleeves. On her straight blonde hair was a floppy straw hat with a wide brim. Two red velvet ribbons hung from her hat to below her shoulders. He was not sure about the flowers, but daisies seemed to linger in what he could remember. She was about twelve years old. She did not sense his presence; at least she did not look his way. Ed stood motionless and spoke very gently. "Little girl, speak to me. Those are lovely flowers." She turned her head rather slowly toward him and smiled. It was a smile of innocence and childhood, but she did not speak. A moment later, she began to fade like an evanescent wraith. "Stay, little girl," he pleaded, "stay awhile longer. You bring me the love and the memories of something I cannot name. Please don't go." He reached out as if to hold the vision a little longer, but she left him all alone, just as his own youth had left him years ago. The dream changed.

He stood rooted to the spot, waiting and hoping for the return of the sheer happiness that had filled his being. He espied two figures standing on the hillock, silhouetted against the deepening twilight sky. They approached without movement, like shadows being zoomed effortlessly into closer vision. In his dream-state he could not tell whether they were short or tall. But they were slender. Their coloring was neither dark nor light, but their facial expressions were remarkable. They appeared to be in a constant state of flux. Never did he see fixed features in either face. The figures came nearer and stopped on the spot where the little girl had left him. Ed stood speechless and motionless and gazed at them. He wondrously felt no fear. Deep within him was a feeling that he should know them. Something told him that he should speak first. "Who are you? From where have you come?" The prescience that he knew them became very strong and puzzling. If only the mobile faces would remain unchanged long enough for him to see and recognize. One of them, the one with the darker, shadowed face, answered, as he stretched out his arm in Ed's direction. "We know you Zalnan of the Deer, and you will know us better. You will come to feel an affection for us as your life extends into the years to come." The deepening dusk was now beginning to transform them into dark shadows. Ed answered, "You call me by a name which is not my own." There was no reply. Then one of them spoke; which one, he could not tell. "Zalnan, I am the Angel of Death. Whoever sees my face shall not live."

Ed asked, "Shall I therefore die?"

"No, you have not seen my face; you will live. But I shall be near those to whom you minister. I shall come on the appointed day to unveil myself to one you try to heal. Without death there can be no life. My mission will often be one of love and compassion for those who cry to see me. I shall embrace these souls. What is an embrace if it is not an act of love? I am truly a messenger of compassion. Remember this, Zalnan, when I take one of yours."

He was gone. The setting sun threw its last rays heavenward as it dipped below the horizon, and dusk was now very deep. A chill crept through Ed's body.

The remaining figure spoke. "I am the Angel of Pain. You know me well. I am wherever you are. We are inseparable. We complement each other's thoughts. In the surgery, in the office, at the bedside—wherever you walk or rest, I stand behind you; I listen as you listen. I am your adversary, even though I am your constant companion. I know that you have come to accept my presence because you acknowledge that I am an inseparable part of the very life which you attempt so faithfully to preserve. You may come to think better of me, Zalnan. It is only in this way that the cleansing can come. Know that I am always with you."

"What cleansing?" he asked. "And why do you call me by this other name? Stay a moment—"

The figure was gone.

Ed stood all alone in the darkness. There came over him a sorrowful weeping. He fell to his knees and with his arms outspread he gave vent to a howling anguish into the darkness around him. He felt a heaviness he could no longer endure. It pressed him to the ground.

Ed tossed restlessly in his bed and awoke with a cry as there echoed down through the valleys and convolutions of his half-awake mind, "ONE YEAR LESS TO LIVE—One Year Less—one year less—less—less . . ."

CHAPTER XXXV

The following day Deutermann and Ed compared notes. Except for the decrease in restlessness, Elena's condition remained grave. She was still semi-conscious and unaware of their presence. At least she was no worse, they agreed.

Since Ed returned during his vacation time, no office appointments had been booked by Karen. After aimlessly wandering through the business section of the town, he made a few small purchases and then drove back to the club. He poured himself a drink and stood staring out of the large window at the acres of shrubs and trees, including an aged sycamore maple whose branches almost brushed against the side of the building. His gaze fell on the shell of a moth clinging to the outside screen. It had been there a long time—he first noticed it last fall—a simple little moth with outspread wings. it had alighted there and fulfilled its amazing life cycle after ensuring the continuation of its species. With its podia still clinging to the netting, its abbreviated life had ended. The sharp winds and snows and sleet of the past winter had failed to dislodge it. So there it remained, a little symbol of what it had been, before it had succumbed after its travails of egg-laying. As if tenacious of life, even in death, it had secured itself in this preserved immobility.

It seemed to Ed that it bore a message. He would not make a move to dislodge it. It had earned its permanent perch. His mood lifted slightly as he turned away from the window.

A few hours later he returned to the hospital. Dr. Herzog was there. "Hello, Michael. What do you think?" The doctor raised his head from studying the chart. "A little better, Ed, a little better. We recovered fat in the urine specimen, I want you to know. She obviously had a shower of fat emboli. As a hematologist, I can tell you that it is rare in your type of case, but it happens. Anything can happen, as you very well know."

Ed examined Elena. Her limbs were less restless. Her eyes appeared to focus a little. Using an ophthalmoscope, he could see the telltale pinpoint hemorrhages in the retina. Over her chest were a few minute hemorrhagic spots. "Did you get any new values on her blood gases?" he asked.

"They are not much better, Ed, but the ratio is not quite so disproportionate. Here comes Deutermann. He'll fill you in on more of what happened while you were away."

"He already has, Michael."

During the next two days the tide gradually turned. Elena began to mumble unintelligible words which sounded like a foreign language--probably her mother tongue. The following day her restlessness disappeared and her eyes opened. Still no intelligible speech but her eyes followed moving objects and people. The same evening she used the hand that was not immobilized by the intravenous tubes—and passed it over her lips and face.

When Ed came in the following day, she recognized him. Her heart rate and respirations were down to almost normal. The nurse had fixed her hair into two long braids that hung down on the pillow.

The endotracheal tube seemed to bother her, particularly when she tried to swallow.

"Is the tube irritating you, Elena?"

She nodded. She looked worn and tired.

"Nurse, will you please disconnect the oxygen outlet."

The nurse did as she was ordered. Ed whispered something to her. She left and soon returned with a small packet. He then gently removed the adaptor from the endotracheal tube. "Elena, listen to me, my dear. I am placing a piece of gauze over the tube opening. Hold it with the fingers of your free hand to close the opening of the tube and try to breathe naturally."

She obeyed—rather apprehensively at first. She found that she could breathe through the normal passageway. This brought a faint smile to her lips.

"Now, Elena, with your fingers still over the opening, try to say something. Something nice."

"Edward—Ed, dear."

That evening the tracheotomy tube was removed and the skin opening was covered with a thin pad of gauze. It would close spontaneously in due time, leaving a small pitted scar.

That evening she spoke to him. "I am not in my room." She was sparing of words and a little out of breath.

"No, Elena," he answered.

"Where am I?"

"You are in I.C.U., Elena—Intensive Care, my dear."

Elena thought about this for a while. It was an effort for her to talk. "Will I be alright?" She took Ed's hand.

"Yes, Elena, you will. You have been away for awhile. Welcome back, my dear." His eyes were brimming. A part of him was alive again. It is doubtful that she heard his last words. She was asleep.

The following day she was transferred back to her own floor.

A curious phenomenon—the diary. the reasons for keeping one are as manifold and varied as human nature itself. Prominent people presumably write with the intention to eventually collate the data into a volume which will someday serve as a source of information, carrying with it implied direction of political and economic action to those who will learn what history can teach. Toynbee, the great historian, despaired that mankind would ever learn.

Ed was not motivated by such altruistic impulses. To him, keeping a diary was simply a personal essential. It served as an extension of thoughts and feelings he experienced during his working hours. His work demanded concentration and meticulous performance; his thoughts crystallized and focused sharply on the problem at hand. Afterwards, he needed a periods of objective reflection and introspective evaluation.

He wrote about Elena's case and was brutal in his self-evaluation:

> ...the confusion and indecision nearly overwhelmed me. The fact that I did not succumb to that state of mind is no consolation. Sheer self-discipline must have accomplished it. My great love for Elena must have played a great part as well.
>
> I keep wondering about my apparently normal outward appearance in spite of the fact that I was being torn within myself.
>
> How many individuals have lived in their own private worlds, unsuspected of harboring internal conflicts, without any visible outward signs of their deep-seated turmoil? Many, I am certain. Many of my patients, so affected, are possibly managing to carry on their lives without ever revealing themselves. There must be a broad spectrum of antagonisms, frustrations, hatreds and yearnings which batter them about silently, but which still remain compatible with everyday "normal" living.
>
> Those who finally cry out in anguish and disorientation of their senses become the mental casualties for the institutions or the psychiatrists.

He put his pen down, poured himself a brandy and dropped into an easy chair. He reached for the memo pad which he habitually kept within reach on a side table. One of the items: DINNER WITH DOTTY AND CLYDE–? He did not even remember jotting it down the night he returned from the airport, with all the other problems he had on his mind. He closed his eyes; Patti's face. After a few moments of indecision, the desire to know more about Patti grew. There was no doubt that she had intellect as well as intelligence. She appeared to have an alcohol (as well as drug?) problem which up to now had not marred her looks or appearance. It was her professional performance that would eventually suffer. He wondered about that.

With the phone on his knees he dialed Dotty's number. It was picked up by her on the first ring—as if she were waiting by the phone expectantly. "Hello, Dotty, this is Ed," he said cheerily, "is it too late to accept the dinner invitation you were kind enough to extend at the airport? You must forgive me for not getting back to you sooner but I have had a trying time at the hospital-but now that the patient is out of danger—" It was as far as Ed got in the explanation when Dotty's voice started to chirp over the phone for a number of minutes while he sipped his drink silently and gratefully. She was explaining that she was just about to call him, which was why she was so near the phone when it rang. Since Patti was leaving the day after, would tomorrow night be alright? While she talked, it struck Ed that she and Stacy must have been very much alike in many ways. He wondered why he had not noticed it before. It explained their close sister-like relationship when Stacy was alive.

Clyde met him at he door, holding a drink as he linked his other arm through Ed's and led him into the den where Patti was leafing through a magazine section devoted to the social activities in their local area. Dotty was pottering busily in the kitchen. Patti stood up as Ed entered. He thought it rather odd, unless it was due to an ingrained professional habit of an attorney rising to meet a prospective client. Since his motive for coming was partly to study her, Patti's gesture seemed to reverse their roles somehow. A few moments later Dotty came in, full of cheer and musical laughter.

Dotty was serving the dinner herself. Clyde was never a great conversationalist but his occasional word and pleasant demeanor rendered his parsimony of words neither uncomfortable nor embarrassing. Which left most of the talk to Ed and Patti. She had been drinking the wine rather steadily and there was a flush to her cheeks. Tilting her head in a coquettish way she spoke to him across the table, "Dotty tells me that you are a surgeon-a good one and very well known, Doctor Rankin. In what particular field does your interest lie?" Her eyes held a hint of amusement. There it is again, the cross-examining lawyer, mused Ed.

"For many years I was interested in all aspects of orthopedic surgery, but in recent years practically all of my time has been devoted to 'failed backs,'" he replied factually, with no hint of bragging.

"Failed backs?"

"Yes. People who have had one or more spinal operations which, unfortunately, have not proved successful," he explained. "We try to rehabilitate them through surgical means, if necessary. I say 'we' because it always involved a team of assistants and technicians, both in the operating room as well as after the surgery."

"I see." It became obvious that Patti did not choose to pursue this line of talk further.

"Do you travel much, Patti?" Ed was trying to bring the conversation back to their recent flight. Patti's smile faded momentarily. She reached for her wineglass. Clyde was busy draining his. Answering directly, she said, "Yes, I have to. The last trip I took, the one we were both on, was after a case I had defended." She emptied the glass. Twirling the glass stem with her fingertips, she looked down into the glass and said slowly with some emotion, "I lost that case, doctor. It was a great disappointment to me." She raised her eyes and looked directly at him. Her eyes said: please understand my drinking-and that other thing. I was depressed and under great strain. Please—please.

"I am sorry," Ed said.

Clyde seemed oblivious to any undercurrent in their conversation. He said blandly, "You can't win them all, Patti."

Dotty caught the tail-end of Patti's words. She said proudly to whoever would listen, "Isn't she terrific! I don't care even if she did lose." Turning to Patti, "I know that the disappointment was great, dear, but I feel that you, dear sister, are a wonderful girl of great accomplishment." Turning to Ed, "Don't you agree?"

"Yes," he said, "I think that she is terrific." He looked at Patti. His eyes said, trust me. Her eyes were pleading and grateful; her hands were trembling. As Dotty went back to fetch the dessert, Patti excused herself and left the room. She was back before Dotty, who fussed around in the kitchen, waiting for the coffee percolator to quit rumbling. Patti's eyes were now round and bright; her hands were no longer trembling. She was a picture of composure and aloof self-assurance. She was "in balance" again.

The rest of the evening passed rather quickly. When it came time to leave, Ed wished Patti a pleasant trip since she was leaving in the morning. Dotty and Clyde saw him to the door. They were so sincere and solicitous in their hospitality that a deep feeling of gratitude toward the two generous and thoughtful friends welled up within him. His countenance showed it and they were happy for it.

Months later, Dotty mentioned to Ed that Patti had achieved a great success in a very important defense case. Ed remembered reading something about it in the newspapers. "I shouldn't have worried," Dotty confessed. "I knew that Patti would eventually—would—"

"I know, Dotty," Ed replied, "you don't have to spell it out for me; I also hoped she would—"

CHAPTER XXXVI

Ed exposed the full sensitivity of his nature to Elena without fear of her believing it a weakness. he felt Elena would understand him.

During his visits he told her about the "silent conversations" he had had with her over the years. Whatever veneer Ed had built up during his professional life was stripped away in his meetings with Elena. It brought them closer, if possible.

They were standing near a window, in her private room, looking down on a beautifully landscaped area donated by a man grateful for his wife's recovery. They had been silent for a while but this was not unusual. She turned her head, looked at Ed for a long moment. He was unaware of her gaze. THE TIME HAD COME TO TELL HIM, SHE DECIDED. She returned to her bed.

She had not spoken much of herself as Ed had freely opened his heart to her. She had been willing to listen. This kind, loving man sitting beside her was content to wait. he was happily in love with the woman she now was. He apparently was not going to question her about her life. He would wait until she was willing to talk. She breathed deeply.

"Ed," she began, "do you remember our last meeting, in Canada?"

"Of course, I remember it very well. How could I forget? We were so much in love and you-you were beautiful and warm and—yes, I remember it very well." He looked at Elena, remembering how things were.

Elena continued, "I have carried that memory all my life for more than our love. Before I left to meet you I was seeing George Waverly occasionally. He was on the teaching staff, part-time, at the university. He was an older man, fifteen years older than I. Very charming and highly principled. We shared many common cultural interests. He was the older member of a faculty group in which I moved and a very interesting dinner companion. Although I did not encourage him, I could see that his interest in me was more than casual. I never allowed the situation to progress to the point where he could feel free to declare his intentions. you see, I was very much in love with someone else." Her eyes became moist.

"At our last meeting, my dear Ed, it became quite clear that your residency and future training would require several years. We never discussed marriage at any time. Our love, in those days, was enough." There was a long pause as Elena relived those days of that time in her life.

"Some time after I returned to the university I realized I was pregnant."

Ed stiffened in his chair. He looked at Elena, his mouth slightly open. No words came. He stared at Elena.

Her face no longer showed the storm of emotions which swept over her in those days long ago. Her voice was calm. "Yes, I was pregnant. In my loneliness I longed terribly for my mother. I felt so vulnerable and confused and terrified. I could not write you, my love, for fear it would disturb you and would interfere with the work so essential to your training. Besides, what could you do? She paused, a faraway look in her eyes.

Ed passed his tongue over his dry lips. He was living through the poignancy of her terrible ordeal.

"When I talked to George, he could tell from my voice that there was something grossly wrong. `I am your friend, Elena. I can be more than a friend, if you will let me,' he pleaded. `I am old enough to have gained some wisdom. Believe me, you can confide in me. You must know how I feel about you, my dear. Please let me come over and tell me all about it. I am sure I can help you, Elena,' he coaxed."

S. H. Nickerson

"There is no point going into detail, Ed. George came over and to my own surprise I unburdened myself to him. He seemed to invite such confidence."

Ed made an unintelligible low sound.

"Elena, Elena, you should have called me or written. I could never understand the abrupt break-off. You should have let me know." Ed's voice was hoarse. "You should have told me."

"—He wanted to marry me as soon as possible although I was carrying another man's child. he proved to be so kind and loving and so helpful and understanding that I grew truly fond of him—"

"We were married a month later. After our marriage I discovered that he was very affluent—the senior partner of a large engineering firm, well-known in our area. His part-time teaching was just a hobby for him. I have not wanted for anything. He was a wonderful father and husband. We did have a son, George Junior, during the second year of our marriage. Both sons were treated alike and given the same love and affection. They both bear his name, of course." Elena stopped here. She gave a deep sigh, sank back against the pillows and closed her eyes.

Her eyes remained closed when she spoke quietly. "—Ed, Lyle Edward is your son. He does not know you are his father. George and I decided that was best. He resembles you."

A profound silence descended upon them.

Ed tried to picture himself in the role of father. He had performed surgery on many handicapped children throughout his professional life. he enjoyed a great rapport with them and had a deep affection for them. The indestructible optimism of a child grunting and struggling with braces and crutches, but walking, probably for the first time, was always touching. The smiling determination of their little faces was reward enough. He loved them as children, but did he ever feel paternal toward any of them, as a father would toward an offspring, he asked himself.

A feeling of deep self-reproach gripped him when he thought of his beloved Elena alone. He was not by her side when his son was born from her labor pains. He was not there to see his son take his first steps. He never took part in the games his child played and enjoyed. He did not supervise his schooling or his education. He knew nothing of Lyle Edward's growing up. But George waverly did. All of it. And he, Edward Rankin, was the father of this man who carried his genes in his body and even looked like him. it was unreal.

What was real to him was Elena's agony and the loneliness and desperation she must have felt when she carried his child. She chose to remain silent and ha worked out her problem—without him. All for his sake; to avoid hurting him or interrupting his career. HIS PRECIOUS CAREER!

The hurt he felt, in the silence which lay between them, showed in his face. It was greater, much greater, than anything he could have felt years ago. If Elena had only known this.

Elena could see what was happening to Ed. She began to weep softly. She wept though she knew it all had to be said; all the past pieces had to fall into place. And now it was done. What now remained was the life, whatever it turned out to be, which lay ahead for both of them. She thought,

> *What manner of fate would have brought us together this way after so many years, if not to carry our love to its fullness in our present union? If only he will come to me now and hold me; just hold me. Everything will have been worthwhile. Some day when he sees his son, who looks like his father did years ago, he will be very proud.*

Elena stopped weeping.

Ed stood up and came close to her. Looking into her eyes, he held her hands. He spoke very softly; his voice sounded tired. "My love, my dear Elena, I was not there when you needed me most. I will never be far from you again." He paused, his eyes became moist. "I wish it were possible to undo, or change much of what happened. I wish. . ." He could not finish.

He held her for a long time. He would never let her go again.

There was new gentleness between them. The knowledge of what Elena revealed to Ed brought a bittersweetness which they both shared and felt deeply.

A few days later, after a final checkup examination, Ed decided that Elena no longer needed hospital care. The incision in her throat was closing. Under ordinary circumstance Ed would have recommended that she return home to the care of the referring doctor—wearing the spinal brace, of course.

After all she had been through, since her operation, the thought of going home had not quite entered Elena's mind. The care and the love she was receiving beguiled her into a feeling that she was already home. Now, for the first time, in a long while, she found herself thinking of the "other" home. However, travel was out of the question. She was not yet ready for a plane trip.

Ed arranged to have Elena transferred to a resident-suite at his club. There were several floors of permanent residents—all members. On the top floor facing the northeast was a suite with a large living room and a tremendous bedroom with adjoining bathroom. Adjoining the living room on the south side was another bedroom and bathroom.

When she was comfortably settled by her bustling private nurse, a bell system wa arranged so that the nurse, who used the other part of the suite, could be summoned if necessary.

Dan McElligott was waiting for Ed when he stepped out of the elevator into the foyer. Dan was the club manager.

"Hello, Dr. Rankin," he started. "I—er—see from Mrs. Waverly's registration that she is a member of a club in her area with whom we have reciprocity of privileges. Should we use the membership number she gave me, or—?"

"No, Dan. Charge it to my club account, please."

"Your account, doctor?"

"Yes, Dan. My account."

Dan was obviously waiting for Ed to say something more. Some further explanation seemed to be in order. He waited politely for Ed to volunteer further information.

"Mrs. Waverly is the mother of-someone close to me and I promised him to give her the best care following her surgery. She is not quite ready for a plane trip home, so what better place than a suite right here to keep her under my supervision. She is my patient."

CONVERSATIONS OF SILENCE
198

Dan McElligott looked positively relieved. The orderliness of things was now restored.

"Very well, Dr. Rankin," he agreed cheerfully. "We'll do everything possible to make her stay enjoyable. Oh-one more thing-about the meals—anything special?"

"No, Dan. She'll call down, or her nurse will. She is not on a special diet."

◆◆◆

Ed, do you remember this one? That was then—such a serious look. Why, Ed, you were looking at me, and not at the camera. Here's another one—again your head is turned towards me! I never noticed it before. You wanted to say more; you never did." Elena looked up at Ed. She could see the lines of fatigue in his sensitive face. He needed a rest.

Elena pulled out a separate packet of snapshots. Neither one could recall the names or the faces. They looked strange now, almost like intruders.

The snapshots passed from her hands to his. A number of the Canadian boys were no longer alive. Dieppe in World Was II had resulted in terrible casualties in the Canadian contingent. All that was left was their smiling faces.

Elena sighed. Such a bad thing, the war! It seemed such a long time ago—all this. Ed was lost in deep reflection when Elena said, "Ed, you haven't been listening. Look at this one—when we were standing in front of the Redford Library. Isn't that Cranston to my left? I remember him as being a genius in your class. I wonder what happened to him."

Ed took the snapshot and studied it for a long moment. "His name was Crandall, Berlowe Crandall."

Ed was reluctant to discuss Crandall.

"Please tell me, Ed, I remember something sad about him."

"Elena, do you remember when we read Kant at the university?" She nodded. "Well, in his Transcendental Logic, he raised the question, *Can we isolate reason? Is it a source of conceptions and judgment which spring from it alone?* You know, Elena, I have often pondered those lines since... since Berlowe Crandall. That is why I have never forgotten them, trying to find an answer to what happened to Berlowe

Crandall. In those days, all that really mattered to us medical students was to acquire as much medical knowledge as possible. We eagerly sought maximum exposure to the daily lectures and revelations by our professors. We learned about the normal and abnormal processes which take place in our bodies—mysteries which became gradually unraveled and revealed. We were enthralled, living and learning in a new world—a circumscribed world nevertheless. Nothing was allowed to intrude.

"It was not an indifference on our part. The apparent lack of concern with what happened to Berlowe was really because of our preoccupation with so much medical knowledge that had to be absorbed and learned. It pre-empted all other considerations.

"Besides, we were young. We were not yet doctors, Elena, with mature understanding and intellect. Not yet. We were neophytes, equipped with the mental and emotional apparatus, consistent with our immaturity. I see you are smiling. Our intellectual capacity for study far outstripped our emotional capacity to respond fully to outside tragedy or mental disintegration. You know, my dear, it is only with the passage of time, when the abrasive assaults of living have peeled away the stout green-husk of our youth, that our deeper, vulnerable sensitivities are exposed and tormented. Along the way we have found that human nature, call it what you will—the spirit within us—can be sublime or degraded, heroic or cowardly, generous or parsimonious, loyal or unfaithful. It can be everything good or bad, Elena.

"Life's endeavors are nothing like the pretty painting symbolizing the harrowing ascent up a steep mountain, where the successful climber finally stands at the summit with arms outstretched in an exultant attitude of victory and freedom, silhouetted by the bright sun in the background!

"It can also be symbolized by someone crawling through a long and tortuous tunnel with many labyrinthine cul de sacs, where the victor *finally* crawls out into the open sunshine. FREEDOM! Psychiatrists would probably have a field day determining why I prefer the picture of the mole-spelunker to the oxygen-deprived mountain climber. But I have a couple of "skinned knees" to prove my point. What does all this have to do with Berlowe Crandall?"

"Skinned knees, Ed? Really—?"

"Humanness is a conglomerate of inconsistencies tethered together by tenuous threads. It is like a slowly weaving Hydra with many heads. The total nature of the host is the body that can keep these straining heads; I almost said furies, in check with greater or lesser degrees of success. The final measure of these contending counter-balances can range from greatest glory to abysmal devastation. Am I pontificating?"

"You do sound like Lambert, our old language professor. Do you remember him? He . . ."

"Berlow Crandall," Ed continued, "must have experienced an almost physical buffeting, Elena. The specter of it still hangs about in my memory."

"He was a genius. Nobody questioned it. He could recall extemporaneously from textbooks which the rest of us had not yet read. We were convinced he would qualify for the best appointment available in any institution. His breadth of acquired knowledge was so wide that, on one occasion that I can remember, he corrected the professor—mind you—in a detail that was obscure to begin with. It had something to do with sarcomatous changes in the small bowel. This same professor's name can be seen as the author of one of the most prestigious textbooks of medicine. Crandall read textbooks we were preparing to read the next semester. He read them and understood them. He was a likable fellow and quite sociable. Always had a friendly smile. He was an enthusiastic participant in our class activities. We all accepted the fact of his amazing receptive mind.

Then something curious happened.

"Sometime in the third academic year, he and I were having a beer in a nearby grill. The tavern was off limits, but the beer was excellent. Without warning and much to my surprise, he ducked under the table and hid there. I had to bend down to talk to him. He seemed unwilling to come out. 'Crandall! What in hell are you doing under there?' He paid no attention to me but appeared to be listening with his ear cocked for something. After apparently satisfying himself, his head gradually came up until his eyes appeared just above the table level. He stopped there and moved his eyes from left to right, to sweep the room. Then again, after once more satisfying himself, with whatever he saw or did not see, he came out from undercover, and we continued our beer drinking.

"I asked, 'What was that all about? Someone chasing you or

something?' He nodded without speaking. When I thought about it afterward, I concluded it must have been a bill collector. It would prove very embarrassing for him to be importuned at that particular time. The easiest way out was 'to make himself scarce.'

"Other incidents began to occur. On one occasion, he dozed off in the amphitheater, even emitted a gentle snore. Absenteeism gradually because a habit. Occasionally, we could see him making an almost physical effort to concentrate. It soon became evident that his determination had the malleability of Turkish Delight. Crandall was in deep trouble, but we were young, enterprising medical students, each with our own goal and with the overriding drive to make good.

"It can be assumed that, during this period, Crandall was carried along on waves of deep confusion, waves which finally tumbled ashore, into a spume of fragmented sanity and disorientation.

"Whatever Crandall experienced was strong enough to take on almost physical form. In desperation he tried to fight it down, to 'swallow it' as it were. In his case he could no more swallow it or destroy it than if it were a sea urchin passing down his gastrointestinal tract. So he succumbed. We never saw him again." Ed paused for a moment and continued, "The years have brought tremendous changes in all branches of medicine and surgery, Elena. Orthopedic surgery is hardly recognizable compared with what it was not so many years ago. The brain, in recent years, has been charted and explored to such an extent that much increased knowledge has been acquired about its function and about its 'silent' areas where many processes, including those of personality traits, reside.

"I often wonder, Elena, if the time will ever come when geniuses like Crandall can be salvaged and saved for the enrichment of mankind, rescued from retrogression into ruin.

"Let's look at the photo again, my dear. Is there anything in Crandall's face or eyes to reveal a sign of the tempest which must have (already) been brewing in his mind?

"Hmmm—I think I look worse than he does. Much worse!"

Ed spent all his time away from work, with Elena. It was an easy matter to just drop in. Elena was now ambulatory most of the day. She managed to get into and out of the brace very well. Her private duty nurse was needed only for the afternoon shift, mostly for her personal needs.

One evening Ed knocked at the door, as usual, and Elena opened it herself instead of using the buzzer. Her hair was put up in the fashion Ed knew so well. She wore a long hostess gown. She looked beautiful. Ed forgot his manners, remained standing on the threshold instead of stepping inside, and simply looked at her. Oh, how he loved her, standing there. She was still in her slippers. Higher-heeled shoes were still taboo for her. She looked like a little girl.

"Ed Rankin," she chided in her slightly hoarse voice, "are you going to just stand there all evening, or have you dropped by just to borrow a cup of sugar?"

Ed laughed and quickly came in. He closed the door behind him. Elena hooked her arm in his as they slowly walked back into the apartment. When they turned to each other he kissed the top of her head which reached up to his chest. they held each other. A nervous trembling passed through Elena. She looked up at Ed questioningly. His eyes told her he understood. With his arm around her waist they walked toward the bedroom. Ed helped her out of her clothes. The brace came last. It had to be removed while lying in bed. Ed joined her quickly.

They were facing each other and studying each other's features. Ed's voice was hoarse with excitement and desire as he gazed at his lovely Elena. She was still trembling uncontrollably.

"Ed, will it be alright to do this? Oh, my love, hold me and tell me that it will—"

"After all, darling," Ed whispered, "how many patients can boast of such personal attention and service from their doctor?" Then, in a more serious and reassuring manner, he whispered, "Just do as I say, my dear, and everything will go well."

Elena and Ed became as one. Their act of love was a union of body and mind. It was a slow, deliberate savoring that carried with it not only the present but all the joy of the long ago. It was an expression of life in its ultimate fulfillment. It was not a violent experience—it was a gentle complete surrender to each other-that knew no holding back.

The day passed into deep twilight. Elena rested in bed with her eyes closed.

Ed went over to the cabinet and poured some sherry for Elena and cognac for himself. When Elena first came from the hospital Ed had gone up to his apartment and returned with the bottles. he made a bit of a ceremony about Elena's "homecoming" at the time.

She sipped her sherry and Ed sat by her holding his snifter and occasionally bringing it to his lips.

He looked into the depths of the amber liquid.

"All my life, Elena," he began in a reflective voice, "I have been traveling on a road. To where? It was always my thought that the direction I took was of my own volition and of my own design, but for quite some time now I have come to realize that we are carried, like the wind, along paths over which we have little control. We compromise and reconcile ourselves to the changes as we go and that is how we manage to make a life of it. The outward appearance, a doctor presents to the world, is a molded personality. An excellent bedside manner is an unconscious affectation. To smile easily is an essential trait. The years work to create a patina, a veneer. The resulting exterior is of a self-possessed, confident and successful doctor. That is what the public sees. This is what the public needs. You might wonder why I am telling you this."

"Yes, Ed, in a way I do. Is it going to be in the form of a general public confession, darling? If so, before you put on your hair shirt, please let me have a little more sherry."

Ed smiled and, after returning to the chair by her side, continued, "The doctor does not consciously engage in subterfuge, this—this putting on a front. It is image—a public image which plays an important part of his interaction with his patients. What I want you to know, my dear, is that my own self-assessment falls far short of the image, Elena, that I tell you this. I want you to know everything about me."

A gentle smile played about Elena's mouth, as if she found the situation somewhat humorous. "—and you wanted me to know this? You felt I had to hear these words? So that you could feel cleansed of all except those things which were basically simple and good. My dear, sensitive Ed. You haven't changed since college days."

Ed looked up at her rather queerly. Was this the "cleansing" he remembered in a dream spoken by a faceless voice?

The smile remained on her face as she said invitingly, "Come to me, my imperfect man and lie down beside me. Tell me how much you love me."

◆◆◆

CONVERSATIONS OF SILENCE

Dotty's hand groped for the ringing phone at her elbow while still engrossed in the letter she was reading. It was Ed on the phone. "Dotty, I am calling to ask you . . ." That was as far as he got. She did not let him finish. Instinctively taking her glasses off she cheerfully exclaimed, "Ed, how nice to hear your voice. Only last night I was telling Clyde that it's been ages since we have heard from you." She was thinking of the "important patient" she had heard he had been spending much of his time with. She also belatedly remembered that it was Ed calling her; not the other way around. "It's so good to hear your voice, Ed," she finished lamely.

"Dotty, I would like you and Clyde to join me at the club for dinner; any time soon will be fine just so it fits in with your plans. I must confess, it has been a long time. Too long."

Dotty closed her eyes. She will never forget her assumed role of surrogate wife to Ed that night.

Ed continued, "I am having a guest I would like you both to meet."

Dotty momentarily experienced an uneasy feeling. Up to now he had been living the life of a bachelor. This was his first mention of someone else.

Ed met them in the foyer. Dotty had been to the hairdresser a few hours earlier. Skillfully applied makeup and an eye-catching dress completed the picture of Dotty at her best. She was a very handsome woman. Clyde was the same old reliable unchanging clyde but he was noticeably thinner. This pleased Ed.

They greeted each other and exchanged pleasantries. Ed hugged Dotty.

"Elena will be down in a few minutes," he remarked, "we can then all go in."

It was the first time that Elena's name was mentioned.

Elena, Dotty mused. The name carried a foreign sound to her ears. To her mind it did not seem to go with Ed although she admitted to herself that it was a strange bit of logic, on her part.

The elevators doors opened.

Elena stepped out, solicitously assisted by the operator. The first impression was of a rather young woman but as she approached it was quickly dispelled by the grey in her hair. Ed stepped forward and offered his arm. She took it in a proprietary way which was not lost on Dotty, or even Clyde.

Elena wore low-heeled sandals which did not go with what she was wearing. So she was Ed's 'important patient!' Dotty forgot her manners long enough to stare at Elena's feet but she managed a smile as they both approached.

Elena spoke first.

"You are Ed's dear friends. He has spoken of you many times. So often, in fact, that I feel you are old friends of mine as well." She gave them a worm disarming smile. Dotty decided that she could like Elena if she got to know her better and felt a pang of jealousy as she saw that Elena was beautiful. As they walked into the dining room Elena leaned closely on Ed's arm. The maitre d' hurried forward to greet them. Fred, the pianist of the dinner ensemble nodded toward them with a smile.

The club, in spite of the changes which came with the passage of time, had retained much of its charm and warmth. Elena was saying to Dotty, ". . . and Ed can be so strict and unsympathetic when he assumes the role of doctor. I won't bore you with the details of the operation but this man, sitting beside me, will not yet let me wear high heels. he tells me that it is not good for my back so I have to wear these silly dreadful things," she finished with a sign of resignation as she gave Ed's arm a gentle squeeze. She spoke rather rapidly which made her accent more pronounced.

Memories of Stacy distracted Dotty as she listened. Nowhere could she fit Elena into the picture, as she and Ed sat close together with an unspoken affinity for each other. In her mind she compared Elena with Stacy. She saw two totally different women who apparently laid claim to much of Ed's life. She came to the surprising conclusion that the incongruous one in her mental picture was herself. It preoccupied her mind as she tried to keep up with the light conversation. It was a disturbing self-revelation that she would have been undeniably happy to continue being Ed's surrogate wife. At the same time it shocked her matronly propriety.

She was brought out of her fantasy by the emphatic remark, "I heartily agree," by Clyde. It momentarily startled her, as if her patient, ever-faithful husband had divined her thoughts. "What's more," Clyde continued, "why on earth he was returned to Congress for another term—" This to Ed. Elena was also an active participant in the discussion. Dotty tried to join in halfheartedly but her interest in political and economic news was restricted to reading the headlines and the captions of the printed media.

Ed noticed that Elena's interest in such matters had not flagged since her university days where she managed to insinuate herself into the middle of most heated arguments. However there was an undeniable shift in her philosophy which had palpably undergone a change, probably influenced by George Waverly, her late husband.

The musicians had left some time ago. There remained only the hum of subdued voices in the half-deserted dining room. After the cordials and brandy all conversation languished. The evening was coming to a close.

As they walked into the foyer Elena took Ed's arm. She walked beside him as he continued chatting with his friends who were now quite aware of the strong bond between him and Elena. It confused them a little; it was all a bit too sudden and recent. They felt excluded, somehow; the circle of warmth between Ed and Elena did not quite reach them. Dotty felt she was losing a close friend. "Goodbye, Ed," she whispered. Clyde caught the sound but chose to remain silent.

They exchanged a few more words in the foyer. Shortly thereafter Ed and Elena were gone.

Dotty and Clyde stared at the closed elevator doors for a few moments longer. They would have to think about the evening a little longer to sort things out.

"Goodbye, Ed," Dotty said, this time to herself.

CHAPTER XXXVII

"The plane arrives in mid-afternoon, Ed. remember, we gain time, so it will be bright daylight and Lyle or George, Jr. will be waiting for me. There is no need to worry about me, and don't act so nervous. You would think I was going on a transatlantic trip, or to the Middle East."

Ed still looked worried and solicitous.

"Yes, dear. I'm sure you will be fine. Don't forget to ask for an extra pillow to sit on. I don't want you sinking way down into the soft seat. Better still, shove one of their bulky magazines under the seat cushion-it will support—"

"Yes, yes, doctor," Elena interrupted. "you have already told me all that. For goodness sake, will you please calm down."

"Yes, but I don't want anything to happen to you. You are my very life, Elena."

She did not answer. Soon the flight departure was announced and after many more reassurances and admonitions, he kissed her and followed her with his eyes until she disappeared into the cabin.

Ed's goals had been undergoing changes. His priorities were turned around. For one thing, being Chief of Service at the hospital was no longer important to him. Deutermann had been assistant long enough and it was time he took over. Elena was the most important thing in his life. His future plans would all revolve around her. For the present, he wanted to divest himself of the directorship of the department. He also wanted to get away for awhile. He hoped to put his thoughts into better perspective. He could not divorce from his mind his obsession with Molly Kyland and the year he gave away. Stacy and Dwight still obstinately clung to him. His son Lyle Edward. His relationship to his son would have to work itself out-between a father and a son who was a stranger to him, a son who was a grown man and well advanced in his own professional career. For now, Ed did not attempt to think further than resigning his directorship and getting away. He picked up the phone and dialed Dr. Frank Deutermann's number.

"But you are right in the middle of a teaching program, Ed," Deutermann protested mildly.

"You can manage very well, Frank," Ed assured him. "You are familiar with my techniques, and besides, I shall give you the entire folder of clinical notes and lectures. I really am very tired and I cannot do my best work feeling this way," Ed finished, "except for a few days I have had no rest for many months."

Remembering that he was the one who had interrupted Ed's vacation, even though for good reason, Frank shrugged
his shoulders and smiled without enthusiasm. "Okay, Ed," he nodded, I don't think there will be any problems."

It was settled. Ed could not wait to get away. All he needed to do was throw a few things into his bag.

CHAPTER XXXVIII

He dropped his bag and proceeded to open the storm shutters. He then pulled the sliding glass doors apart and stepped outdoors. The scene that greeted his eyes was unchanged from when he left. It was as if the panorama had been frozen in time, in total immobility, needing only his gaze to activate it back to life.

Only he had changed.

He looked inside the refrigerator and found it well stocked. Good thing he thought to call Daisy and Tyrone to put in the usual foodstuffs. They were generous on their shopping expeditions. He mixed a vodka with some orange juice and inserted a cassette of Tchaikovsky and Rimsky Korsakoff selections into the tape deck. He carried one of the stereo speaker attachments out onto the sunporch. Dropping into a beach chair, he let out a long sigh. He was now ready to relax.

He thought of Elena—and Stacy. The memories of both intertwined in a confusing pattern. Stacy was lost forever. She was in the heaven she always sought—and hoped for. It was strange that Stacy should enter his thoughts so frequently lately. Perhaps this was the beginning of what he hoped would happen—the unburdening and disgorging of obsessions which had remained too long like a cancer, in the back of his mind, Stacy and Dwight. To bring it out into the light of day, to look it over and then to let the wind catch it and blow it out to sea, a weightless wisp of something that happened long ago.

Ed rose early the next morning planning to walk along the beach. It was always pleasurable to go barefoot in the sand. He was in his shorts when Tyrone knocked at the door. He poked his head in. "Everything o.k. Dr. Rankin?" he inquired. "Just dropped by to check." He gave Ed an appraising look of approval. In truth, Ed looked ten years younger than his age. Skiing, tennis, and swimming in his earlier years, combined with simple exercise and careful weight vigilance in his later years paid dividends.

Tyrone continued, "The missus say for you to look in the 'frigerator; anything you don't see, you need, let her know."

Daisy and Tyrone were an elderly couple who seemed to come with the place. They were originally recommended by the previous owner when he and Stacy bought the beach house. Tyrone was the less articulate of the two, but nonetheless made it clear that he was the dominant member of the couple, a domestic status to which Daisy happily acceded.

Tyrone was a superstitious man in some ways. Last year, when Ed talked to him about a tornado which had touched down a few miles away, Tyrone remarked, "I knew it goin' happen."

"You did? How?" Ed had asked.

"The trees. They tell me. The leaves was shaking and trembling, like they fear sump'n. The leaves, they show me their undersides, like they wanna tell me. They say sump'n coming, sure enough. They tell me all that."

Ed listened, slightly skeptical. Since he was not acquainted with tree language, he let it go at that. Tyrone was very serious, however. He liked to sing while cleaning up around the house, particularly when trimming the shrubs. He had a deep bass voice. It was always the same song slowly rising and with deep feeling. It carried a nostalgic quality. The words were almost unintelligible, vaguely understood.

Ed sat on the limb of a long-dead, sun-bleached tree. Its trunk had disappeared and reappeared from time to time, like a recurring resurrection, depending on the vagaries of the tropical storms and high tides which washed out or carried in huge quantities of sand. The old limb still possessed some resilience and it imparted a rocker-like motion which felt pleasant to Ed as he gazed out on the ocean. The water glittered and sparkled as it caught the reflection of a bright sum which gave the sea life as it did to all living things. Small puffs of clouds floated in a sky of sun-blazoned blue.

It was a peaceful time for Ed. The turbulence of recent happenings was gradually simmering down. It was being replaced by a languor which he recognized and nurtured. It was a feeling which he had rarely experienced and the pleasant lassitude filled him with a sense of peace. He remained almost immobile as he studied the ocean, for fear that the feeling would flee if he disturbed it by any physical or mental act.

He watched the small moving dots in the distance grow larger as the pelicans came into view. From habit, he counted them as they went by with slow beat and long glide above the water, skirting the coastline and surveying the shallow water where the gentle surf was breaking into frilled frothy ruffles of white, hissing and sighing into the sand.

The birds were on their daily forage for fish. He noticed absent-mindedly that the second bird was pressing the leader while the other birds kept their respective distances. Their flight was effortless and beautifully graceful. He wondered what silent communication among them occasionally prompted them to move into a V-formation during flight. It lent a military, regimented appearance which was further enhanced when their aerial reconnaissance revealed a school of fish below and they banked into dive-bombing formation. They were expert fishermen and rarely missed a strike.

Ed sat there a long time. It was soon early evening. A gentle, pleasant breeze came in from the east. A sensuously peaceful feeling had settled upon him and had remained with him all day. His mood was in harmony with the "betwixt-and between" hour—that magical part of the day between early twilight and yet-to-come nightfall. He could not remember when he last felt so content and free from burden.

And then he thought of Molly Kyland and his year of life he gave away. When would this self-flagellation end, he asked himself.

Soon afterward he turned back toward the house.

CHAPTER XXXIX

Ed stirred restlessly in his sleep. He dreamt that he was writing in a book which was beautifully bound in leather. On its red cover was an undecipherable design embossed in gold. He knew he had been writing for some time, steadily, and with clear forceful purpose. His thinking was precise and he was recording his thoughts with crystal clarity. But his writing began to falter. As the assembly-line of his thoughts wound down to a halt, his hand stopped for want of image-material to record. He had somehow lost his train of thought. Looking back at the pages he had already filled, he was surprised to find that they were still blank—as if the thoughts he had already recorded had been washed away so the expunged words would not be there to read.

He was mildly surprised, but his reaction was not the extreme feeling that such an impossible finding would have provoked in a waking state. In the dream-world the wanderer experiences emotions and reactions which are erratically bizarre, extreme or illogical, but they all wear a cloak of plausibility which renders the perceptions un-extreme and quite logical. It is a temporary schizophrenia which evaporates, the moment the dreamer emerges from the fuliginous dimness of this other-world into the dull safety of wakefulness.

Still dreaming, he studies the blank pages before him-the ones over which he had labored. His thoughts had been transmuted into bold, purposeful words onto pages which somehow remained stubbornly blank. It was as if he subconsciously did not wish anyone, perhaps even himself, to read them. What had he been writing, he asked himself. A few moments ago it was a concise idea with a plan. It had all slipped away—the idea, the plan. It was about—what?

"It was about one year less," a voice behind him suggested. "The year that you gave away a long time ago. I see it is still bugging you, if I may borrow a colloquialism."

"It does occur to me from time to time," Ed agreed. "I wonder about it—usually at the most irrelevant times," he added somberly. "By the way, who are you? You seem to know a lot about me." Ed moved to confront his visitor.

"Do not turn around. No need to look" the voice ordered, "We've met before. Look in the mirror in front of you. What do you see?"

"I see no one except myself."

"Precisely," the voice replied. "When you see yourself, you see me. I am your alter ego. But—back to your—er—writing. I would prefer to avoid this sensitive subject, but you did promise, you know. You made a bargain...and your patient did very well. I recall many of your conversations in the past—the ones with Stacy—forgive me—for instance. You were always preaching about Heaven, so why all the foot-dragging now?"

Ed was thoughtful for a long time. Would he be held to a promise made in a moment of desperation. He wanted to say the most appropriate and cogent words. He began, "I offered to give a way something which was not mine to offer or to give. It was the precious gift of Life." He was growing accustomed to conversing with a voice. "—to enjoy the colors of the flowers; to watch an ocean expanse, or to be awed by the towering majesty of a snowcrested, sun-gilded mountain; to hear the sighing of the wind through the forest; to touch people; to hold things—" His words came more easily. "—to taste the sweetness and goodness of living; to look up into a fantastically blue sky; to feel the warmth and joy of love; to . . . to just live and immerse myself in all the joyous vibrant sensations that the amazing body can feel; but . . ."

"But what?" the voice asked.

". . . But this shadow passes over me every now and then, and . . . I remember. I ask myself if the bargain is irrevocable. Stacy knew about it. I have never told Elena."

"You shall never tell Elena," the voice repeated doggedly.

"You sound like an echo. Besides, do not, I beg you, be so blooming positive about everything. I want you to help me find the answer. Frankly, you are of no help at all. I am getting slightly tired of you—or me—or whatever you are. Just an echo, nothing more!"

No answer. Then, "You have a point there." Silence again.

"When I was young," Ed reminisced, life to me was a deep well from which the living draught could be endlessly drawn. I was so profligate with the years I thought I had them to spare. Now, it all seems like yesterday."

"Well-?"

"Well . . . I do not know what else to say. It is the Primal feeling of approaching blackness, densely closing in from all sides. It enters the body and quickly spreads like a venom, poisoning all the physical and mental senses. I want to cry out but cannot. I want to run but it is hopeless to run from it. I can only curl up in a dark corner, wrap my arms, in protection around my agonized belly and head, and grieve silently—unwept and unlamented." Ed curled up tightly in his deep sleep.

"Life," he continued, "—anything and everything—has become precious to me beyond words. Perhaps this primal feeling is the price I have been made to pay . . . this primal pain. Even the description of physical pain which can transcend any word in the human vocabulary has lost its mystery. I feel it. It can be no worse than the final parting from all that is dearly loved." He lapsed into silence.

"Tell me," Ed continued, "which year will it be? Before next year? After five years? Ten?"

No answer.

"Will you at least look at what I have written and read it back to me. I feel that I should know."

The voice answered loftily, "This is not the time for levity or humor. You know as well as I that what you cannot see, I cannot see. Please do not misjudge, however. You have my sympathy and understanding. We are in complete rapport. Remember that." The voice trailed off.

When Ed awoke, the early light of sunrise appeared over the ocean's edge and emblazoned the wall facing the east windows. He finally bestirred himself and decided to walk along the beach. He would set out for the lighthouse whose beam flooded his room at regular intervals at night. He felt that something had been lifted from him last night. The answer, he knew, would come in good time.

He was ravenous this morning. He looked into the refrigerator. Daisy and Tyrone had provided him with plenty of provisions. He carted his orange juice, toast and coffee out on the balcony where he could sit and enjoy the view of the ocean and the friendly lighthouse.

As he drank his coffee the answer came.

IT WAS THE PRIMAL PAIN that mattered.

The belief, that he had sealed a bargain, had goaded and pricked him like an indestructible gadfly. Over all the years he had not only given up one year, but had, in effect, given it up many times over. Every time he thought about it, he had endured the loss anew, inflicting a fresh wound upon all the earlier scars.

He knew that he had paid the price in full.

It would have been wonderful here with Elena, he thought.

He walked north on the beach toward the lighthouse. The sand felt warm under his bare feet. The sun was quite high and slightly behind him, creating a shortened shadow which preceded him. He felt wonderfully free. It had been a long time.

In the distance, a lone person was walking toward him—a woman. In the past, he would wonder about the approaching figure. There was always a vague feeling of anticipation as they slowly came closer to each other. It had the fantasized quality of a clandestine meeting—two people would meet, look at each other and somehow . . . He stopped in his tracks. The approaching woman reminded him of Elena. She really looked like Elena! He walked a little faster. But from a short distance away, she turned into a sunburnt stranger. They passed each other with a slight nod.

The lighthouse loomed large and tall although it was still quite a distance away. Ed noticed it had a fresh coat of paint—upper half black, lower half white. It looked beautiful; he felt a genuine fondness for it. A long spit of hand stabbed into the ocean south of it. As its tip a grine built of coral rock served as an observation point. It provided a breathtaking sweep of the ocean and the miles of beach both north and south of it. Near its tip a woman stood shading her eyes with her hand, peering out to sea. She also reminded him of Elena. he did not move any closer. He wanted to love the unknown woman who reminded him of her. He could not approach and suffer the disenchantment.

That evening he wrote in his diary.

> *In this solitary place I am never alone. Elena is always with me. I see her everywhere. In the past she remained only as a memory until I found her again. Now she fills my life. If I should lose her now, I know my life would never be the same. She means more than the young beautiful singing Elena I once loved. Long ago I offered one year of my life for someone and felt it was perhaps too much to give. Now I would give my life without question so that Elena might live.*
>
> *Not until I have her with me shall I feel whole again. Without each other, she and I are not complete.*

Ed felt that he had stayed away too long.

When he returned from his trip, he stopped by to pick up the accumulated mail at the club. He called Karen. She was glad to hear his voice and he was cheered by hers. They decided when to resume office hours. Ed was glad to hear there were no pressing problems. He told her to notify the hospital telephone operator of his return.

When Karen finally said happily, "Doctor, I am so-o-o glad you are back." Ed was sure she meant more than his mere physical return.

He went through the mail, laying aside what he knew could wait. He stopped. An envelope in Elena's handwriting. It must have been waiting for him for almost a week. He opened it hurriedly and read:

"As you know, we took the trip in fine shape. I am now able to do some light work about the house and to potter around in our greenhouse.

The tingling in the fingertips is practically gone and, except for the occasional fuzziness of speech which has not knocked out my silly little accent, I am as good as new.

I feel like a pincushion from Dr. Winthrop's injections, but as long as you say so I shall dutifully keep going in for them.

I guess I will never know all the details but there is a period of five days—so you told me—which are a total blank, except for some shadows and whisperings in dark corners.

Part of the time I dreamed I was with my mother. She was still young and I was her child, but I seemed to be grown-up.

Dearest Ed,
it is all behind me now and, although Dr. Winthrop tells me I am quite sound, I feel my heart go bumpa, bumpa whenever I think of you. So, I think you had better come out to look me over and tell me what you think.
Love,
Elena

When Ed dropped into the Administrator's office and handed her his resignation, she was shocked. He suggested to her that Dr. Deutermann was the logical man to head the department. He added that there was no question of his reconsidering the move. however, he assured her, he would continue to admit his private patients. The international character it imparted to the hospital would be preserved, which pleased the administrator. Later, the hospital Board suggested a testimonial dinner but Ed scotched the idea by firmly stating he would not appear. A short time late a bronze plaque was hung in the operating room suite as a testimonial to his services. Ed capriciously remarked that it was the first time he had viewed a plaque at the hospital which had not been put up posthumously. The staff photographer took a few pictures and Ed was free at last.

The plane circled before landing. As he caught sight of Elena he could not help but remember that other plane trip he hurriedly took from the south, after receiving Deutermann's distress call about her. As they approached each other Ed felt like a weary traveler arriving home after a long tortuous journey. They held each other without words.

Lyle must have been close by although Ed had not noticed. The young man stepped forward with a friendly smile. With his left arm still enfolding Elena, Ed shook his hand. Lyle's eyes were blue-grey. He was tall. He had a sensitive face, which Ed studied, searching for some sign of recognition-that his son would somehow know it was his father's hand he was holding. He hoped, illogically, it might happen by virtue of his genes the young man carried in his body. It became a long moment, so long that Elena spoke, to relieve the awkwardness. "Lyle Edward has been head of the engineering firm ever since George died." She put her arm through Lyle's and smiled proudly at him. Lyle looked at his mother wondering mildly at the use of both his Christian names. He could not remember the last time she did so.

Ed did not seem to be aware of his own unusual behavior. "I should have known you long ago, Lyle," he said impulsively, almost irrationally. The compulsion to say the words lay beyond his control. Elena raised her eyebrows, as she glanced sideways at Ed. There was a look in his eyes she had never seen there before.

Lyle's composure never wavered although he did not quite know what to say. Diplomatically, he nodded vaguely in agreement. Anxious to change the subject he suggested, turning to his mother, "I'm sure you two have much to talk about. Suppose I drop by, later, for an after-dinner drink." Turning to Ed, "Mother keeps the very best cognac at the house; I am the only one who drinks it. My brother, George, never touches it."

"We will have a drink together," Ed murmured. "By the way, I brought a little package I want you to have." He thrust it into Lyle's hands.

Lyle turned to leave, hesitated, turned back to his mother and gently place a kiss on her cheek. He looked thoughtful.

To Elena the kiss carried a message. *He suspects. He knows. The resemblance to his father is inescapable. He knows.*

Strange, she felt no panic. Actually a feeling akin to relief.

Ed gazed at the back of his son's retreating figure. He felt a touch of sadness, a longing for the wasted empty years. Smiling young Lyle bore a remarkable resemblance, had stood before him and engaged in polite talk-as a total stranger; a man who was the product of another man's devotion and love during the formative years. It was an irretrievable loss, an emptiness which would remain with him always. The memory of Lyle's smile gladdened him, however. The reflection of himself in his son could not be taken away from him. At least he had that.

Lyle sat in the cab deep in thought. His feelings were a blend of surprise and confusion, laced with excitement. *I feel–I know-that his life and mine are joined somehow, somewhere, in the past. The way he looked at me, the words he spoke, mother's solicitude.*

The plaintive, "You want I should open the door for you, mister?" brought him back with a start. He stepped out quickly. His abstraction remained with him as he passed through the open elevator doors. It seemed a mere moment the express elevator reached his floor. He stepped out barely in time to avoid being brushed by the closing doors. Standing there the realization, which he had been skirting, crystallized sharply in his mind. His lips formed the soundless words. MY FATHER?

Absorbed in thought, he walked past the usual office greetings, barely nodding. He closed the office door very softly behind him. No noise, no intrusion. He had to think. He stared out on the busy traffic many floors below, returned to his desk.

His brother dropped in.

"Lyle."

"George."

He thought, *What about George? Do I tell him that I have just met my father? Do I say anything? Maybe not ever. I feel like a "Waverly." I am a "Waverly." We have been close all our lives. Nothing must separate us or erect a barrier between us.*

CONVERSATIONS OF SILENCE

George noticed his older brother's preoccupation as he sat drumming his fingers on the desk, a faraway look in his eyes. He suspected it was the Polchofsky electrical contract. It had been bothering him lately about the penalty clause for late completion. he searched through a drawer, retrieved a file and left, banging the door behind him.

With a sigh Lyle turned to the papers on his desk and buzzed for his secretary. Remembering Ed's gift, he tore the package open.

It was a diary.

◆◆◆

"Ed, darling. He knows. When he kissed me on the cheek, I knew." She was sitting in a hard chair since she was still wearing the brace.

"Perhaps you are right. A mother's intuition. I hope so."

Thoughts about their own future were pre-empted by what had transpired at the airport. It had been like a tableau orchestrated by an invisible hand. Ed experienced a feeling of helplessness in the face of inevitability. Thinking out aloud he said. "It had to happen. It has to be played out." Elena did not reply.

"I think—" he paused, "—that since we all know, it would be better to put discussion aside when he comes tonight. If he brings the subject up, asks questions, we will answer and disclose freely. Perhaps he will choose otherwise. At least until he has relegated his new-found "father" (Ed smiled wryly) to the proper place in his mind and can deal with it. I know how he feels. I feel the same. Here we were at the airport—both strangers—meeting each other for the first time—a meeting complicated by a binding circumstance thrust into our lives, which, by its very Father-Son nature, demands a resolution of sorts." He paused.

"I am glad that I came. Meeting my son has given me great pleasure. I cannot call it paternal love or joy. Not yet. It is too early— or too late-depending on how the evening will go. Much will depend on how Lyle sorts things out between us. For his sake, perhaps, it would have been better if I had not come. I have placed an unnecessary burden upon him. I cannot shake off a guilty feeling that I have intruded into a good man's life and complicated it."

Elena remained silent. She rose and walked over to Ed who took her proffered hand. They walked out onto the terrace, his arm around her waist. The view of Lake St. Clair was beautiful. It was that time of year when the shrubs and flowers were in full landscape magnificence. He pulled her to him and held her gently, firmly. It gave them a sense of support and comfort, of the rightness of things. It was an overpowering bond between them.

That evening she met Lyle at the door. They kissed each other and walked into the living room, Elena hanging on his arm. Lyle appeared stimulated and over-attentive.

"You're looking wonderful, mother. Hope the doctor—er-Ed will let you get rid of the brace soon. What did he say? The huskiness is practically gone from your voice. you have no pain? and—and—oh-yes, —George and Jacqueline send their love. They are—"

With a laugh, she gently shook his arm. "Whoa! Lyle, slow down! You're running over with words!"

Lyle stopped. He had the penitent look of the mother-small boy kind.

"There, that's better. Sit down right here." She patted the back of the chair. She was also acting over-solicitous and she knew it. "You know where the cognac and brandy are. Help yourself while I call Ed."

Near the doorway she turned and spoke to him across the room.

"Your mother understands, Lyle. I want you to know that Ed, you father, (*how strange the word!*) feels as you do. He also is in an emotional limbo, like yourself. As for me, Lyle, the story is not a sordid one. On the contrary, it is warm and beautiful." Her face lighted up as she spoke. "Please try to remember this." She turned and left. leaving Lyle looking at he spot where she had stood.

On her way she thought, *This is not going the way we planned.* She was out of breath and realized she was walking too fast.

Lyle was still in his chair when they entered. They came forward, warm smiles on their faces. Lyle rose, came toward them, hand outstretched. Strained feelings lay just beneath the surface. The scene took on a brittle quality which they tried to dispel. The effusiveness was a trifle forced.

Ed and Lyle shook hands and studied each other, searching for something they could reach or say.

Something spontaneous and unpremeditated passed between them. Ed's pleading look impelled Lyle to tentatively place his hand on Ed's shoulder. Ed did the same. A moment later they were hugging each other and resoundingly patting each other's back. Soon, they parted looking a little self-conscious of the emotional display between two grown men who still needed to know much more about each other. But that would come in good time.

Elena sniffled unabashedly, putting her minuscule handkerchief to good use. She was the first to bring the situation down to a calm level. She assumed a practical voice when she suggested, "You two boys (BOYS! *she was carried away*) talk to each other while I fetch the cheese tray." Still sniffling, with the handkerchief to her nose, she gestured to Ed, "Ed, Lyle will show you were to find to cognac. Ed's favorite is Hennessy X.O. I'm sure there is a bottle somewhere." As an afterthought, "you both love cognac." her tone suggested that this was a revelation of the first magnitude.

When she returned she found the men seated. Lyle was listening; Ed appeared to be doing all the talking. Elena chose for herself a white wine, a Montrachet. By the time they were well into their second drink the group seemed at ease and presented a typical family scene. Ed had been talking for a long tie, bringing events up to the present. It was a long narration. He was coming to a close, "–loved your mother ever since university days. Times were different then. Life was different. I am not sure that its quality has improved much since those times." He looked at Elena She raised her eyebrows, a questioning look, but chose not to comment.

Ed noticed, irrelevantly, that Lyle preferred to warm the snifter over a spirit flame before pouring the cognac. He was content to twirl it around in the glass against the warmth of his hand. He continued, "There is too much to tell in one night. I am hoping we will get to know each other better in time, Lyle, to understand and to–" He was about to say 'love each other' but an instinctive restraint stopped him. It was too soon. It was rushing it. Lyle could guess what remained unsaid. he understood Ed's hesitance. he pretended not to notice the lapse. Ed became absorbed with his drink. Elena toyed with her wine glass. They were all talked out. Silence in the room. Each with private thoughts; cogent thoughts.

Ed broke the silence, "You never married, Lyle?"

Lyle exchanged glances with his mother. Her protective instinct prompted her to answer for him. It was still too painful for him. "Angela was a beautiful generous person. We all loved her–" She looked at Lyle.

"Leukemia," he said. "the worst kind."

"I'm sorry," Ed replied in a whisper. The entire clinical picture was clear in his mind.

Lyle had not planned to stay as long as he did but he was glad he came. As much had been made clear to him; much remained unsaid, perhaps never to be revealed. His mother still retained much of the beauty of her younger years. Part of her life would forever be a closed book to him but it was a good beginning. He was hopeful that everything would eventually fall into place.

The latter part of the evening passed quickly. It was, surprisingly, monopolized by Elena. Since the men were generally silent she was impelled to fill the hiatus. Irresolute at first, she soon gained momentum chatting and chattering, mostly about Lyle's growing up. The men were content to be good listeners. Ed, as usual, loved the sound of her voice.

Lyle stood up. "Work tomorrow." It was time to leave.

They both saw Lyle to the door. In the foyer Lyle turned to his mother. "We should take Ed to Al Green's, or the Little Club. Perhaps to the Country Club. Why don't you call and make arrangements, mother. He must not go back without celebrating our--our reunion."

"I would like that," said Ed. He again clasped Lyle's shoulder. Lyle patted his. Elena let Lyle out, after a perfunctory maternal kiss.

Elena leaned against the closed door, her eyes closed. She rested there a few moments. Although she had appeared to be in control the evening had held the potential for a stressful and tense time. She heaved a deep sigh and took Ed's hand. They moved slowly toward the staircase turning the downstairs lights off on the way. Elena held Ed's hand and led the way. Her hand trembled slightly in his. He knew the signs. Their lives had been put aside for Lyle. Tonight they would again live for each other, have each other. It would be a night of total giving. Of silent communication. Of few words. They entered her bedroom.

They were all at the airport including George with his young bride Jacqueline. Elena fluttered around the group, her laughter like the tinkling of fine crystal. It was a minor celebration of sorts that she was finally able to discard her brace. It never ceased to surprise her that her doctor-lover retained his two distinct identities in her case. She had accused him with a chuckle, more than once, of harboring a split-personality.

She looked at Lyle and was jubilant that things had turned out so well. He appeared to have recovered from what might have been confusing, disturbing, perhaps shattering, revelations. At least he looked calm, a slight smile on his face. She wondered, Has he told George. She returned to Ed's side and put her arm through his. *The children will have to become accustomed to their mother's display of affection for a man who is practically a stranger to them, she thought, but who always has been a living part of my life.*

"—the work has been piling up. I have to get back—," this in answer to Lyle's question. The P.A. system came alive announcing his flight. He picked up his tote bag and leaned over to kiss Elena. She whispered something in his ear. He kissed her again. She looked beautiful. The little group noticed the glow on her face. They all watched Ed until he disappeared through the gate.

Ed was in deep thought by the time the plane had reached cruising speed. It was an early morning flight, much too early for a drink but he had one contrary to his usual practice. His thoughts turned to his office, ever-loyal Karen, his work. There passed, in a parade of memories a kaleidoscope of so much that had happened since the beginning—his Elena, the others, Stacy, the war years, his work—always his work.

But now it would be Elena. He had finally found the lost part of himself. He was content. He could live peacefully with it now.

He recalled the words Elena had whispered in his ear, at the airport. 'Like Ruth of long ago, wither thou goest I will go.'

It was good. Everything up to now was merely a prelude for what lay ahead.

It was the end of the beginning.

CHAPTER XL

They faced each other. They barely heard the voice of the clergyman...

"—in sickness and in health—?"

He was again in the Intensive Care unit, Elena near death, gasping for air, a tube feeding oxygen through an opening in her windpipe. He looked at her, reassured.

"—do you, Edward, take Elena to be your wife—?"

He was seeing Elena at the Alliance Française. He loved her that first day. It was only yesterday.

"I do."

"—Elena, take Edward to be your husband—?"

She was back on Playfair Island, with Ed, skipping stones, when he gently held her, told her he loved her. The first kiss, their first embrace. It was only yesterday.

"I do."

It was a beautiful fall day, the leaves in full color. They had cocktails and champagne outdoors on the terrace. It had been a quiet ceremony, the wedding group was small. Present, were Dotty and Clyde, Lyle, George and Jacqueline. Also, Karen his secretary and a few of his associates with their wives. Karen's Scottish burr could be heard over the hum of voices. It was a happy scene.

Elena and Dotty were in deep conversation. George and Lyle were listening to Karen's recital of great surgical exploits performed by Ed. Most certainly exaggerated, but who could fault Karen's enthusiasm?

Clyde was with some of the doctors, drinking.

Ed and Elena presently stole away. It was done so unobtrusively the guests did not guess that it was not spontaneous but pre-arranged. They hardly missed them.

It was an uncommon kind of honeymoon, their going back in time, to relive some of the past. They hoped that what had gone before, might be once more savored, experienced and "rounded out." Afterward, to let all things glide back into the dimness of reminiscence. At least, Elena and Ed agreed it was possible. It explained their return to the place where their jointly woven lives began. Theirs was no planned schedule. Much of their visit would be as separate individuals, dictated by their personal memories. Ed stood across the street and looked at the building which was once his 'home.' It looked in need of repair. He walked up to the Medical building where he saw old class pictures, including those of himself. Only strangers gazed back at him. Elena revisited the women's college.

Later, she thought of a small restaurant she often visited, in the early days before she knew Ed. The owners were husband and wife. They did the cooking and serving. The dishes were of her native country. She thought of the many hours she spent at a corner table drinking coffee while studying from a book. Occasionally, one or the other owner would drop by, sit down, talk to her in her native tongue, over a cup of coffee . . .

To her delight, she found the restaurant still there. The parents were gone but one of the sons had carried on the business and the tradition. They definitely had prospered over the years. The astonishing finding was the menu. It was exactly the same as in the old days; the same dishes made in the same traditional way. She sat in her old corner, now remodeled. She thought, with a warm feeling, of the old owners and their friendly gossip, especially the wife with her free motherly advice. For a few sweet moments she recaptured the old carefree Elena of long ago. The feeling stayed with her as she finally reluctantly decided to leave. At the door, she looked back toward the corner where she had sat and again saw herself as the young girl whose unknown future was of little concern to her in those days. She left.

It was the day before they were planning to leave. They strolled, arm in arm, through the campus. It was a cold morning and Ed was glad he had brought his tweed jacket. Elena was happy with her new slacks and Russian boots, particularly with the high heels which she was now allowed to wear. She practically strutted in them. She stopped walking, as something occurred to her. Ed looked at her questioningly. She disengaged her arm, walked away from him, while glancing over her shoulder at him, with a mischievous look in her eyes. She headed toward a mound of fallen leaves and proceeded to kick them vigorously in all directions. To Ed, she was again the young Elena, the woman-child, a free spirit. She had indeed reached the past, retouched it and "rounded it out." The memory of his young Elena was so real, it aroused in Ed a feeling of almost unbearable poignancy mingled with pleasure.

She stopped as suddenly as she began. She returned to Ed's side. Arm in arm, they walked away.

www.ingramcontent.com/pod-product-compliance
Lightning Source LLC
Chambersburg PA
CBHW030107170426
43198CB00009B/527